Fly-Fishing the Rocky Mountain Backcountry

Rich Osthoff

STACKPOLE BOOKS

0 11557 02766 2

Published by
STACKPOLE BOOKS
5067 Ritter Road
Mechanicsburg, PA 17055
www.stackpolebooks.com

Printed in the United States

First edition

10 9 8 7 6 5 4

Cover design by Caroline Stover

Cover photos by the author

The author wishes to thank Abenaki Publishers for permission to reprint portions of articles that first appeared in *American Angler* and *Fly Tyer* magazines.

Library of Congress Cataloging-in-Publication Data

Osthoff, Rich
    Fly-fishing the Rocky Mountain backcountry/Rich Osthoff.—1st ed.
      p.   cm.
    Includes bibliographical references and index.
    ISBN 0-8117-2766-1 (pbk.)
    1. Fly fishing—Rocky Mountains—Guidebooks. 2. Backpack fishing—Rocky Mountains—Guidebooks. 3. Rocky Mountains—Guidebooks. I. Title.
    SH464.R63078   1998
    799. 1'757'0978—dc21   98-26356
                                                                              CIP

ISBN 978-0-8117-2766-2

Contents

DESTINATIONS

To Dick and Elmer,
who took the time to take me fishing.
And to Dawn for letting me go.

A Vast, Untapped Fishery

Give me trout, give me trout water, and I inherit the most beautiful country on earth.

I can think of no better reason to fish than to wander the pure and wild places where trout live. If sentiment alone can carry an angler over several thousand miles of wilderness trails, then this sentiment has carried me as I've fly-fished throughout the Rocky Mountain backcountry in search of trout that rarely, if ever, see humans.

Among the towering peaks, yawning canyons, and black-timbered slopes of the Rocky Mountain backcountry lies a vast fishery that few anglers have experienced and fewer still have explored. You could fish a lifetime and never see a fraction of this fishery or weary of its haunting beauty.

I speak of roadless westslope rivers where hefty native cutthroats still rise eagerly to hairwing dry flies—rivers like the South Fork of the Flathead in the Bob Marshall Wilderness of northern Montana and Big Creek in the Frank Church Wilderness of western Idaho. There is still superb, uncrowded angling on rivers in Yellowstone Park where roads, with their attendant hordes of tourists, don't penetrate; you can drift a gnat on a 7X tippet to spooky rainbows in the glassy Bechler Meadows or float Green Drakes to throngs of migrating cutthroats in the Yellowstone headwaters far above Yellowstone Lake. East of Yellowstone in the rugged Beartooths of Montana, I know a brook trout lake that's good for a couple dozen obscenely obese squaretails a day. South of Yellowstone the mighty Wind River Range of Wyoming straddles the Continental Divide for 100 miles and harbors an estimated seven hundred trout lakes, including the finest golden trout waters in the world; you can lace on your hiking boots and climb to shimmering tarns among the clouds to cast to outsize goldens that are every bit as powerful and elusive as they are dazzling. If you'd rather float than hike, you can raft the Middle Fork of the Salmon River in central Idaho and cast to chrome-bright cutts, soak in hot springs, and nap on white sandbars in the shade of towering ponderosa pines. If sliding on your butt while groping for handholds sounds exhilarating, you can scramble 2,800 feet straight down an eroded gully into the bowels of Colorado's Black Canyon of the Gunnison and battle leaping rainbows that glint like molten silver against the ebony canyon walls. And these outstanding backcountry waters are but a few of those I've been fortunate enough to fish.

It's ironic that in an era in which unspoiled trout fishing is at a premium and anglers drop considerable sums on guides, rod fees, and airfare to far-flung fishing meccas, a major American fishery open to free public use is being relatively ignored. Yet in the case of the Rocky Mountain backcountry fishery, it's happening.

Much of this fishery is difficult to access. Unlike remote regions of Alaska or New Zealand, where well-heeled anglers can drop in by plane or chopper, much of the Rocky Mountain backcountry lies within designated wilderness areas and parks, where motorized equipment is prohibited. Access is primarily by foot or horse over steep, rocky terrain at high elevations, and anglers who tackle this spectacular country on their own need specialized gear, plus a measure of woodsmanship and ambition not required for roadside or fly-in angling. There's no sugarcoating it—the logistics and physical demands of traveling and fishing much of this backcountry are considerable. But then anglers who are willing to work for their fish count this as a blessing, because they know it's the inaccessibility of the backcountry that keeps the angling crowds at bay. My longest backpack fishing trips have spanned nearly two weeks and covered more than 140 miles of rugged terrain. Yet not all backcountry fishing is so demanding—I've also enjoyed solitary angling on dozens of worthwhile waters that are well within the range of an average hiker with just a few days to spend.

Many anglers avoid the backcountry because they've bought into the notion that high-country trout are invariably small. Angling writers who've never experienced the broad scope of this fishery often repeat the old refrain that at high elevations food is too scarce and the winters are too long for trout to grow much. It's true that small trout abound in the backcountry and that stringers of pan-size fish can be caught at will from many wilderness waters. Yet the largest brook, rainbow, cutthroat, bull, and golden trout I've taken in the Rockies have all come from backcountry waters. And I know waters above 10,000 feet in elevation where mature trout average 20 inches and grow hog fat—just like trout in the West's most heralded spring creeks and tailwaters.

Many anglers also believe that backcountry trout are too gullible to challenge an accomplished fly fisher. They mistakenly assume that wariness and selectivity are qualities drummed into trout solely by heavy fishing pressure. But backcountry trout descended from generations of wild stock are often extremely wary of natural predators, shadows, vibrations, or anything that seems out of kilter in their crystalline environment. Selectivity by trout toward a specific food form is, likewise, a perfectly natural behavior that allows them to feed efficiently. In my experience backcountry trout—especially wild, trophy trout living in balance with their food supply—are often extremely wary and selective.

Still other fly fishers bypass the backcountry because they believe it's primarily a stillwater fishery. This bias against fishing lakes is unfortunate, because the small, intimate lakes that abound in the backcountry are fascinating to explore and fish. Besides, the backcountry teems with restless, tumbling waters. Most lakes have substantial inlet and outlet streams, which attract trout like magnets during feeding and spawning periods. Many major rivers have headwaters in or flow partially through wilderness areas. And much of the backcountry is laced with sparkling creeks that are tailor-made for light fly rods and wandering souls.

And finally, many fly fishers overlook the backcountry because there's a scarcity of reliable information about its fisheries. Whereas the forest service manages land, timber, and water in much of the backcountry, state wildlife agencies bear primary responsibility for managing fish. As a result, the forest service is rarely a dependable source of information on fish size, quantity, or distribution. A few state fisheries managers may be able and willing to point you toward promising waters, but many managers are new to their regions or have limited time and resources to commit to large backcountry fisheries; they actually rely on backcountry anglers for much of their information. Surprisingly, even fishing guides who work near the finest backcountry fishing in the West are often unfamiliar with local waters that can't be easily accessed. Some outfitters can horsepack anglers to fine wilderness fishing, yet many outfitters cater primarily to hunters and don't know the productivity of local waters or the particulars of fly-fishing them successfully. Most books and articles have dealt only superficially with the angling opportunities available in vast roadless areas.

This book is devoted to the Rocky Mountain backcountry fishery and to the ambitious fly fishers who want to tackle it—for a weekend, a week, a summer, or a lifetime of summers. It examines the superb fishing opportunities available in the backcountry and addresses the special skills, knowledge, and equipment required to fish it successfully. Any attempt to be truly comprehensive is doomed, for there are far more worthwhile waters scattered across the backcountry than anyone can possibly find and fish in a lifetime. There are—and I hope always will be—excellent waters waiting to be discovered or rediscovered by anglers willing to make the effort.

Part of my goal in writing this book is to shine light on a neglected fishery. In an era of shrinking natural bounty and growing private exploitation of publicly owned fish and wildlife, it's crucial that this priceless public fishery be recognized, more effectively managed, and adequately protected for future anglers.

In truth, the Rocky Mountain backcountry supports a fishery that is more productive, challenging, and diverse than all but a handful of anglers realize—a fishery that in the hectic years ahead is bound to be discovered by an increasing number of fly fishers who seek the very best our sport has to offer: the chance to fish for wild trout in wild, unspoiled country.

Rich Osthoff
April 1998

Gear and Strategies

CHAPTER 1

Travel Options

When I look back on nearly twenty summers of fishing remote waters throughout the Rockies, I recall scores of memorable fish. But my many carefree weeks of wandering through wonderful country shine just as brightly. Backcountry angling is a package deal: The fishing and the traveling go hand in hand. Fishing may be the focus of your trip, but traveling wild country will be much of your reward. Of course, in backcountry angling, just getting to the water is also much of the challenge. Whether you're going to tackle the country on your own or hire an outfitter is a primary consideration.

The affordability and challenge of fishing the Rocky Mountain backcountry on my own have always appealed to me, and I can do so for about $500 a month, including fishing licenses and road expenses between treks. Fully outfitted and guided horseback trips cost around $1,000 per person per week. That's a bargain compared with the price of guided trips to Alaska or more exotic locales. Still, a thrifty, self-guided angler can easily fish the Rockies for an entire summer on a grand.

Guided horseback trips are available to most backcountry waters in the Rockies, and some anglers haul their own stock from distant states. Horses can transport anglers beyond their comfortable hiking range, making a horse trip an attractive option for families and other groups with limited time or backpacking experience. But skilled anglers who are strong hikers will find advantages to hiking on their own.

A fit hiker can cruise mountain trails at better than 2 miles an hour—nearly as fast as a horse string. And even an average backpacker can negotiate dense timber, blowdowns, boulder fields, and steep slopes that no horse can handle. Reaching the very best highcountry lakes often requires some off-trail travel.

Horse outfitters tend to establish base camps on lakes that are accessible by trail and have firewood, spacious campsites, and grass for the stock. Clients who want to fish other waters must often take lengthy rides or day hikes from base camp. When I trek on my own to a remote lake that holds trophy trout, however, I take every edge I can get. I camp right on my target lake so I can watch for cruising or rising fish, even while I eat. In that magical last hour of daylight when big fish are on the prowl, I'm fishing rather than riding or hiking back to base camp. When bad weather blows in, I can pop out of the tent between icy downpours and fire a few casts, which might produce the biggest fish of my trip.

Because horses can pack a lot of stuff, they usually do. I'm talking heavy wall tents, cooking tarps, cots, Dutch ovens, and food-laden grub boxes that backpackers can only fantasize about. Much of this cargo translates into comfortable living and fine dining, but some of it translates into lost fishing time. On travel days, breaking down a horse camp and loading the animals can burn up an entire morning. A backpacker can break camp and hit the trail in fifteen minutes.

Outfitted trips are usually scheduled months in advance and lock you into fishing a specific area at a specific time—but high-altitude conditions vary widely from year to year. Self-guided anglers who can scrap one destination at the last minute and adopt another have a better chance of hitting hot fishing. I was set to fish near Mount St. Helens the year she blew, for instance; in this case the fishing sounded a little too hot, so I headed elsewhere. In the horrendous fire season of 1988, when Yellowstone and the surrounding forests were an inferno, I hiked and fished all of August in the greater Yellowstone area simply by going where the fires weren't. On my last trip that summer, I hiked over a pass just beyond a closed fire zone and enjoyed the finest golden trout fishing of my life. And in 1992 spring runoff was over a month ahead of normal on the westslope cutthroat rivers of Idaho. So I pushed my departure date up to mid-June, before most people had scheduled their vacations, and enjoyed two weeks of superb fishing in solitude on the roadless sections of the St. Joe River and Kelly Creek. I plan and research my backcountry trips in advance, but as a trip approaches I follow snowpack, runoff, and fire conditions, and I'm always prepared to juggle dates or switch destinations.

Horse outfitters throughout the West cater primarily to hunters in fall and to a mixed clientele of families, sightseers, and casual anglers in summer. Llama outfitters also handle a mixed clientele. Experienced outfitters can generally deliver an enjoyable ride through scenic country, a comfortable camp, and good fishing for small to average trout. If you're after exceptional fly angling, however, you want an outfitter experienced at guiding fly fishers on one of the premier backcountry waters. Such outfitters often advertise in fly-fishing magazines. Western fly shops may also be able to suggest qualified outfitters, and state guide associations publish listings of licensed guides and describe their services (state tourism departments usually have these listings).

Many fine backcountry fisheries are not served by outfitters who specialize in fly-fishing trips. If an outfitter isn't going to double as a valuable fishing guide, a drop trip might be your best option. On such a trip, the outfitter hauls your party and gear into the wilderness, drops you off, and rides out with the stock. You camp and fish on your own. At the end of the trip, the outfitter rides back in to pick you up, or you walk out. A drop trip costs only a fraction of a fully outfitted and guided trip yet quickly puts you in very high or remote country. If you choose a drop trip, it's your responsibility to research and select the waters you'll fish.

Float angling is another option. Float anglers have some definite advantages over hikers: They're on the water full-time, and they see the entire river, including heavily timbered areas and canyons tough for backpackers to access. An outfitted and guided river float is an excellent option for families or groups that include nonanglers. Everyone can thrill to the whitewater ride while the anglers get in plenty of fishing.

Outfitting is like every other business—there are both top-flight and fly-by-night operations. Before you hire an outfitter, ask specific questions about the gear and service he'll provide. Know what you're buying. And remember, money won't buy everything. Even if you pay top dollar for a guided trip to excellent water, expect to work at the fishing. Often guides deliver their end of the deal, but clients lack the stamina or angling skill to fish effectively.

Wyoming requires nonresidents to hire a licensed guide in order to hunt big game in a classified wilderness. Fortunately, there's no similar regulation in any state limiting the fishing rights of nonresidents. Except for Indian reservations, the Rocky Mountain backcountry is mostly federal land open to any angler who wants to tackle it on his own. I hope it will always be so. There's something indescribably sweet about great wilderness fishing earned by your own toil and resourcefulness.

CHAPTER 2

Making a Group Trip Click

There are many good reasons to fish the backcountry with family or friends. Shared experiences and memories should be part of every sporting life. But a group trip that isn't carefully planned can quickly disintegrate into a trip you'd rather forget.

I've met dozens of dispirited parties straggling along mountain trails. Some of those groups weren't equipped to handle wet, cold weather, but many others were doomed from the start, because a gung-ho leader had chosen a route too difficult for some members of the party. Whenever a group is composed of hikers of widely varying ability, the route should be geared to the slowest hikers in the group. To push inexperienced hikers beyond their comfortable limits in rough country is to invite dissension. It's also dangerous. Once fatigue sets in, coordination and concentration plummet and a simple misstep can put an entire party in a fix.

With kids, and even with adults who are seeing backcountry for the first time, there's no need to push deep into wilderness. Hiking just a few miles beyond the trailhead is enough to excite the senses and convince everyone that they're really roughing it. Just ease into the country, pitch a comfortable base camp, and save the bulk of your energy for fishing, day hiking, and playing. Kids in particular are more likely to connect with the outdoors if they're allowed to explore at their own pace for at least part of the trip.

My own kids, Dale and Dana, are several years away from buckling on a backpack and hitting the trail with me, but on their baptismal trip

I'll show them some quiet corner of the backcountry that's an easy hike. We'll almost certainly be fishing for small brook trout or pan-size cutthroats, not big golden trout, but when it comes to fishing with kids, action beats size every time. On solo trips I blow by countless waters that are overpopulated with small fish, but these are precisely the waters that kids and inexperienced anglers enjoy the most and learn the most from.

I made my first backpack trip as a teenager with my dad and two younger brothers. We hiked only 20 miles into the Wind River Range, but we were in our own little corner of heaven catching 8-inch brook trout hand over fist from a meadow stream, and stringers of snaky cutthroats from a lake that I now routinely bypass without wetting a line. Just being in the mountains for the first time and fishing those sparkling waters whetted my appetite. Right after that trip I started college and worked straight through the summers. I didn't get back to the mountains for four years, but the summer after I graduated I made a beeline for the Rockies and spent two months hiking alone in the Wind River Range. After that summer I was gut-hooked on fishing the backcountry.

A lot of very good backcountry angling can be reached by round-trip hikes of 20 to 40 miles. Given decent trails and a reasonable pace, most adolescents and adults in fair condition can handle trips of this length. For these middle-distance trips, I prefer to travel with no more than a few partners who are decent hikers, avid anglers, and enjoyable companions. With larger groups every meal and move becomes a major production. Also, big groups—like the scout troop that unwittingly pitched its camp almost on top of mine on the Flat Tops Plateau—shatter the tranquility for other wilderness users. Large groups that have several capable leaders should split into small groups for the benefit of everyone.

Long-distance trekking for trophy trout is, in my view, at most a two-person proposition, and partners should be virtual clones in hiking ability. Some of my favorite high lakes are over 30 tough miles from the nearest trailhead, and just reaching them takes two days of hard hiking. Even if the hiking goes according to schedule, I'm left with only three days for fishing on a weeklong trip. For those three precious, hard-earned days, I haunt the water and barely take time out from fishing to eat. Frankly, anglers who attack the sport at this level will have a tough time finding a truly compatible fishing partner and should consider going solo.

CHAPTER 3

The Joy of Going Solo

Never travel alone—it's a rule found on nearly every list of wilderness dos and don'ts. It's also a rule I violate regularly. Since 1977 I've taken well over a hundred backcountry fishing trips throughout the Rockies, and roughly 80 percent were taken alone. At first I usually traveled alone because none of my buddies were willing to devote an entire summer to hiking and fishing. As I developed into an experienced backcountry angler, I began to prefer traveling solo much of the time. My log shows that of the fifty-nine backcountry trips I've made in the Rockies since 1986, two were with my brother Eric, and the rest were solo.

There are immense practical advantages to traveling alone if you're comfortable doing it. All of the choices are yours. You hike at your own pace. When you're feeling strong, you can step out and really cover some ground. If you want to hike until dark, bolt down a cold supper, and hit the trail again at first light, you just do it.

You plan your own route and go exactly where you please. If you elect to blow by a dozen inviting lakes to invest all of your fishing time in a specific one, you can. If a lake you've targeted doesn't pan out, you're free to explore in any direction you please without consulting a committee. If you choose to ration your food so you can stay in the backcountry an extra day and see a lake you'd otherwise miss, you just tighten your own belt. I did this on one trip and discovered a lake that yielded many of my biggest golden trout on return trips.

When you travel alone, you're free to indulge your own hiking and fishing style, even if it's a tad antisocial. For instance, I often carry dinner in my vest so I can fish right through the prime evening hours without returning to camp to eat. And when I'm alone, I usually dispense with the evening campfire routine. Summer days in the Rockies have sixteen hours of daylight, and after going hard all day I like to hit the hay at dark so I'm ready to roll at sunup.

And when it comes to the fishing, there are definite advantages to chasing trophy trout alone. High-altitude lakes with exceptionally big trout often have very low fish densities, and the best fishing tends to be concentrated in narrow zones. Fishing alone simply gives you more undisturbed cracks at the best water. That may sound selfish, but it's really just sensible. Think about it—you wouldn't bust your tail locating and patterning a big whitetail buck, and then invite a couple of buddies to sit close to your stand where they might spook or intercept him. Well, big trout are as shy and elusive as big bucks—too much commotion puts them on their guard or puts them down entirely.

Ultimately, though, hiking and fishing alone offer much more than practical advantages. Consider the things you go to wilderness to find—independence, self-sufficiency, release from daily routines, the quiet to hear yourself think (or not think), the opportunity to see and absorb wild country. All of these experiences are enhanced by traveling alone.

For me, hiking alone fosters a heightened awareness of my surroundings—just as hiking in grizzly country does. When the big bears are about, their presence colors my perspective, and whether or not I see bears, I look at the land differently. Hiking alone is like that—there's an edge to it that alters how I perceive the country. When I travel alone, the sky is bigger, the peaks are bolder, and the wind howls more forlornly. And much of the time I like it like that.

Of course, backpacking alone in remote country requires constant vigilance. If you mess up and get hurt, there's nobody around to bail you out. But I've never believed that hiking alone is inherently more dangerous than hiking with a group. On the contrary, groups typically include inexperienced or reckless members who are far more likely to encounter serious trouble than a single, skilled hiker is.

The more you travel alone, the more comfortable you'll become doing it. If you travel alone often enough, you'll come to appreciate that it's a uniquely rewarding way to go.

CHAPTER 4

The Extended Summer

Fishing the backcountry can be very time-consuming. Just hiking to and from remote water can chew up the better part of a week. Exploring a single large mountain range with hundreds of lakes and streams can take a lifetime of two-week vacations. To fish extensively throughout the Rocky Mountain backcountry requires a hefty investment of time.

From 1976 to the present I've fished this backcountry for one to three months nearly every summer; I've missed just three years. In my travels and my many talks on fishing the backcountry, I'm frequently asked how I find the time. The question misses the mark. I don't find the time, I make the time.

For a decade after college, I was single and life was simple. I fished all summer, every summer—that was just a given. October through June I sold outdoor sporting goods for a couple of bucks an hour over minimum wage. I did it well enough that my employers usually granted me summer leaves rather than lose me altogether. After I was married, at age thirty-two, I continued to hike and fish extensively. My wife, Dawn, tolerated having a fishing bum for a husband remarkably well, but as I worked my way upward in pay and responsibility, my employers became less flexible. When I was denied unpaid leave one summer, I walked away from my job as head copywriter for a major outdoor sporting catalog. That didn't win me points with many people.

The next few years—as our two young children reach school age and I become firmly established in my self-employment ventures—

won't be the peak of my backcountry fishing career, but I do look forward to hitting the trail again for some extended summers. Of course, everyone has his responsibilities and priorities; still, if you *can* free up a good chunk of summer to hike and fish, do it. The rewards and practical advantages are many.

When you have several weeks, you can start with shorter shakedown cruises. A couple of three- to five-day trips of 20 to 40 miles will toughen you and get you acclimated to hiking at high altitudes. Once you've found your legs and wind, you can tackle the long, tough trips that you couldn't handle comfortably on a two-week vacation. Regardless of your physical condition going in, hiking for an entire summer will leave you leaner and meaner.

An extended summer affords you the leisure to truly explore. When you have only a week to fish, you tend to go where the fishing is a known quantity—probably a place you've already been. But if you'll be taking several hikes, you can gamble a couple of them on exploring new country. If the fishing turns out to be a bust on one trip, you'll make up for it on the others. Over time those exploratory trips will be the ones that turn up hot new waters and expand your backcountry knowledge. Many of my favorite high lakes I initially stumbled upon while exploring. Some are waters I've never read or heard a remarkable word about in my extensive research, and I wouldn't have found them any other way.

Anglers on short vacations must basically choose between the backcountry and the famous roadside waters of the West. On an extended trip, you can fish both. I often recuperate between backcountry trips by treating myself to a few days of fishing on one of the West's premier roadside rivers. Compared with the rigors of backpacking, camping and fishing out of a car is a life of luxury—you can sleep with a real pillow and eat peaches out of 16-ounce cans. Fishing for sophisticated trout on catch-and-release rivers will unquestionably make you a better angler. I've gotten to know rivers, including the Madison, the upper Missouri, the Green, and the San Juan quite well by fishing them repeatedly for short stints between backpacking trips. I can camp cheaply along all of these rivers and fish them effectively on foot, without a guide. Over the years I've found ways to escape the brunt of the crowds even during the summer tourist season. When I've seen enough of other anglers, I'm ready to hit the backcountry again.

Hiking and fishing for a week or two is a nice vacation. But fishing the backcountry for a couple of months is a grand adventure of your own design. Being a fishing bum for the summer might sound as easy as falling out of bed, but creating a big void of free time and then milking it for all it's worth is a challenge. I know anglers who set out to fish the backcountry for a summer but quit after a couple of weeks and haven't tried it again.

When you dream and scheme of a summer in the mountains, you envision endless blue skies wafting over postcard-perfect country, and fish that are built like footballs. But over the long haul, you're going to pay the piper for every peak moment. En route to those 5-pound golden trout, you'll endure lung-busting climbs of better than a mile in elevation, feet beaten to a pulp by rocky terrain, swarms of biting bugs, and every climatic extreme from sweltering heat to stinging sleet. When the fish turn out to be built more like snakes than footballs and a storm front pins you in a tent that's no larger than a coffin for a couple of interminable days, self-doubt has a way of welling up. At some point the country and the weather are going to grind you down and strip away your romanticized notions, and your dream summer is going to become a gut check. You're going to find out whether chucking that job, or that relationship, or whatever to go fishing was such a bright idea. You're going to find out whether you have any real affinity for living in wild country for long stints.

If you hike and fish for an entire summer, there's a good chance you'll do it alone. It's just tough to find a truly compatible partner who's willing to make such a major investment of time. In our hectic world, many people may yearn for a little solitude, but very few actually thrive on long periods of isolation. Being completely alone in big country is intimidating. A week of this kind of solitude is going to satiate most people. To come off an exhausting trip, resupply, and head right back into the mountains alone, again and again, all summer long, takes drive and a little practice.

Going into a summer, I like to plan an itinerary of six to eight trips. Nothing is set in stone, but having a game plan helps me maintain momentum and use my summer efficiently. I do the groundwork for each backcountry trip before I leave home: I research the fisheries, gather maps, and plan my routes. This way, when I come off a trip, tired and sore, the homework for my next journey is already done. I can enjoy a short break, restock my pack, and be ready to ramble.

Rather than spend a whole summer in one region, I like to bounce around. Over a summer I often hit several states and fish everything from gaping river canyons to headwater rivers and lakes above timberline. The variety pulls me through the season in anticipation of that next trip in different and fascinating country.

At some point every successful summer takes on a momentum of its own. Whatever its tribulations, toward the end a summer of fishing the backcountry never seems long enough. Hiking into September lets you savor summer right to its bittersweet end. The biting bugs vanish. The tourists clear out. And by then you're as tough as nails. Just when you start to believe you could drift across the mountains forever, though, the days grow shorter, the aspens light up, and there's ice in your water bottle each morning. One afternoon you find yourself hiking head-down into sheets of wind-driven snowflakes the size of half dollars, and in a palpable instant the summer is over.

Even after it is over, a summer of fishing the backcountry stays with you. There are nearly twenty such summers tucked away in my mind, and each stands out distinctly for the country I covered and the fish I caught. They all came with trade-offs, but there are very few things I would trade a single one of those summers for.

CHAPTER 5

Backpacking Gear for Anglers

To reach out and explore the remote mountains where fast fishing is the rule requires faith in both your abilities and your equipment. When bad weather blows in, good gear allows you to ride it through in relative comfort. Assembling a dependable backpacking outfit means knowing the demands that will be placed on each item, and then selecting gear equal to the task. This chapter is not a complete discussion of backpacking gear; it's simply intended to point you in the right direction as you select major gear items.

BACKPACKS

Backcountry anglers should be able to tote 40- to 60-pound loads efficiently over distances. The key word here is *efficiently*. Many packs have a large capacity, but not all packs allow you to walk in a natural and efficient manner.

Two types of large-capacity packs dominate the market—internal-frames and external-frames. Internal-frame packs are streamlined, close fitting, and somewhat flexible, making them popular with mountain climbers and expedition skiers, who must snug the pack close to the body for control and balance during difficult maneuvers. Despite some very sophisticated harness and suspension systems, though, internal-frame packs bear much of the load on the shoulders. Over long distances, supporting the load with the shoulders tightens the upper body, impedes arm swing, and pitches the torso forward, upsetting the natural, relaxed rhythm of walking. Once you're forced out of your natural stride, your efficiency plummets and fatigue quickly sets in.

External-frame packs have visible frames, usually constructed of welded aluminum tubing. The frame serves as a rigid skeleton that transfers the load to the hips. When properly adjusted, the weight of an external-frame pack is suspended almost entirely from the hip belt; the shoulder straps simply prevent the pack from tipping backward. With the load settled squarely on your hips, you're free to walk in a natural, upright manner. Over a long hike with a heavy load, you can maintain a relaxed posture and efficient stride. I feel that external-frame packs are clearly the best choice for all hiking that does not include technical climbing.

External-frame packs have other advantages. A nylon-mesh back band stretched over the pack frame keeps the pack bag off your back so that air circulates freely and objects within the pack don't dig into you. Most external-frames can be fitted with a top bar—a horizontal frame extension that's handy for lashing on bulky items like a float tube, waders, or a wet tent. A top bar also acts as a power handle for swinging a heavy pack onto your back.

Considering that a pack is shouldered a couple dozen times a day, it's worth learning to do smoothly, yet I see hikers who actually sit down to buckle into the harness, and then stagger to their feet. To get into a heavy pack properly, begin by facing the frame. If you're right-handed, grip the middle of the top bar with your left hand (palm down) and the top of what will be the right shoulder strap with your right hand (palm up). (Left-handers should reverse all these directions.) As you lift and swing the pack toward your right shoulder, maintain both handholds and simply flex your right elbow and shoot it through the shoulder strap. In one smooth motion, you're into the right shoulder strap and the pack is up and under control. Now reach up and grab the top bar with your right hand while you thread your left arm back through the left shoulder strap, just like getting into a coat sleeve. You're into both shoulder straps. To transfer the weight to your hips, shrug your shoulders as you cinch the hip belt. As you relax, the load will settle onto your hips.

A good external-frame pack has an adjustable suspension system. The hip belt and shoulder straps can be raised or lowered, and the back band can be adjusted to conform to your back contours. To fine-tune a pack, load it, carry it, and play with the adjustments until it rides comfortably.

Most external-frame packs have two large main compartments and several side pockets. I pack food in the bottom main compartment and carry bulky equipment, including my tent, clothing, cooking gear, and fishing vest, in the top main compartment. I strap my sleeping bag to the frame below the pack bag. Small items are carried in side pockets for easy access. Some pack bags have ski tunnels behind the side pockets, which also carry fly-rod tubes very nicely. I like a pack bag that offers top access to the main compartment. Camp Trails makes an extendable top-loading bag that completely blocks rain, even when the pack is loaded beyond normal capacity.

Carry a new pack on a few shakedown cruises to look for potential problems. For instance, with the hip belt unbuckled, could the buckle slip completely off the belt strap and be lost? If so, double over and sew the end of the strap to create a lip that the buckle can't bypass. As a pack ages, it should be checked for wear before each trip. Particularly watch for failure where the hip belt connects to the frame—this connection bears the full weight of the load and is susceptible to wear. If stitching, grommets, or belt tabs are tearing loose, replace the hip belt. I typically go through two hip belts during the life of a pack, so I buy a spare one when I purchase the pack. Most pack bags are attached to the frame by metal pins secured with wire split-rings. I wrap each ring with electrical tape so it can't snag on brush or clothing and pull out.

Pack bags are primarily made in dark colors—probably because these hide dirt better. Unfortunately, dark packs also absorb sunlight and heat the pack contents. Given a choice, select a pack in a neutral color. Camo is probably the most readily available neutral pack color in external-frames. Mark a camo pack carefully when you drop it to scout for fish or routes; I once laid a camo pack on the ground while I scouted for a way off a ridge, and I had a tough time finding it again. Prolonged exposure to sunlight weakens pack fabrics and waterproof coatings; in camp I use a light-colored pack cover to shield it from sun and rain.

TENTS

Backpacking tents vary widely in design, yet all good ones meet certain criteria: They're lightweight and easy to erect; they shed precipitation while allowing most respiration vapor to escape; they're self-supporting and stable in the wind.

If you hike alone, a bivy shelter is an attractive option. These are little more than erect sleeping bag covers. At first glance they appear very confining, but because you spend most of your time in a tent lying down, the lack of sitting-up room in a bivy is not a great drawback. Bivy tents are more quickly pitched than any other kind of tent. They hug the ground, so even above timberline they can be pitched in the lee of a rock or other windbreak. Best of all, solo bivies weigh under 3 pounds and pack smaller than a loaf of bread. For most of my solo hiking, I carry a bivy. My favorite is roomy enough at the head that I can prop myself on my elbows to read. This bivy also has a full-length screen on top, and on clear mountain nights, or in arid canyons, I roll back the waterproof fly to reveal the stars or admit a breeze.

Dome tents have captured a large share of the two- and three-person tent market. On the plus side, they're roomy and extremely stable in wind. On the minus, they're relatively heavy and complex to pitch, and they collect more moisture under the fly than other designs.

The standard in two-person backpacking tents has long been the double-ended A-frame design with ridgepole (typified by the Eureka Timberline series). This simple design is quickly pitched, ventilates well, and is fairly light. Some tents are a basic A-frame with a center hoop added to expand and stabilize the sidewalls. This design retains the simplicity, lightness, and breathability of the A-frame yet approaches a dome tent in stability and roominess. My favorite two-person tent is a compact, expedition-grade model built on the A-frame with center hoop design. At just over 5 pounds, it sleeps two adults, yet it's light enough to carry on solo trips when I want more room than a bivy provides.

Beyond the common tent designs, there are some truly innovative options. If you're willing to spend top dollar and research the market, you can take your pick of well-built, lightweight tents. A good rule of thumb is to allow about 3 pounds of tent per person. Groups are better off carrying several small tents than one big model. Small tents handle wind better, and small, level tent sites are much easier to find than large ones.

Among tents with similar designs, you'll see substantial price differences. High-grade anodized aluminum poles drive up the price of a backpacking tent by around $100 but are much lighter than fiberglass poles and much stronger than cheap metal poles. An expedition-grade tent with top-notch poles, materials, and reinforcements at all stress points costs more initially but will be a bargain in the long run. When the jet stream howls across the peaks, you'll be glad you didn't skimp on your tent.

Nearly all poles are now shock-corded to speed assembly. Shock-corded pole sections are also less likely to be misplaced, but it pays to deliberately count and bag your tent poles each time you break camp. If a tent comes with soft, wire stakes, replace them with hardened aluminum stakes that are light and resistant to bending.

Tent fabrics are waterproofed before they're stitched. Unless seams were taped by the manufacturer, though, you need to seal them to plug the holes created by stitching. Seam sealants are prone to drying and peeling; they last longer when applied to inside surfaces.

After extended use, even an expedition-grade tent fly will begin to leak rain through the fabric. Spraying a weathered fly liberally with silicone waterproofing solution will boost water repellency greatly for several weeks.

Many hikers pitch their tents on plastic ground cloths to protect the bottom from dirt, moisture, and abrasion, but I've never bothered with ground tarps and I've never seen significant damage to my tent floors.

In the early morning tents are typically wet from rain or dew. On travel days, when I break camp early, I roll a wet tent loosely and lash it to the top bar of my pack. At my first sunny rest stop, I dry the tent and pack it away.

BOOTS

When I was in college, in the mid-1970s, waffle stompers were the rage in campus footwear. Students were tromping to class in big-time mountaineering boots that had heavy leather uppers, stiff steel shanks, and thick lug soles. Breaking in a pair of these babies was a long-term commitment. I plunked down $200 of busboy earnings for some boots that were still stiff as boards after a winter of everyday wear. I finally got tired of abusing my feet and dumped the boots on a buddy for $25. I think he wore them for drinking beer on Friday nights.

Today backpackers can choose anything from heavy-duty mountaineering boots to ultralight day hikers that are little more than high-top running shoes. For general backpacking I shy away from both extremes. Heavy mountaineering boots are generally too stiff for comfortable hiking, and ultralight hiking boots don't provide enough protection or support. I like medium-weight hiking boots with soles that flex naturally right out of the box. Uppers will break in with wear, but boots with rigid shanks will remain stiff in the soles.

Some medium-weight hiking boots have all-leather uppers, but combination leather-nylon uppers have become more common. Leather-nylon uppers are light and break in quickly, but cactus spines whistle through nylon panels, and nylon can't be sealed with waterproofing waxes. Most good hiking boots now have built-in waterproof, breathable membranes and are totally waterproof when new, but in my experience, waterproof membranes fail from stress long before the boots wear out. Once that happens, all-leather boots can still be waterproofed with wax. Until boots need supplemental waterproofing, go easy on the waxing. Too much wax, especially with natural fats and oils, degrades leather and stitching.

Buy boots that are a bit wide. When backpacking, your feet spread more than normal and will swell significantly over a long day. Thoroughly break in boots before a trip. If your boots are already comfortably broken in, you should still walk in them before a trip to condition your feet.

I wear a single sock rather than a layered-sock system. I like synthetic socks with good moisture-wicking properties and reinforced toes and heels. When I rotate socks, I rinse and thoroughly dry the soiled pair in case I need them later in the trip. I pack four pairs for a weeklong trip.

I carry lightweight sandals and wear them for traction and protection on stream crossings and for limited wet wading. I also wear sandals around camp while my boots are drying or just to give my feet some air.

SLEEPING BAGS AND PADS

In the high country, cold, wet weather can strike at any time. But if you pack a good sleeping bag and keep it dry, you can handle bad weather comfortably, even if you're pinned in your tent for a couple of days.

The warmest, lightest bags have goose down insulation. Even the best synthetic insulations don't equal goose down for loft, warmth-to-weight ratio, and compressibility. A well-designed goose down bag rated to 15 degrees Fahrenheit weighs under 2½ pounds, stuffs compactly, and is tough to beat for June through September in the high Rockies.

A common knock on goose down is that it loses insulating ability when wet. To that I reply, "Don't get it wet." A waterproof stuff sack protects the bag while you hike, and a watertight tent protects it while you camp. In summer, when you get frequent opportunities to dry body-generated moisture from a bag, there's really no excuse for having a wet bag.

Don't confuse prime goose down with inferior waterfowl insulations that contain coarse feathers. Goose down is rated by cubic inches of loft per ounce, and high-quality down bags state the "fill power" of the down utilized. Good bags contain down with a loft of 550 cubic inches per ounce or higher.

Since down is a loose fill rather than a batting, it's prone to shifting. High-quality down bags are built with sophisticated baffle systems to keep the fill evenly distributed and eliminate cold spots. Shaking a down bag after removing it from a stuff sack helps fluff and distribute the down. For long-term storage, a down bag should be hung or loosely folded rather than compressed.

As down becomes soiled, the plumes mat and lose insulating efficiency. Down bags should be washed as needed using warm water, a delicate cycle, and a mild detergent formulated specifically for down. I run the bag through an extra rinse cycle to remove all soap residue. Down bags should be tumbled dry on very low heat or air-dried. Sleeping bare inside a bag when you're working hard and not bathing daily will quickly soil it. To keep a bag clean over an entire summer, I sleep in a clean T-shirt and very light polypropylene long-john bottoms. A good down bag is expensive initially, but with care it will perform well over a decade of frequent use.

Tapered bags are more efficient insulators than rectangular bags, so they dominate the hiking market. Mummy bags are restrictive, though. Most nights I use my bag as a blanket and toss a T-shirt over my head. It has to be cold before I zip the bag, and it has to be really cold before I cinch the hood over my head in true mummy fashion.

A sleeping pad cushions and insulates you from the ground. Closed-cell foam pads are light, inexpensive, and good insulators, but self-inflating sleeping pads such as the Therm-A-Rest are infinitely more comfortable. This brand has an open-cell foam core and an airtight nylon shell. When inflated, the backpacking model is only an inch thick, yet it supports an adult completely off the ground, hip bones and all. A three-quarter-length pad weighs about a pound and rolls compactly for travel.

To round out my sleeping gear, I carry a small, homemade pillow— a block of open-cell foam stuffed into the bottom of an old khaki pant leg, which I can remove for washing.

I pack my sleeping pad, bag, pillow, and rain suit in a single waterproof stuff sack, which I strap to my pack frame below the pack bag. To do this, I roll the pad, insert it in the stuff sack, and bush it out to create a center cavity; there I stuff my bag, my pillow, and finally my rain suit. If it starts raining on the trail, I can grab my suit without opening my pack. If it's raining as I make camp, I throw the stuff sack into my tent and unpack my bedding inside.

RAINWEAR

High mountains create their own weather—much of it bad. Rain, sleet, snow, and gale-force winds can strike at any time. Even a bluebird day can quickly sour. Many times I've departed camp under sunny skies to explore surrounding waters, only to see the weather swiftly deteriorate. Now I seldom wander even a few hundred yards from camp without stashing my rain suit in my fishing vest. As long as I have this suit, I can weather a storm in relative comfort, even if I'm caught several miles from camp.

Waterproof, breathable rainwear has captured much of the hiking market. Most breathable rainwear uses a microporous membrane sandwiched between various materials—often a sheer nylon lining and a polyester-cotton shell. Microporous membranes allow water vapor to escape yet prevent water drops from entering, protecting you from perspiration buildup and external moisture.

I've owned two high-tech breathable rain suits, but in recent years I've returned to well-made polyurethane-coated nylon rainwear. Coated rainwear keeps me absolutely dry even if I'm fishing in driving rain. When hiking in light rain, I vent my coated raincoat by leaving the zipper open and fastening just a couple of the chest snaps. Coated rainwear built with a single layer of nylon fabric is lighter, absorbs less water, and dries faster than most multilayer breathable rainwear. It's much less expensive, too.

In the high country, a rain suit often does double duty as a windbreaker. Layering a raincoat over a down vest or fleece jacket keeps you snug in the coldest mountain weather you're likely to encounter from June through September. When fishing on blustery evenings, I often wear my rain pants to stem heat loss from my legs. Rain suits for angling should be in camo or neutral tones.

HATS

I once spent a week roaming the Wind River Range with a T-shirt wrapped around my head turban-style, after a gust of wind plucked my hat from my head as I was crossing a rushing creek. I didn't fully appreciate the protection that a hat afforded me until then.

A hiking and fishing hat should protect your face, your ears, and the back of your neck from the powerful high-altitude sun. It should have a sturdy brim to shield your eyes from driving rain and to block glare when you're fishing directly into a low sun. A hat also affords protection against biting insects, especially deerflies, which are fond of biting balding humans, like me, squarely atop the head.

For a while I wore a felt hat with a circular brim, but it vented poorly while I was hiking, and I don't like using a chin strap in the wind. Eventually I switched to a saltwater-flats-style fishing cap with an extended bill and a rear flap that shades my neck and ears. Functionally, this cap is pretty close to perfect—it's built of breathable, fast-drying cotton-poly cloth, and the adjustable headband cinches in the wind. In a driving rain, I pull my raincoat hood right over the cap, and the extended brim shields my face. Lately I've been fishing in a baseball-style cap that I've modified to perform like my flats cap by sewing in a lightweight flap that drops to cover my neck and ears. For street wear, or for photos, I tuck the flap up inside the cap. I also sewed a safety cord tipped with an alligator clip to the back of my cap and clip it to my shirt collar so I'll never lose another one.

CLOTHING

High-country anglers must handle a variety of fast-changing weather conditions with only a few pounds of clothing. Garments must perform well when used alone or layered with other clothing.

For comfort and breathability, I like cotton T-shirts. I fish and hike in long-sleeved T-shirts. With the sleeves pushed up, they're as cool as short-sleeved shirts; with the sleeves down, they protect my arms from sun, wind, and bugs. On hot days I wet the sleeves for a cooling effect. On an extended trip I rotate two T-shirts. When one gets sweaty, I rinse and dry it so it's ready for reuse. For sleeping I pack a separate short-sleeved T-shirt. Some hikers like lightweight polypropylene underwear shirts for general wear, but I find them too warm for summer hiking, and when you're sweating, polypropylene gets ripe in a hurry.

When it's too cool or breezy for just a T-shirt, I add a lightweight, long-sleeved flannel shirt. Shirts should have snaps rather than buttons, which tend to snag on pack straps. When it's cold, I add a fleece jacket with a stand-up collar. If it's cold and windy, I add my raincoat as a windbreaker.

For hiking I stick to loose-fitting cotton or cotton-polyester pants. They're lightweight, breathable, fast drying, and nonbinding. Blue jeans fail miserably in all performance categories except durability. I sleep in lightweight polypropylene long-john bottoms. In cold or wet weather, I often wear the polypropylene bottoms under my rain pants. I rarely hike in shorts, although I do pack running shorts for swimming and limited wet wading and for catching a little sun around camp. For week-long trips I take two pairs of hiking pants. Cotton and poplin pants are both prone to splitting, so I reinforce the crotch and seat seams with high-strength thread.

A bandanna serves as a towel, washrag, and pot holder. It keeps the sun and bugs off my neck and cools me in blistering heat. And I've landed some of my biggest backcountry trout with a bandanna wrapped around my palm for a secure grip on the tail.

MISCELLANEOUS GEAR
As a rule of thumb, if you don't use a piece of equipment almost daily, you don't need it. A first-aid kit is the exception. Other than that, purge your pack of gadgets. You'll cut weight and keep your pack organized.

One nonessential I always carry, however, is a book. I usually read myself to sleep, and when bad weather hits, a good book is a welcome companion. For reading in my tent, I wear a headband that holds a small flashlight. It puts light right on the pages and frees my hands for unwrapping root beer barrels.

CHAPTER 6

Eating Simply in the Backcountry

I like to eat as much as the next person, but I trek into the mountains primarily to fish, not to eat, so my eating is tailored around my fishing. In fact, I've developed an alternative style of eating in the backcountry— one that affords me total flexibility and increased fishing time.

My approach to eating in the backcountry has changed over the years. Early in my hiking career, I dined on freeze-dried chicken cacciatore, noodles-in-a-cup, herbal tea, and all the trendy stuff that backpackers eat. But I never became a fan of freeze-dried dinners. They're expensive and consist mainly of processed rice or noodles with a heavy dose of seasoning. For a fraction of the cost, you can get the same nutrition from macaroni, egg noodles, ramen, or white rice, all of which are readily available, even in the small general stores scattered around the West.

And when you get right down to it, instant rice and noodles provide marginal nutrition anyway, especially over an extended summer. Whole-wheat breads and crackers are more nutritious and require no cooking. Once that light went on in my head, my approach to eating in the backcountry changed radically. Since I rarely cooked breakfast or lunch anyway, I concluded that it was foolish to carry several pounds of cooking-related gear just to heat a dinner that was primarily rice or noodles. After a few summers of backpacking, I made a rash decision that I've never regretted—I got rid of my stove and a host of cooking-related items, including fuel bottles, pots, frying pan, spatula, cooking oil, fish batter, dish soap, and dish pad. I began eating whole-wheat bread or crackers with canned fish or meat as my dinner entrée.

Canned meat? Gee, that sounds heavy. Many backpackers think I'm joking when I tell them I pack canned food, but a backpacking dinner menu built around canned protein is fairly light. The canned meats and fish I carry weigh roughly three cans to the pound, including the metal. Seven cans for a weeklong trip weigh just over 2 pounds. Salami and cheese can be used to reduce the number of cans carried. I pack a couple of loaves of whole-grain bread to cover most of my dinners, and whole-wheat crackers for the last couple of nights. My dinner entrées for a week weigh about 5 pounds. That's as light as a freeze-dried dinner menu when the weight of a stove, fuel, and cooking gear are factored in. For many years now, my cook kit has consisted of a fork, a few squares of tinfoil for baking trout, and a GI can opener. That's it.

Whole-grain breads are high in fiber and carbohydrates. My dinners typically include canned salmon, tuna, or chicken and are definitely higher in protein than standard backpacking fare. Over an extended summer, I stay stronger on canned dinners than I do on freeze-dried, and I find canned meals tastier and more satisfying. Various sauces liven up any canned meat or fish. I've been known to visit fast-food restaurants just to stock up on house-brand packaged condiments. Ketchup, mustard, barbecue sauce, soy sauce, taco sauce, horseradish, tartar sauce, jams, honey, salad dressing, and mayo are all available in individual packets.

For ease of preparation, a canned dinner can't be beat—I just break off a hunk of bread and eat my meat or fish right out of the can. I can toss dinner in the back of my fishing vest and eat on the water without returning to camp. That gives me the flexibility to fish right through the prime evening hours, when most anglers are returning to camp to cook. Eliminating the evening cooking ritual pays off with some superb fishing, especially when you're working trophy-trout lakes with low fish densities. I know golden trout lakes that are typically dead on summer days, but as soon as the evening shade hits the water, big fish move onto the shallow feeding flats; you can set your watch by their arrival. A few fleeting hours when the big fish are in range and feeding—that's what all of my planning, travel, and sweat often come down to, and I milk those peak periods for all they're worth. Believe me, the backpacking dinner has yet to be concocted that could make me forsake a crack at a 5-pound golden trout.

Eliminating cooking is also an advantage on travel days. When I'm putting the hammer down to reach remote water, I can hike until last light and then eat a quick dinner. Because I don't need excess water for cooking or cleanup, I can camp wherever darkness overtakes me. Likewise, in bad weather I can eat in a jiffy without having to cook.

My dinners are usually rounded out with a little fresh produce. In the backcountry I get intense cravings for fresh fruits and veggies, and eating some each day supplies valuable vitamins and eases those cravings. I'm not talking about packing watermelons. Plums, nectarines, avocados, carrots, cherry tomatoes, cucumbers, green peppers, and small heads of red cabbage travel well and keep several days without refrigeration. For each trip I toss in a couple of small cans of kidney beans for nights when I'm really hungry—they're tasty right out of the can and are very filling. Dessert is usually nuts or cookies.

Trout are the only food I cook in the backcountry. Most literature cautions backpackers not to depend on fish for food, but a decent angler hiking in almost any of the country covered in this book could rely on fish as a sole source of protein and rarely go hungry. Early in my hiking career, I almost lived on trout. I still enjoy dining on firm trout flesh just minutes removed from pristine water, but these days I eat trout only about once a trip, and then it's usually for lunch on a nontravel day when I'm not losing prime fishing time.

Always study local regulations before killing any fish. Few backcountry lakes have special regulations, but quite a few major backcountry streams and rivers are under catch-and-release or slot-size regulations. These days some anglers attach a stigma to killing any trout, but many backcountry waters have so many fish that eating some benefits the survivors by easing the intense competition for food. On the other hand, I rarely kill a single trout from trophy lakes with low fish densities—here even the small fish are destined to become brutes, and it's vital to let them grow. Trophy lakes often have connecting streams or nearby lakes with smaller fish, and a short foray to neighboring waters usually yields enough trout for a meal.

I prefer eating small or average trout—they're less fatty than the big ones and easier to cook. I love trout fried to a crisp, golden brown, but baked trout are excellent and are healthier fare on a steady basis. Since I quit packing cooking gear, I've baked all my backcountry trout in foil. To prepare them for baking, I gut them, leaving the heads intact; there's just something more regal about a dead trout that's not decapitated. After examining its stomach contents, I toss the remains in deep or moving water away from campsites to erase bear-attracting odors. It's impossible to clean fish away from shore and bury the remains without leaving scent. Fish die in all waters and decompose naturally or are consumed by small organisms, so I don't consider a few fish entrails to be pollution.

If I have good firewood, I burn it down to coals and bake the fish on the glowing embers, flipping them after five minutes of audible sizzling. If wood is scarce, I build a flaming bed of small sticks and set the foil packs directly on the fire. Even above timberline I can usually scrape up enough twigs from beneath dwarfed shrubbery to bake fish.

There's a bit of technique to eating a trout. Start by prying away all fins and their attached bones. Split the skin along the back and peel it completely from the top side of the fish (lightly baked skin is mushy, but well-baked skin can be crisp and delicious). Dust the exposed fish with salt, pepper, and lemon juice; mayo mixed with a few pinches of powdered Gatorade makes an excellent glaze for trout. The tail section is meaty and free of small bones. The chest cavity has small bones extending at right angles from the spine; insert your fork at the lateral line and lift gently to pry away the back meat without disturbing these bones. The thin flesh hugging the rib cage is most easily peeled away with your fingers. After eating the top side of a trout, break the spine just ahead of the tail and slowly lift the entire skeleton. Hold the boned flesh down with your fork as you pull the skeleton forward. The remaining side of fish is boneless.

After a meal of baked trout, I rekindle my fire and burn the heads, skins, and skeletons. I set the cooking foil facedown on the flames and completely burn away any attached skin, flesh, and scent. A hot fire will burn the foil partially away as well. I crush the remaining foil into a ball and pack it out. While I have a fire going, I burn any combustible food wrappers from my pack, and I toss my empty cans into the fire to burn away labels and scent. I flatten the cooled cans and pack them out.

Many wilderness areas are becoming increasingly scarred by fire rings. One advantage of cooking fish in foil is that it can be done on a small fire without building a ring of rocks to support a grate or frying pan. Just scrape or dig a small depression and save the topsoil so you can replace it. Build a fire that's about a foot in diameter. Afterward, scatter the cold embers and replace the topsoil. I like to build no-trace fires if only for the selfish reason that it reduces the chance that other anglers will discover and use my campsites. On very remote trophy-trout lakes that I visit regularly, I can roughly gauge fishing pressure by monitoring the number and condition of fire rings. When new rings appear on certain lakes, I'm concerned, because it takes only a few fish hogs to seriously dent some trophy-fish populations.

When I roll out of the sack on a travel day, I eat breakfast, break camp, and hit the trail within twenty minutes. Breakfast is usually granola bars and a handful of raisins or dried fruit washed down with water. For variety I sometimes substitute Fig or Apple Newtons for the granola bars. Cheese- and fruit-filled croissants hit the spot and pack well for a couple of days. Banana bread or bagels smeared with cream cheese are a fast, hearty trail breakfast. Some cereals, such as Frosted Mini-Wheats, are high in fiber and pretty tasty when eaten dry. Since most backpacking diets are lean in vitamin-rich foods, I take a multiple-vitamin supplement with breakfast.

Summer days are long. To keep my energy level constant, I snack throughout the day rather than eating a big lunch. For snacks I combine quick-energy foods with more complex foods that release energy more slowly.

Dried pears, apricots, bananas, pineapple, and chopped dates are excellent for snacking and are available in most groceries. Dried cherries and cranberries are produced in my home state of Wisconsin, and I buy several pounds of each to see me through a summer. Tomato slices dried in a home dehydrator are very zesty. Cashews and almonds are extremely nutritious and are among my favorite snacks. Various forms of jerky, including individually wrapped kippered beef steaks, are hearty snacks. Cheese is a good source of calcium. Individually sealed sticks of string cheese keep the longest without refrigeration. Tortilla chips are a tasty, lightweight source of carbohydrates; to reduce their bulk, pound on them before transferring them to a plastic bag. I always carry plenty of trail mix made from granola, dried fruit, and nuts.

A word of warning: If you leave reserve food in the trunk of your car, secure it against mice by storing it in an empty cooler. I once returned from a trip to find much of my reserve food in shambles. A pair of baited traps set in my car trunk produced four white-footed mice in under an hour.

Dehydration has a way of sneaking up on you in cool, arid mountain country. It causes general fatigue and cramps, and can be a contributing factor in altitude sickness. When you're hiking, drink at regular intervals, even if you're not thirsty. I down at least a pint of water every one to two hours on the trail, plus a quart at breakfast and another at dinner. Infrequent passage of small amounts of dark urine is a clear sign of dehydration. If you see this, boost your water intake.

Quenching a thirst with cold, sparkling mountain water is one of the simple pleasures of backpacking. I enjoy mountain water so much that I rarely mess with powdered drinks. I do carry some powdered Gatorade to cover up the taste of chemically treated water. (See pages 34–35 for more on water purification.) Tea and coffee are diuretics that can remove more fluid from your system than they replace. Alcohol should play a very limited role in the backcountry, where your safety depends on an alert mind and good coordination.

Backcountry anglers can supplement their diet with a few wild foods other than trout. I know for a fact that in a "survival" situation, spruce, blue, and ruffed grouse can be taken with rocks. On one trip a friend killed and decapitated a 3-foot-long rattlesnake, which made a tasty appetizer, but it would take a big rattler to make a substantial meal, and I don't mess with rattlers of any size.

I'd rather fish than forage for edible (and potentially dangerous) mushrooms, onions, greens, or seeds, but I'm a sucker for a good berry patch. After midsummer huckleberries can abound at elevations to 8,000 feet, and I've seen smatterings at 10,000 feet. Huckleberries grow on low bushes and look much like blueberries but are shinier and have a reddish tint. Fresh, firm huckleberries pop into your mouth and are easily the most delicious berries I've eaten. On lush western slopes in the northern Rockies, I've found them so plentiful that I've filled a quart bag from a few bushes. Remember, though, that where huckleberries abound, bears are probably near as well; I often catch the sweet scent of berries before I spot them, and bears can smell berries from great distances. Stay alert while picking. If a berry patch has fresh bear sign, such as scat or branches stripped of leaves and berries, vacate the premises. (There's more information on bear safety on pages 37–42.)

Red and black raspberries are common along stream corridors at moderate elevations, and I've seen stragglers near timberline. In western Idaho and eastern Oregon I've encountered superb patches of huge black raspberries in river corridors. At lower elevations they often grow around jumbled boulders that are prime rattlesnake habitat, so be careful where you step or reach.

CHAPTER 7

Backcountry Hazards

Every year bad things happen to a tiny percentage of wilderness travelers. Many of those killed or badly injured are involved in high-risk sports such as rock climbing. Most other injuries occur out of inexperience or recklessness, but even a cautious and competent wilderness traveler faces risks. In the backcountry you should be alert to the dangers you're exposed to, and cut your risks as much as possible.

LIGHTNING

Lightning scares me like no other high-country hazard. Mountains generate afternoon thunderstorms almost daily in summer. Anyone who spends much time above timberline will encounter lightning close up and personally. Because anglers carry long rods and travel open shorelines, they're particularly vulnerable. Over the years I've emerged from the backcountry twice to learn that nearby anglers had been killed by lightning.

My closest brush with a bolt came in the San Juans of southwestern Colorado. I was fishing above timberline at well over 11,000 feet on Twin Lakes. The surrounding peaks were nearly 1,000 feet higher, but the basin itself was wide open and not a place I'd choose to weather an electrical storm. Just as I completed a tour around the lakes, I heard the first roll of distant thunder. I promptly headed for my pack; I wanted to descend a few hundred feet into timber before the storm blew in, and it looked like I had plenty of time to do so.

31

I was skirting the base of the small knoll where I'd dropped my pack when a bolt zinged out of the blue. The strobelike flash and deafening crack were simultaneous. My graphite fly rod came alive in my hand. I jumped instinctively and released the rod, but not quickly enough to escape the jolt that traveled up my arm. Then I was back on the ground and taking stock. My first realization was that I was still standing. My second was that I had not taken a direct hit but had absorbed a ground charge. I believe the bolt hit the top of the small knoll, a mere 30 yards away. My rod, carried low to the ground, transmitted the juice up my right arm, which remained numb for about an hour. Eerily, that bolt was the first to strike within several square miles and wasn't followed by another in the vicinity for a half hour.

It's well known that lightning tends to align on the highest object in an area. What's less appreciated is that lightning frequently discharges as clouds roll over ground that's quite low in relation to the surrounding topography. While sitting out storms on passes, I've seen lightning strike well below my position, and many times I've seen lightning strike basin floors that were girded by massive peaks. High-country anglers need to appreciate that standing in a treeless meadow 1,000 feet below the summit of a towering peak leaves you dangerously exposed. If lightning discharges as clouds pass over the meadow, it may very well align on you as the highest point in the vicinity. The neighboring peak affords no protection, because it's outside the immediate area. Always consider your degree of exposure relative to your immediate surroundings.

Fishing often picks up as rain begins, and it can be tempting to fish through lightning, but wading, tubing, or casting from shore during an electrical storm is foolish. Open expanses above timberline and big meadows below it are also dangerous. If you're caught in the open, find a depression in the landscape and sit or squat until the storm passes. Don't seek shelter in the lee of isolated rocks or trees. Aluminum-frame backpacks and all fishing rods should be dropped flat at a distance.

When pitching camp in sunny weather, consider how exposed you'll be to wind and lightning if a storm hits. In open country pitch camp in depressions that can't flash-flood. In timbered country pitch camp in small clearings or under trees of uniform height. Avoid camping within a half dozen lengths of trees that tower over the surroundings.

Daily thunderstorm activity over mountains is fairly predictable. When it's hot in the outlying basins, expect thunderhead formation over the peaks by afternoon. By evening the basins cool and the thunderheads begin to disperse; by the following morning there's often not a wisp of cloud in the sky. You can work around daily storms by crossing passes and exposed areas in the morning. When day hiking out from a base camp to fish or scout outlying waters, it's safer to stay in the same drainage. If you pop over an exposed pass and an electrical storm develops, it could be a long wait until you can return safely.

To estimate your distance in miles from lightning, observe a flash, count the seconds until you hear thunder, and divide by five. If your count is ten, for instance, lightning is only 2 miles away.

If you feel an electrical charge flowing through you—if your scalp tingles or your hair stands on end—you're in immediate danger. Your best bet is drop to the ground or squat to avoid taking a direct hit.

But even then you should remember that energy from a cloud-to-ground lightning stroke surges through the surrounding terrain. If you can limit your contact with the ground to a single point—by squatting on one foot or sitting with your knees pulled to your chest and your feet off the ground—you'll reduce the chance that a ground charge will route through the core of your body. If you're in a tent when lightning is bombarding the immediate area, sit on your air mattress and avoid contact with the ground or tent poles.

Lightning follows some definite patterns. Understanding these patterns and limiting your exposure greatly reduce your chance of being struck, but nobody can anticipate precisely when or where lightning will strike. In this sense traveling the high country where lightning is so common is a bit of a crap shoot. That day in the San Juans, I believed I had plenty of time to clear out ahead of any localized lightning, and I could have easily chosen to cross over that innocent-looking knoll rather than skirting its base. If I had, I might well have become a statistic.

HYPOTHERMIA

Hypothermia is the biggest killer of hikers. When it's wet and windy, hypothermia can occur at temperatures as high as 60 degrees Fahrenheit. Even in summer the mountains produce plenty of wet weather with temperatures near freezing. Everyone who travels the high country should have dependable gear and a strategy for staying dry and warm.

If you get wet or chilled near camp, it's simple to change into dry clothes or dive into a dry tent and sleeping bag. As you range away from camp to fish or explore, however, it becomes more critical that you avoid getting wet or chilled. You may think you're within easy striking distance of camp—but what if you blow a knee? What if fog or darkness delays your return trip? What if you get lost? Can you handle a cold, wet night if you can't get back to your camp? That's what you need to prepare for. Most victims of exposure perish because they become lost or injured and aren't prepared for bad weather.

Mountain weather can change from sunlight to storm in less than an hour, and when you're tucked in a basin, you can't see what's looming behind a ridge. Even when I venture only a few hundred yards from camp, I carry my rain suit so I can stay dry and fish right through an unexpected cloudburst—as long as there's no lightning.

If I depart camp to fish a neighboring lake or distant stretch of river, I also pack a fleece jacket, a water bottle and food, maps and compass, matches, a first-aid kit, a water filter, and two flashlights (by carrying a pair of flashlights with interchangeable parts and batteries, I'm just about guaranteed of having one functioning light). Still, I rarely wander more than 5 miles from camp, and 3 miles is a more comfortable distance.

A drop of just a few degrees in your core body temperature triggers involuntary responses designed to stabilize that core temperature. The first such response is reduced blood flow to your skin and extremities as your circulation concentrates around vital organs; numbness and loss of dexterity in the fingers and toes are symptoms. If reduction of blood flow to the skin fails to boost core temperature, shivering begins—an involuntary exercise that increases metabolic activity. When intense shivering sets in, you should help warm yourself by boosting activity or decreasing exposure. Prolonged shivering signals that your core temperature is still dropping.

As hypothermia sets in, victims have trouble thinking coherently, speaking clearly, and walking without stumbling. As hypothermia advances, victims grow rigid, turn blue, and curl up. By the stumbling stage, a solo hiker is in real trouble and may be incapable of acting to save his own life. If a companion becomes incapacitated, strip his wet clothes and get him into dry clothing. If sleeping bags are at hand, get into a bag with the victim and share your body heat.

WATER PURIFICATION

Sparkling mountain waters may look perfectly safe to drink, but *Giardia* and other parasitic protozoans, flukes, tapeworm eggs, bacteria, and even viruses can inhabit any given gulp of surface water.

Giardia is the most common waterborne threat in North America and is especially prevalent in cool waters. Its cysts are spread between watersheds by beaver and other mammals. A backpacker who drinks untreated water can easily ingest the few cysts needed to contract the disease, known as giardiasis. Once ingested, the cysts attach to the small intestine and begin reproducing. Symptoms usually occur one to three weeks after ingestion; many hikers are out of the mountains when they fall sick. The symptoms can include bloating, gas, abdominal cramps, diarrhea, nausea, vomiting, and headaches. Severe dehydration and weakness can occur. Most victims require medication, and a few need hospitalization.

Water can be rendered free of *Giardia* and most other waterborne pathogens by boiling, chemical treatment, or filtering. Boiling is effective, but it's impractical to boil at frequent intervals or to carry a full day's supply of boiled water. Iodine tablets affect the taste of water, and you should wait at least fifteen to thirty minutes before drinking (the colder the water, the longer your wait). Iodine tablets are also unstable—they should be stored in an airtight bottle and replaced at the first sign of discoloration or deterioration. Only filtering produces cold, clean-tasting water that can be consumed immediately. Because most mountain country is laced with lakes and streams, using a filter usually eliminates the need to pack water.

Filters screen out debris and organisms over a given size. The pear-shaped *Giardia* cyst is roughly 8 by 12 microns, but it's pliable enough to slip through smaller openings. A filter with a pore size of 2 microns is effective in filtering out *Giardia*. Units classified as microfilters generally screen to the 0.2-micron level to eliminate these cysts as well as most bacteria. Units classified as purifiers typically combine microfiltering with an iodine resin (which affects taste) to eliminate virtually all pathogens, including viruses. I pack a microfilter. When I drink from a tail-water river or any other water of dubious quality, I microfilter *and* use iodine tablets. On extended day hikes, I sometimes purify with tablets so I don't have to carry my filter. Iodine tablets also serve as a backup in the event you break, lose, or forget to pack a filter (although I've never had that happen).

For carrying water I reuse clear plastic beverage bottles. They're light, tough, and available to fit any pocket configuration. Beverage bottles don't impart a plastic taste to water, as most canteens do. If a beverage bottle develops deposits from powdered drink mixes or iodine tablets, I just replace it.

HIGH-ALTITUDE SICKNESS

All forms of altitude sickness are caused by lack of oxygen. Oxygen occupies 21 percent of the air by volume at any altitude, but as altitude increases, the density of air (barometric pressure) decreases, so you inhale less oxygen with each breath. The risk of developing altitude sickness is greatest after a rapid ascent to unaccustomed elevations; the problem can strike anyone, regardless of age, physical condition, or experience. Veteran mountain climbers in top condition have been stricken at elevations that they've previously exceeded many times.

There are three types of high-altitude sickness, each with distinct symptoms. Acute mountain sickness (AMS) is the most common and least serious form, and can occur anywhere above 7,000 feet. AMS usually develops within several hours of rapid ascent. Symptoms include headache, nausea, general weakness, shortness of breath, and sometimes vomiting. If you experience several of these symptoms, drink plenty of fluids and reduce strenuous activity until you feel better. If your symptoms don't diminish in one to two days, then it's wise to descend.

High-altitude pulmonary edema (HAPE) is a less common but very serious form of altitude sickness that usually occurs above 10,000 feet. Symptoms include extreme weakness, shortness of breath, and most notably, a persistent cough beginning twelve hours to two days after rapid ascent. HAPE is caused by the buildup of blood serum and fluid in the lungs. By the time congestion is advanced enough to be heard as wheezing or rattled coughing, or to produce pink phlegm, victims are in real trouble and could be too weak to travel within hours. Without rapid descent, increased oxygen, and medical treatment to eliminate fluid from the lungs, victims become increasingly weak, lapse into a coma, and eventually drown in their own fluids. Because HAPE is so debilitating, it's imperative that you descend and seek medical treatment without delay if symptoms develop. In the early stages of HAPE, a descent of a few thousand feet can be very beneficial. Delaying descent for a day to see if a victim's condition improves can be fatal.

Cerebral edema (CE) is less common than HAPE but just as deadly. CE usually occurs above 12,000 feet but can also occur at lower elevations. It's caused by an excessive accumulation of fluid in the brain and usually develops one to three days after rapid ascent or following strenuous exertion at extreme elevations. Depending on the areas of the brain affected, symptoms may include severe headache, double vision, hallucinations, extreme weakness, and stumbling or loss of motor skills. Without rapid descent and medical treatment, victims lapse into a coma and die. Even with medical treatment, many CE victims experience brain damage or recover slowly. You should descend immediately if symptoms occur. As with HAPE, a delay to see if the condition improves can be fatal.

The surest way to prevent altitude sickness is to climb slowly. Some experts recommend allowing a full day for each 1,000-foot increase in elevation above 7,000 feet. That's largely impractical, though, because many routes climb several thousand feet in less than 10 miles. When I hike out of a trailhead that's near or above timberline, I like to camp at a similar elevation the night before I start my trip. This gives my body a night to acclimate before I start working.

Of course, not every headache or bout of fatigue experienced in the mountains signals altitude sickness. Hauling a pack 20 miles over rough terrain will drain even a well-acclimated hiker. During the first few days of a trip, or anytime you really spend yourself at high elevations, some shortness of breath and headaches are to be expected. Just be alert to serious symptoms, and if they occur, descend while you can.

BEARS

At some of my talks on fishing the wild areas of the Rockies, I field as many questions about bears as I do about fishing. Bears, especially grizzlies, inspire fear and paranoia all out of proportion to the number of attacks they make. All bears are powerful and potentially dangerous, but if you follow a few rules, you have little chance of an ugly encounter. In twenty summers of hiking the Rockies, I've never had a bear act aggressively toward me or raid my gear. In fact, most bears I've seen in the backcountry were on the run by the time I spotted them, or fled as soon as they became aware of me. I'm sure that many more bears have smelled or heard me approaching and slipped away unseen.

Black bears range over most of the Rockies; grizzlies primarily roam Yellowstone, Glacier, and the surrounding forestlands. Grizzlies are more powerful and aggressive, but black bears exist in far greater numbers over a broader range, so they raid a lot more camps and actually attack more humans than grizzlies do.

Both species hibernate and have a tremendous drive to eat and store fat during the brief mountain summer. Not surprisingly, bears are the most omnivorous of the large predators, consuming everything from elk calves, spawning cutthroat trout, and carrion to insects, berries, and green grass. This drive to eat gets some bears in trouble. Once a bear overcomes its fear of humans and raids a campsite or eats trash, it's likely to deteriorate into a camp robber or garbage bear.

In national forest and wilderness areas throughout the Rockies, black bears are legally hunted, and that goes a long way toward keeping them honest. A bad bear can turn up anywhere, but I've never seen widespread, systematic camp robbing by black bears in areas with significant hunting pressure. Problem bears are more likely to be encountered in parks that are closed to hunting or on Indian lands that don't have significant hunting in the backcountry. This doesn't mean all refuges are crawling with problem bears. Yellowstone and Glacier hold many black bears plus the bulk of the surviving grizzlies in the lower forty-eight, and the bears in both parks are well managed. Policies include daily hauling of garbage beyond park boundaries, a ban on roadside feeding, strict food-storage rules for all campers, and elimination of persistent problem bears. Backcountry camping in national parks is usually by written permit at designated campsites. Hikers are advised of known bear activity, and areas frequented by grizzlies are periodically closed. When you're hiking in areas that don't require a permit, talk to rangers and scan the bulletin boards at trailheads for reports of bear activity.

Most bear trouble occurs when animals are lured into camp by careless food handling. Cook, eat, and wash dishes well away from camp. Avoid getting cooking odors on your clothes; in bear country you must also break the habit of drying your hands on your clothing after releasing a fish. My no-cook method of backcountry dining eliminates the grease and powerful cooking odors that can attract bears from a distance. All food and garbage should be stored in zippered plastic bags to minimize odors. Don't take snacks into your tent, and remember that nonfood products such as sunscreen and toothpaste may smell like candy to a bear. When you break camp, don't dump cooking grease on the ground or leave partially burned food scraps in a fire ring. Any food or scent you leave behind endangers the campers who'll use the site after you. Besides, you don't want a bear eating your scraps, even after you're long gone, because any taste of human food could lead to trouble for that animal and other hikers.

At night or when leaving camp, hang your food. I carry 50 feet of rope and I usually hang my entire pack. Boat rope slides over limbs without fraying or grabbing, unknots easily, and doesn't absorb water.

Mature grizzlies are not nimble tree climbers, but black bears are skilled climbers and ingenious pack robbers. If a black bear can get a paw on a pack, it will hook the material with its claws and rip the pack open. While in college I worked summers for a canoe outfitter in northern Minnesota, where bear raids on campsites were common, and I saw many food packs that had been disemboweled in this fashion. Designated campsites in national parks often have poles for hanging food; in wilderness areas you generally have to find a suitable tree. Ideally, food should be suspended at least 4 feet below a horizontal tree limb, 4 feet out from the tree trunk, and 10 feet above the ground. In lodgepole forests where there are no sizable horizontal limbs, I often hang my pack from a "leaner"—an uprooted tree supported by standing trees at about a 45-degree angle.

Above timberline you'll have to leave your pack on the ground, unless a bear pole has been provided. There's not much natural forage for bears above timberline, so few of them hang out this high for long; still, they do ramble through. Whenever I leave my pack on the ground or hang it in a vulnerable position, I knot a sweaty T-shirt or a pair of ripe hiking socks to it on the theory that a strong dose of human scent should deter an honest bear.

When bears smell food, they normally approach from downwind to investigate. When possible, store food and cook downwind of your tent site so that an approaching bear doesn't have to go right past you to reach your food. From evening through early morning, when bears are most active, sinking thermals carry scent downhill, so sleep uphill from your food cache when you can. Avoid camping directly on riverbanks, lakeshores, and game trails—all are natural travel corridors for bears. Don't camp near obvious bear food sources such as animal carcasses or berry patches.

I like to store my pack away from camp, but not so far away that it's disassociated with human scents and sounds; 30 to 60 yards is a comfortable distance. I hang a bell from my pack to alert me if a bear bothers it. To prevent the bell from swinging in the wind and sounding false alarms, I snug it to the pack so that it takes a real jolt to ring it.

Most confrontations outside of camp occur when bears are surprised by humans at close range. Bears have excellent noses, good hearing, and better eyesight than is commonly believed, and they'll normally detect people and clear out in advance. But in high winds, along noisy rivers, or in dense cover, a bear could have trouble detecting your approach. To decrease your chances of surprising one, talk or hang a loud bell from your pack, and make extra noise when passing through dense willows. Don't mess with the little tinkle bells commonly sold as bear bells. Get a real noisemaker. My bear bell is a baseball-size jingle bell from a sleigh harness; when I want it to really sing, I rig it to bounce against my thigh or pack with every stride. (A ranger in Glacier once told me it was by far the loudest bear bell she'd ever heard.) Finally, don't hike after dark, when bears are most active. In grizzly country I make it a point to be near my camp by dark.

As you travel, be on the lookout for an abundance of fresh tracks and scat, which indicate heavy bear use of an area. If you spot or smell an animal carcass, give it a wide berth; bears have likely found the carcass before you and may defend it. If you spot a bear feeding along your route, skirt it widely and upwind, if terrain permits. If a bear is heading toward you but is unaware of you, speak to it in a normal voice. Every unaware bear I've talked to has fled immediately.

If a surprised bear charges, your response may influence the outcome. According to researchers who have studied bear body language, an animal that huffs and charges with its head high and its hair flared is probably bluffing; it will likely stop short of attacking if you don't run. Raising your arms and shouting may back it down. Bears, especially grizzlies, are swift runners capable of staying with deer and elk for short bursts. I've watched an adult grizzly run flat out, and it's an impressive sight. Running from a charging bear is futile and may inspire an animal that's just bluffing to press an attack.

If a bear charges with its head low and its ears laid back, it will probably keep coming. If you're unarmed and caught in the open, experts say your best bet is to hit the dirt and curl up; clench your hands over the back of your neck and your arms tightly around your face and head to minimize serious injuries during a short attack. A surprised bear that elects to run over you may be bent primarily on escape; if you drop to the ground in a submissive posture, it may cuff or chomp you only briefly before fleeing. Charging bears have sometimes completely bypassed people in the fetal position.

Some of the fatal maulings in the Rockies in recent years have occurred at night; the victims were attacked in their sleep, dragged from their tents, and partially eaten. This is pretty clear evidence that grizzlies, in particular, do occasionally prey on people. In such a scenario, a bear is unlikely to break off its attack quickly. During prolonged attacks, some victims have survived by playing dead. I'd defend myself if I had the option.

There are differing views on whether backpackers should carry guns. In the national parks, firearms are prohibited, so in most of the prime grizzly country in the Rockies, carrying a gun is not an option. Non-Indians also can't carry guns on some Indian reservations. Guns are allowed on most national forest lands. I carry a handgun in prime grizzly country outside the parks; otherwise, I'm not willing to lug nearly 5 pounds of revolver, holster, and ammo. As a hunter, I'm pretty experienced with long guns, but I'm not confident that I could KO an enraged bear with a handgun, in a melee, in the dark. Even the big magnum handguns have less power than rifles considered too light for grizzlies, and handguns are less accurate. In Alaska, where anglers regularly fish in proximity to brown bears, the guides carry high-powered rifles or shotguns loaded with slugs (that says a lot about where handguns rate as grizzly medicine). If you do carry a handgun, handle it safely and use it on a bear only as a last resort. Don't use a gun as a license to run a messy camp, and don't annoy or alarm other hikers by target shooting in the backcountry.

Pepper spray is lightweight, affordable, simple to use, and can be carried in the national parks—factors that make it popular with backpackers. Research and field incidents have shown that pepper spray is a fast-acting, effective deterrent if a bear is hit directly in the face with a heavy blast.

Bear repellents contain about 10 percent oleoresin capsicum (red pepper) and are sold in pressurized cans that operate like small fire extinguishers. Most repellents include a belt holster for keeping the spray handy at all times; this is important, because most bear attacks happen with little warning. A 10-ounce can typically delivers six one-second bursts with an effective range of about 25 feet. The spray is delivered in a shotgunlike fog rather than a stream. A coloring agent lets you see where the repellent hits. When I began packing bear spray, I burned up a $50 can test-firing on trees and was impressed with the range, coverage, and accuracy of my blasts. I now pack spray on every trip, and I buy a fresh can every few years (use your old one for target practice).

Knowing that grizzlies are prowling the landscape can make it difficult to sleep, but seeing a grizzly in the backcountry, especially in the lower forty-eight, where only several hundred survive, is more likely to be a thrill than a nightmare. I saw my first grizzly in the Teton Wilderness south of Yellowstone Park in my second summer of hiking. I was camped alone on a grassy ridge with scattered stands of lodgepole pine. While tending a small fire on a misty evening, I glanced up and saw a large, brown bear angling toward me at less than 100 yards. I'd seen black bears before, and I knew at a glance that this wasn't one. This was a big, mature grizzly, probably a boar, that walked with an awesome rippling of his shoulders. I spoke to let him know I was there, and he bolted for the timber. It was a treat to watch that bear run—the bulging power, the improbable grace, the unexpected speed. His neck whipped to and fro as he fled. His great head swiveled in a frenzy, trying to pinpoint me. Then he was simply gone back into the timber.

As fleeting as our encounter was, that bear will always be with me. When I haven't been in the mountains for a while, I sometimes see that grizzly barreling across that misty ridge. Two decades of roaming the Rockies have not produced a more indelible image.

SNAKES

The vast majority of hikers struck by rattlesnakes are hit below the knee. That makes guarding against snakebite pretty straightforward: Wear snake protection to the knee, be careful where you put your hands, and don't fool around with snakes. Even experts eventually get nailed while handling them.

Leather or thick Cordura hiking boots will protect your feet. My snake leggings are double-layered 1,000-denier Cordura nylon. I made them by cutting a pair of heavy-duty bird-hunting chaps at the knees. The leggings are baggy and open at the top so air circulates freely, and they ride down over my boot tops by their own weight.

Western diamondbacks are found throughout the West, particularly in the hot, arid low elevations. Most of the rattlers I've seen while fishing the backcountry have been in the river canyons of Idaho, but they also inhabit the foothills abutting most mountain ranges.

A snake lying in direct sunlight on a hot day would quickly stew in its own juices. When the sun is high and hot, rattlesnakes retreat to the shade of rocks and brush, and then emerge to hunt mice and other small rodents in the cooler hours or at night. In snake country, however, you can bump into a rattler anytime. In Hells Canyon on a sunny afternoon that was well over 100 degrees Fahrenheit, I came within a stride of stepping on a thick diamondback coiled on the trail in the shade of a small bush. That's as close as I've come to field-testing my snake leggings.

Snakes can't hear airborne sounds, but they can detect minute vibrations and usually seek cover as a large animal approaches. Some snakes hold their ground, however, and most rattlesnakes don't rattle before striking. The striking range of a coiled rattler is about half its body length. Diamondbacks can exceed 6 feet in length, although most are less than a yard.

In the United States, few snakebites are fatal, because most victims reach hospitals quickly. But in the backcountry, where treatment is a long way off, prevention is definitely the best policy.

AVOIDING INJURY

I'm fortunate enough that in twenty summers of backpacking the Rockies, I've never blown a knee or busted a leg. With all the boulder fields, downed timber, and rotting snow I've scrambled over, there have been plenty of chances. If my wheels had come off in a remote spot, it would have been a while before anyone came looking. For the first ten summers I fished the backcountry, I hitchhiked all over the Rockies, and often nobody knew what state I was in, much less my hiking itinerary.

To be sure, I've taken my share of tumbles. Anyone who totes a heavy pack over rough terrain and who fishes wet, rocky shorelines is going to go down. It's a matter of when, not if. And when you do fall, it's likely to be on rocks, slopes, or other nasty terrain, with the added weight of a pack driving you down. The key to avoiding injury, then, lies in controlling a fall. This might sound like a contradiction, but how you fall makes a difference.

Above all, stay relaxed. A relaxed body reacts faster and is much more supple than a tense one. Extending a stiff arm or leg to break a fall is the quickest way to snap a bone. If you're going down, do what you can to protect yourself and then ride it out as relaxed as possible.

In a fall a backpack can act as added weight that drives you down or as a big cushion to fall on. As you fall you can often twist around or sit back so that you land on your pack; just be sure your feet aren't wedged before you make any sharp twists.

Arm swing plays a big part in maintaining balance. I backpack with my hands empty so my arms are free to grab for support or to counteract a stumble before it turns into a fall. When carrying my pack, I keep my rods packed away even if I'm making frequent stops to fish. Trying to snake a fly rod through timber takes my attention away from my footing, where it should be.

Hiking above timberline presents plenty of opportunities to boulder-hop. Many off-trail passes have a nice, grassy slope on one side and a junkyard of watermelon- to car-size boulders on the other. Lakes tucked in cirques usually have some jumbled shoreline. Boulder fields are intimidating, but crossing them can be safe and easy. Pick a route with a gradual contour so you can hop between rocks with only slight vertical differences. With practice you'll get into a rhythm and zigzag across boulder fields while making good time. Watch for flat rocks, though—they're prone to tipping under your weight. If you start to lose your balance on rocks or while crossing a log, squat to lower your center of gravity and bring your weight under control.

Steep downhill hiking with a heavy pack is a tremendous strain on the knees. You have to brake with every stride to check your momentum. On a long grade, your knees can fade and buckle. Downhill falls are particularly dangerous, because they're often headfirst with lots of momentum. When hiking down steep, off-trail slopes, be patient. Cut your stride length. Look at the lay of the land and switchback down in a serpentine course that follows the easiest contours. On slopes that are littered with loose talus, keep your weight back so that you can sit right down if your feet shoot out. When I'm in good condition, my ascent time on a long, steep grade is often faster than my descent time. Going up, you can attack a slope; coming down, you need to stay under control.

In rough country it's easy to plant a foot wrong and turn an ankle. As you feel an ankle begin to roll, you can avoid a sprain or ligament damage by buckling your knee instantly to relieve weight on your ankle while you transfer your weight to your other foot. This reaction can be honed with a little practice at walking speed. I've rolled my ankles many times in the mountains without injury.

If you do strain, sprain, or twist something, ice it in cold mountain water to limit the swelling (after a long day of hiking, I routinely ice my feet anyway). On the South Fork of the Flathead, deep in the Bob Marshall Wilderness, I once had an Achilles tendon tighten so badly that I was reduced to hobbling. A day of rest in camp did nothing to improve it. The next day I limped out from camp to fish and see if the tendon would loosen up. Things were looking grim until I happened on a sandy slough of tepid water cut off from the river by an exposed gravel bar. I pulled off my boots and waded slowly up and down the slough, and I was amazed how quickly and completely my tendon relaxed. After several sessions of wet wading, I had very little tightness, and the next day I carried my pack with no problems.

Speaking of wet wading, nobody likes to hike in wet boots, but on swift, rocky stream crossings, I wear my hiking boots to protect my feet against cuts and bruises and to decrease the chances that I'll stumble and fall. After crossing I wear my wet socks and remove them periodically for wringing. When my boots are sponged fairly dry, I put on dry socks.

Frozen water presents its own problems. Some years heavy snowpack hangs on in the high country into July. Hiking over deep, rotten snow is tiring and tricky. At times you bust through on every step, and covering even a couple hundred yards is an ordeal. Other times you skim over the top for long stretches, then bust through unexpectedly. One leg may punch through right to the hip, or you may bust through pack and all. Busting through is always dangerous, because your feet, shins, and knees careen off buried rocks and splay or wedge in awkward positions. As you punch through, stay relaxed and flexible so that you can adjust to any rocks you strike. When crossing snowfields, swing wide of rocks that project above the snow—they absorb sunlight and transfer heat under the snow to create hidden cavities.

Strangely, the worst fall I've taken in the mountains happened while I was releasing a small trout on the Middle Fork of the Salmon. It was raining and the shoreline rocks were slick. As I bent to slip a hand under the trout, my feet splayed outward, like a giraffe on glare ice. I went down hard on the jagged rocks. Just before my head hit, I managed to twist my face to the side and shoot a palm under my chest to partially break my fall. Then my skull erupted with a loud ringing. I scrambled to my feet, dazed, dripping wet, and cussing at myself. My right temple throbbed and was sticky with blood where I'd struck a pointed rock. The simple act of releasing a fish had nearly left me unconscious and facedown in the river. That incident taught me to be alert to subtle dangers. Even a little slip can have big consequences.

Unless you have strong, stable legs, hiking into remote country, especially alone, is a risky proposition. If you value your ability to tackle tough country, then avoid risky sports, like downhill skiing, which invite nasty knee injuries. A couple of friends have tried to talk me into downhill skiing, and both times it was a pretty short conversation.

SUNBURN

The hazards of long-term sun exposure have been well publicized. Just be aware that it takes less time to sunburn at high altitudes, and that anglers take an extra dose of sun reflecting off water. The best policy is to wear protective clothing and apply sunscreen to your face, the backs of your hands, and other exposed skin. When I hike for several weeks, I usually grow a beard to help protect my face. Shaving in the backcountry isn't worth the bother, and if I'm going a week or more between shaves, I'd just as soon grow a beard and get beyond that itchy stage.

Like everyone else, I've taken more sun than I should on occasion. I can vouch that toting a pack on a sunburned back or plowing through dense willows with broasted thighs is no picnic. Sun doesn't just burn—it also saps you of energy. Backpacking for long stints while clad in nothing but shorts leaves me totally drained, and I doubt that heavy sun exposure enhances anyone's hiking ability.

INSECTS

Mosquitoes usually boom in the first half of the short mountain summer. The best lake country is often pocked with shallow potholes and wet meadows that serve as mosquito factories. At times there's just no escaping the buggers—I've been swarmed atop windy passes at over 11,000 feet.

Mosquito-borne diseases are relatively rare in the Rockies, so the bugs are primarily a nuisance. When they're tormenting me, I wear as much protective clothing as I can tolerate and apply repellent to exposed skin. Be careful how you handle repellents—they're death on synthetics, including fly lines and rain suits. Ultrathon, a repellent lotion made by 3M, is not as messy as liquids to handle and doesn't leak from the tube.

Head nets are an alternative to repellents. Commercial head nets are usually made of very fine mesh to screen out biting gnats. Such nets are invariably stuffy and restrict visibility. I replaced the face panel on mine with a piece of white wedding veil, which blocks mosquitoes while allowing improved airflow and visibility.

Biting gnats are less common than mosquitoes, but they can be bad on streams or lakes, even at extreme elevations. Unlike mosquitoes, which are most active in the evening, gnats are invigorated by sun. Gnats pack a mean bite and are fond of biting around the mouth, nose, and ears. Tucking pant legs into the tops of hiking socks prevents gnats from gnawing on shins. Mosquito dope doesn't work on gnats, but vanilla extract smeared on exposed skin repels some species remarkably well.

Deerflies are most common along meadow streams at modest elevations. Like gnats, they're energized by sun. I haven't found an effective repellent. Deerflies will follow and torment a hiker for a considerable distance, so I actively ambush pesky individuals. Deerflies like to land on the highest available skin, and I take advantage of this habit with a little trick: I hold my left hand overhead, and when they land on it, I cuff them with a quick right. In bright sun you can see the shadow of a deerfly and kill it the instant it lands.

Horseflies behave much like deerflies but are bigger and tend to bite lower. I've had horseflies bloody my shoulders by biting right through T-shirts. They're relatively easy to kill if you know they've landed, but they tend to zip directly in and start cutting. Once, while crossing a meadow in the Teton Wilderness, I was nailing horseflies left and right when a cowbird winged in behind me and started gobbling the bugs as fast as I killed them. When I stopped at a stream crossing for lunch, the bird hopped up on one of my boots and took a horsefly right from my fingertips. So at least somebody out there loves horseflies.

Ticks spread several diseases, which are treatable with antibiotics if diagnosed early. The most common serious tick disease, Lyme, is not prevalent in the Rockies. Rocky Mountain spotted fever and relapsing fever do occur, however. I pick up many ticks while hunting in Wisconsin, which is a hotbed of Lyme disease, so I check myself pretty religiously. In the Rockies I've found only a few ticks hitching a ride. I can detect these bugs walking on my skin. When I feel that slight sensation, I always check it out, and usually there's a tick looking for a place to burrow. Tick-removal kits come with instructions for removing attached ticks correctly—without squeezing.

A severe allergic reaction to an insect bite or sting would be big trouble in the backcountry. If you've ever had such a reaction, talk to your doctor about prescription medications that you can pack for emergency use.

Speaking of things that sting, I bumped into the mother lode of bees along the Selway River in Idaho; several big meadows were riddled with holes in the ground, and bees were streaming out of the earth by the tens of thousands. Walking through those immense swarms was a little unnerving.

And speaking of unnerving, have I mentioned the scorpion I almost sat on in Utah, or the huge, hairy spider that popped out of my pack in Colorado? Look alive out there.

CHAPTER 8

Backpacking Conditioning

I hitchhiked south out of Dubois, Wyoming, early that August morning, heading for the Glacier Trailhead a dozen miles from town. From there I'd hike a serpentine route of better than 100 miles before exiting at Pinedale on the opposite side of the Wind River Range. En route I'd fish some of my favorite golden trout lakes, ford glacial streams, scale off-trail passes, and explore the remote Brown Cliffs region, where few people ventured.

I hoped to reach the trailhead quickly that morning. The Glacier Trail climbs nearly 4,000 feet in its first 7 miles, and I wanted to tackle the climb while I was fresh. I caught a short ride with a local rancher, who dropped me on the highway where a rocky road veered into Whiskey Basin. The dirt track wound through parched grasslands that served as wintering range for bighorn sheep and past a series of sage-bordered lakes before terminating at the trailhead some 8 miles distant. With luck I'd catch a ride from another hiker driving to the trailhead.

I'd just started walking when I heard an engine and turned to see a van bouncing toward me. As the vehicle neared, I saw it was loaded with teenage boys and backpacks—a scout troop or church group, probably. I stuck out my thumb with confidence. The situation was pretty obvious. I was a backpacker. They were backpackers. This was a dead-end road. We were all going to the same trailhead. As the van bounced by, the driver nodded and the boys laughed and waved. But the van kept rolling.

That was it. No more vehicles drove up the road that morning.

It was pushing noon and 90 degrees Fahrenheit by the time I reached the trailhead. I was a little irritated to see the van parked right where I'd expected and caked with dust, except where someone had scrawled GANNETT OR BUST! on a back window. That caught my eye because it told me the troop was on my route.

I put the hammer down on the trail, and the troop came back to me quickly. I caught them only 4 miles up, shortly after the trail broke out of the timber. They were strung out and blowing hard; even the front runners were climbing at a snail's pace. I skipped on by, smiling broadly, commenting on the bluebird weather, and showing them what my rear end looked like going over the horizon. By evening I was camped 20 miles beyond the trailhead in a sandy meadow just a few miles below Gannett Peak, and in excellent position to reach a terrific golden trout lake, another 15 miles distant, by the following afternoon.

Average hikers can reach a lot of fine backcountry fishing. But strong hikers can explore far more territory or blow deep into the mountains to waters that see only a handful of anglers each season—and they can get there quickly with plenty of time and energy to fish. If you can haul a 50-pound pack 35 miles in two days over rugged terrain at high elevations and still feel fairly chipper, you can effectively fish any backcountry water in the Rockies that you set your sights on.

Several elements go into making a strong backpacker. Conditioning is important, but it's not everything. I've seen plenty of people with good muscle tone who were not good hikers. Endurance, body type, and hiking experience enter into the mix, too. As we age, each of us inevitably deals with changes in weight and fitness.

When I delved into backpack fishing right out of college, in 1977, I was a lanky 6 feet tall and 170 pounds with a background in distance running. As a high school sophomore, without any training under my belt, I ran varsity on the state-champion cross-country team. In my last two years of cross country, I finished second and fifth in the conference, so I had some natural stamina that running enhanced.

In my first five summers of hiking, I put on 15 pounds, mostly in my legs. In those years I was touring the West on $500 a summer, hitchhiking between mountain ranges. I walked between rides, so when I wasn't hiking in the mountains, I was usually hoofing across some sweltering basin. Those summers of toting a heavy pack every day built up my legs and made me a much more powerful backpacker. They also taught me that piling up a lot of miles in a day is a matter of hitting your cruising speed early on and sticking to it long after your feet are pounded. No matter how many miles you have in your legs, as you push past the 20-mile mark under a heavy pack, your dogs are going to be howling.

In my midthirties I'd come off a summer of hiking at about 190 pounds. Being fairly big has advantages. A 60-pound pack loaded with food for a lengthy trip is less than a third of my legitimate body weight, which is still a comfortable ratio. A 45-pound pack depleted of food is a light load. Being big in the legs provides more power going uphill and more control coming down. And over an extended summer, I always feel my legs getting stronger rather than wearing down. One of the big allures of backpacking is reaching the point where your legs are firing like pistons and you can charge up a 1,500-foot slope without taking a breather. When the pack feels like part of your body and you just eat up the miles, hiking is as rhythmic and as enjoyable as fly casting. That's when you feel like you really belong in the mountains.

These days, as I approach forty-five, my cruising speed has dropped a notch and my weight tends to drift higher than I like in the off season, but I still get where I want to go. Now I'll come off a month or more of hiking at about 195 pounds. At this weight I'm nearly the hiker I was at thirty, and I can still put in a 20-mile day without crippling myself.

For conditioning I run outdoors for a half hour about three times a week from March through October. From April through September, I bike 30 to 60 miles a week when I'm not hiking. I hunt a day or two a week from October through February, so I walk quite a bit over hills, thick cover, and snow. In spring I carry my pack for a couple of half-day hikes to get the feel of it again. In the month leading up to a backpack trip, I carry my pack a couple of times a week for at least an hour. That's not the training regimen of a triathlete, but it keeps my legs and wind in decent shape for backpacking.

I once hiked 145 miles through the Salmon River country on my first trip of the summer. Those days are gone. Now I take a shakedown cruise of around 30 miles over about four days to toughen my feet, shed a few pounds, work through any initial soreness, and acclimate to high altitude. Then I'm ready for a more ambitious trip. As you hit middle age, the shakedown cruise should be part of your hiking strategy, and it's not a bad idea for younger hikers as well.

In some ways backpacking is for the young. If you set up a check-point 20 miles from any trailhead in the Rockies, 90 percent of the hikers passing through would probably be under forty. Still, this doesn't mean you can't backpack effectively beyond middle age. I've hiked with two men in their midfifties who led fairly sedentary lives, and both were able to backpack 50 miles in a week and still enjoy the fishing. If you pick your destinations carefully, you can find some fine angling less than 10 miles into the backcountry, and I hope to have that much hiking range when I'm seventy. By then some of the trout I released last summer should be dandies.

PART TWO
Research and Planning

CHAPTER 9

Researching Backcountry Fisheries

In my early summers of fishing the backcountry, when I had time and energy to burn, I'd often just pick an area, lace on my hiking boots, and visit dozens of lakes and streams on foot. I thought nothing of hiking 100 miles in a week and scouting several waters a day. I found a lot of decent waters and stumbled onto some gems this way, but few anglers have the time or inclination to scout vast areas on foot.

These days I do most of my scouting by phone, by mail, and by reading every scrap of information I can unearth. Information on backcountry waters tends to be sketchy and scattered, but if you're inquisitive and resourceful, you can identify promising waters through research.

BUILDING A MAP COLLECTION
Building an extensive map collection goes hand in hand with researching backcountry fisheries. In fact, collecting and studying maps will alert you to the existence of scores of wilderness waters and pique your curiosity about them. Even if I don't plan to fish an area in the near future, I like to obtain and study maps to get a feel for the spot's size and ruggedness and how its waters are distributed. As I contact fisheries managers or other information sources, having a map in hand also helps me ask pertinent questions and pinpoint any waters they suggest. For information on obtaining maps, see Resources, page 293.

Topographic Maps

The United States Geological Survey publishes detailed topographic maps of nearly all areas in the Rockies. A few recreational map publishers also offer topographic maps of various national parks and wilderness areas. Topographic maps are a huge advantage for cross-country travel. They let you determine the easiest approach to off-trail waters, and they reveal shortcuts between trails and drainages. As you work with topo maps and compare them with actual terrain, you'll learn to predict pretty reliably, just by looking at a map, whether a steep slope can be negotiated without climbing equipment. As you learn to spot places on topos where you can cross a divide or get on or off a ridge, you'll be able to trim significant mileage between many points by abandoning established trails. Keep in mind, however, that though a topo map shows the gradient of a slope, it doesn't show what's on the ground. A slope above timberline could be covered with grass, boulders, or loose scree. A timbered slope could support anything from clean lodgepole forest to a maze of blowdowns.

Given a topo map, it would be difficult to stay lost for long in the mountains. Prominent landmarks can easily be matched to the map. Most mountain lakes are small enough that from above you can see their precise shape and position in relation to other lakes. Many peaks and walls are also distinctively shaped.

Topo maps also show the magnetic declination for an area—the difference between true north and magnetic north on a compass. In much of the Rockies, this difference is around 15 degrees and is worth taking into account, especially when timber or low clouds restrict visibility and force you to follow a compass bearing.

National Forest Maps

A national forest visitor map shows you an overview of an entire forest. Though these maps usually lack sufficient detail for cross-country navigation, they do give you the big picture at a glance, and that's equally valuable in your route planning. On trips I always carry a forest map, even if I also have topo maps of my planned route. Plans can change in midtrip; if I decide to explore additional waters or exit by an unplanned route, the forest map becomes my primary map. Some forest maps also cover parts or all of adjacent national monuments and recreation areas.

National Park Maps

Topographic maps of national parks in the Rockies are published by the United States Geological Survey and by private recreational map companies. Parks usually sell these maps by mail; contact the park superintendent for a map order form. While you're at it, you can also request an order form for books pertaining to the park, such as hiking, fishing, historical, and nature guidebooks. Also ask for current fishing and backcountry camping regulations.

PUBLIC INFORMATION

Take a four-color map of the Beartooths, the Bitterroots, the Winds, or another major range in the Rockies and spread it out. What do you see? Well, if you're an angler, your eyes will naturally gravitate to the mosaic of blue lakes and streams that dot and crisscross the high country like raindrops and rivulets on a windshield. Big ranges have hundreds of trout waters spread over hundreds of square miles. So how do you begin to decipher which of those blue splotches have the best fishing?

Forest Service

As you begin researching any area, you'll need forest service maps. While rounding them up, also ask the forest service offices for any available information on backcountry fisheries. In national forests, it's state wildlife agencies, not the forest service, that are primarily responsible for fish management, so the forest service often provides only very generalized information about fishing. Still, it sometimes has a listing of lakes and streams with the species of trout found in each and, occasionally, information on fish sizes for specific waters. As I discuss destinations in the second section of this book, I'll mention some worthwhile forest service fishery publications.

Fisheries Supervisors

The most specific public information about backcountry angling comes from state fisheries supervisors. The wildlife department of any or all Rocky Mountain states can tell you how to contact each area fisheries supervisor (state headquarters are listed in Resources). At the same time, request a copy of the state fishing regulations so you'll be familiar with special regulations and nonresident licensing options.

Most western states have only six to eight fisheries supervisors, who oversee fish management on all waters in and out of the backcountry. Roadside waters generate most license revenue and naturally receive more attention than backcountry waters. If a supervisor is fairly new to his region, he may know little about its wilderness waters. On the other hand, if he's been stationed there for years, he may have a handle on the productivity of many waters.

How you approach fisheries personnel makes a difference. They get lots of inquiries about wilderness waters from anglers of all stripes, and most ask the same question: "Where can I catch the big one?" Many fisheries managers are reluctant to "hot-spot" big-fish waters, because they don't want to concentrate fishing pressure, especially on small lakes that are easily overfished. If you tell a manager that you're a catch-and-release fly fisher and that you travel alone or in a small party, he might put you onto a lake he doesn't mention to everyone. But in general, bluntly asking where you can catch the big one is a real conversation killer. As someone who speaks and writes about the backcountry, I get this type of question a lot myself, and it always leaves me a little cold, especially if I suspect that an angler has done zero research on his own and is trying to use me as a one-stop information source.

Fish managers are more approachable if you demonstrate some knowledge of the country and engage them in conversation. Often I tell a manager about some of the places I've fished and what I've caught in his area. That gets a conversation rolling and gives him some feedback on his own waters. If I've done well on a particular lake, I ask if he knows of any comparable spots. If I've done well on some species but not others, I might ask a specific question—maybe "Any lakes in your area producing nice brook trout?" If I've heard a rumor about a specific lake, I'll ask what he's heard about it. I frequently ask managers about lakes I know well; this helps me gauge what they tell me about lakes I've never been to.

If I talk to a manager who knows quite a bit about a range, I make several contacts over a couple of years and let him know how I've been doing on some of the waters he's suggested. Often this leads to more suggestions. I corresponded with one fish manager for a few years, and just before he retired, he sent me a series of maps with fish species and sizes penciled in for dozens of lakes in several remote drainages.

Wildlife personnel periodically gillnet or shock some waters to determine fish size and density. Official data—including netting and shocking results, stocking records, and written management plans for specific waters—are pretty much yours for the asking. I often request fisheries data for waters that I have little information about. Be reasonable and limit your requests at any one time to data on specific waters. Official data pertaining to fish size should be taken with a grain of salt. A gill-netting session often produces less than a dozen fish, and I've caught trout in a number of lakes that were much bigger than any fish taken in netting surveys or mentioned in other fisheries data.

It's best to contact a fisheries supervisor in fall or early winter, well ahead of the upcoming season. At this point his field work is pretty well over for the year, fishing reports from the previous summer are still fresh in his mind, and he's not getting hammered with a lot of angling inquiries, so he's likely to be more receptive to yours. A call or a letter can work—I've had excellent and disappointing results both ways. When I write a fish manager, I do so in questionnaire form, leaving a blank space following each question where the manager can jot information. I enclose a stamped, self-addressed envelope for returning the questionnaire. This approach gives me carefully considered replies yet keeps paperwork for the manager to a minimum.

Other Sources

In general, the outstanding backcountry streams and rivers are easy to identify. Most of the better wild rivers are major fisheries with considerable mileage. As such, they receive some publicity from the angling press or from outfitters who openly advertise the quality of the fishing. Many top rivers have special lure and harvest regulations and can be identified by reading regulation pamphlets. Researching rivers is largely a matter of determining the most productive stretches and the best times to fish in relation to runoff, insect hatches, and seasonal fish migrations.

Lakes are another story. Small, remote lakes with big fish are almost invariably known to only a handful of anglers, who are all tight lipped about their pet waters. To generate leads on exceptional lakes, you have to be resourceful and pan plenty of dirt for every nugget.

Write to outfitters for their brochures. Outfitters operate in specific areas. If a brochure pictures big trout taken from a high lake, and the photos don't look too dated, then that area is certainly worth researching. Outfitters are in the guiding business, not the information business, but there's nothing wrong with describing the type of fishing experience you're interested in and asking an outfitter whether he can provide it.

Stop in local sport shops and scan the bragging boards for photos of big trout taken from high lakes. Visit general sporting goods shops as well as fly shops. Taxidermy studios in foothill towns may also have photos or mounts of outstanding fish taken from neighboring mountains. Just as with fisheries managers, engaging shop owners in conversation (and buying some maps, film, bug dope, or tackle) is more likely to produce usable information than bluntly asking where a big fish came from.

Get a list of record fish from each western state, as well as a list of International Game Fish Association line-class records. Both types of records usually name the body of water where each fish was taken. Big golden trout live exclusively in high lakes, and if a record golden recently came from a certain lake, bigger goldens probably swim there. I caught and released an unofficial state-record golden trout of better than 21 inches from a lake that I gleaned from a state-record list. Another record list recently alerted me to a golden lake that I've been within a mile of several times but have never fished—you can bet I'll swing by it on my next trip to the region.

Talk to anglers you meet on the trail; any one of them may have logged many trips in the surrounding mountains. Talk to spin fishers as well as fly fishers; I've bumped into a few anglers from both camps who knew a great deal about the productivity of various waters. I'm always amazed when other backpack anglers fail to pump me for information. Even in areas I know well, I always talk to other anglers just to see where they've been. And even nonanglers may know something: Once, a hiker who didn't pack a rod but had happened to see some big trout steered me toward a lake where I've since caught many of my biggest goldens.

Often other anglers won't actually name an outstanding lake they've fished; still, they may brag about what they've caught. If I think someone knows of a hot lake I haven't been to, I may offer to trade him a lake from my A-list for one from his.

As you travel the West, grab free tourist newsletters, which sometimes describe off-road fishing opportunities in nearby mountains. Magazines run occasional articles on backcountry fishing destinations; clip all of these and file them for reference. Several books have been published that include brief descriptions or basic data for hundreds of backcountry waters in a given state. Much of the information in these books is gleaned from wildlife department files. As such, it's often incomplete or outdated, but browsing through with a discerning eye and conducting some follow-up research can pay.

A few books have been published that describe backcountry waters in some detail for a given range or region. As I discuss specific areas, I'll mention these books.

In your research, don't overlook off-trail lakes that are close to roads. A lake that requires a 3-mile cross-country hike to reach may see fewer anglers than one 20 miles into the backcountry but right on a main trail.

If you do your homework, you can compile a lot of information in just a few seasons. I currently have leads on more promising waters than I can visit. Remember, a lead is just a lead—you never know what it's worth until you check it out. Once you do find a good backcountry lake or stream, though, it's almost like owning private water. Just a handful of such spots can give you great angling for years to come.

CHAPTER 10

Trip Planning

Once you have maps in hand and have identified water you want to fish, you can plan your route. This might seem like a simple matter, but seriously studying maps, including various cross-country options, can reveal excellent routes that aren't obvious. For example, a group of my favorite golden trout lakes sits on the east slope of the Wind River Range, but studying maps revealed that the fastest approach is from a trailhead on the west slope via an off-trail pass.

Most backcountry trips begin at an established trailhead. Most trailheads are accessed by improved dirt roads suitable for two-wheel-drive vehicles once the snow melts. If you question whether a road is passable with your vehicle, call the local ranger district. At the trailhead, lock your vehicle and store any enticing equipment out of sight. Theft from parked vehicles is uncommon in the Rockies, and I've never had a break-in, but there are occasional problems.

In my hitchhiking years, I enjoyed one huge advantage over backcountry anglers who had wheels—I didn't have to return to a vehicle. I could enter on one side of a range and exit on the other, and see twice as much water and country as I could on a round-trip. On some through-trips I exited more than 200 miles (by road) from my entry point. Through-trips are intriguing to plan, because they offer so many possible routes. I still do an occasional such trip and hitchhike back to my vehicle. A group of anglers can easily leave an extra vehicle at a separate entry point and route a through-trip. A solo angler with a helpful friend can do the same.

In planning a trip, it's easy to bite off too much mileage and leave yourself short on fishing time. As you become familiar with your hiking range and learn to accurately interpret the length and difficulty of a route by reading maps, you'll strike the right balance between travel and fishing time.

If getting to your target water takes longer than anticipated, don't panic. You can probably make up for lost time on your trip out. I've often hiked in a single day out of a spot that took the better part of two days to reach. Coming out, your pack is at least 10 pounds lighter, there's usually a big net drop in elevation, and you can really extend yourself physically on the final day of a trip.

As a cushion I pack an extra day's worth of food on each trip. If bad weather slows me up, if a route is tougher than I'd envisioned, if I want to explore additional water, or if the fishing is simply too good to walk away from, I have the flexibility to stay longer than planned.

The rule is that when you're hiking, you should be sure a friend or relative knows your route and the time you're due back. This is another rule I violate regularly. I give my wife a general description of where I'm going and an estimate of when I'll call home, but that's all it is—an estimate. She doesn't call out the National Guard if I'm a bit tardy. And I don't limit my options or expose myself to dangerous conditions by having to be out by a fixed time.

Timing a trip right is a critical factor. In the Rockies conditions are highly variable from one summer to the next. I saw both extremes in my first two summers of fishing the backcountry (both spent primarily in Wyoming). In my first summer, 1977, the high trails and passes were free of snow and I could hike anywhere in the Wind River Range by mid-June. I haven't seen another year quite like it since, but at the time I thought I was seeing a normal summer. The next year I was back in Wyoming in mid-June and ready to ramble, but in 1978 the northern Rockies experienced a severe winter and cool spring. Deep snow gripped the high country into late July. By then I'd been floundering around in rotten snow and fishing partially frozen lakes for almost six weeks, and I was one frustrated, but enlightened, hiker.

The Rockies cover a lot of latitude, but the Colorado Rockies are much higher than the Montana Rockies, so summer doesn't necessarily come earlier in the south. Winter snowfall and spring weather vary widely from range to range and year to year. Conditions are totally dependent on regional weather. If you plan a trip for early in the season, stay on top of weather conditions and be prepared to switch destinations if the snow hangs on in your selected area. You can get a fix on snow, ice, and runoff conditions by calling the local ranger district right up to your departure date. Usually rangers have flown over the backcountry or are receiving daily reports on conditions from outfitters and hikers.

If trails are passable and ice is off the water, you should find good lake fishing. In fact, right after ice-out, trout often congregate in the shallows, which are the first areas to warm. In early August 1993 my brother Eric and I arrived at a favorite brook trout lake that sits at 10,300 feet in the Beartooths of Montana. We found shelf ice still drifting about and 36-degree Fahrenheit water in the shallows. On sunny afternoons, though, the shoreline pockets were jammed with nice brook trout, which hung just under the surface as if attempting to thaw after nine months under ice.

On high lakes the bulk of the spawning activity by cutthroats, rainbows, and goldens takes place within a few weeks of ice-out, so the earlier you go, the more likely you are to encounter spawning fish. I find the fishing more interesting and challenging once spawning is complete and fish have dispersed into a lake and resumed their normal feeding routines. In recent years I've scheduled the bulk of my high-lake trips for August or early September to miss spawning. On occasion, however, I've encountered spring-spawning species of trout still spawning into August in lakes above timberline, so this strategy doesn't always work.

If you have to schedule a high-lake trip well in advance, it's wise to shoot for mid- to late summer. By August you're just about guaranteed that trails will be free of snow, ice will be off lakes, and spawning will be completed. If it happens to be an extremely hot, dry summer, like the string of summers we saw in the late 1980s, you may be dealing with campfire bans, and the trout may vanish to deep, cool water when the sun is high, but at least you'll be able to reach and fish your target lake. In the mid-1990s we've seen snowy winters and cool springs, with much of the high country remaining unfishable before mid-July.

On the back end of summer, decent high-lake conditions usually prevail until mid-September. By then the peaks are picking up regular dustings of snow, and temperatures dip below freezing at night, but the days can still be comfortable. The two weeks immediately after Labor

Day are a special time to fish the high lakes. The bulk of the summer tourists are gone, biting bugs are virtually nonexistent, the aspens and willows are turning, and the onset of autumn invigorates the fish.

Most of the larger backcountry streams and rivers are at low to modest elevations. Though trails may be passable in June, snowmelt from the surrounding mountains can keep rivers running high and dirty well into July. Stay on top of local conditions and be prepared to change either your trip date or your destination if runoff is raging. If peak runoff in a region ends exceptionally early—say, by late June—you have a great opportunity to move your trip date forward and go fish the rivers in virtual solitude (you'll beat the influx of anglers who have locked into more traditional vacation times). On some westslope cutthroat rivers in Montana and Idaho, trout migrate considerable distances between spring and fall. Early summer will find fish concentrated in the headwaters and spawning tributaries high in wilderness areas. By mid–September many cutts will have dropped below wilderness boundaries in search of large pools to winter in. In general, the best time to fish backcountry rivers is shortly after spring runoff, when most fish are in the wilderness portions of drainages, and aquatic insect hatches are popping.

As a native midwesterner, I needed several seasons of fishing the high country to appreciate just how late summer can come to the Rockies. By July my home area of southern Wisconsin has usually seen several weeks of high heat and humidity, the corn is chest high, and the local trout fishing is entering the summer doldrums. It can be tough to believe that at the same latitude, just 1,000 miles west, the snow is chest high, lakes are frozen, and rivers are roaring with spring runoff. But altitude can do that.

PART THREE

Fishing Gear and Strategies

CHAPTER 11

Fly-Fishing Gear for the Backcountry

There's nothing terribly specialized about fly-fishing gear for the backcountry; if you already fly-fish for trout, you probably own most of what you need. But as you assemble your outfit, don't buy into the hokum, which I've read a dozen times, that all of your backcountry tackle should fit in a shirt pocket. There aren't any fly shops out there. I carry more flies in the backcountry than I do on roadside waters. I take a selection of leaders and a spare spool of tippet material in sizes 3X through 6X; a working assortment of split shot and strike indicators; nippers and a forceps, so I can save my teeth for chewing jerky; a hook sharpener, so I'm not fishing a dull hook when a 22-inch golden trout plucks a Mega Scud off a rocky bottom; plus line dressing and fly floatant. And all of my flies, tools, and terminal tackle combined weigh under 2 pounds. Don't be a pound-wise backpacker and an ounce-foolish angler. If fishing is your chief pursuit, take what you need to fish effectively.

RODS

My primary fly rod for the backcountry is a 9-foot 6-weight with plenty of punch. High lakes and river canyons are breezy places, and the fishing often requires longer-than-average casts. A rod that's a bit on the power end of the spectrum will cast and mend a long line, present a big streamer or a heavily weighted nymph, and buck some wind. If I'm working a brawling river canyon, like the Gunnison, or a high lake that I know will require very long casts, I occasionally pack a 7-weight as my primary rod. To make long casts or drive a fly line into the wind, you must be able to double-haul. If the double-haul isn't in your casting repertoire, spend a few hours with a good instructor or buy a video, and put in some prac-tice time. Within a week you'll grasp the fundamentals of the cast and see a significant jump in your line speed and casting distance.

I never hike into remote country without a backup rod, which is usually a 4-weight with a light action. If I run into glassy lakes and rising fish that require a delicate presentation, I go to my light rod. Sometimes those rumors of big trout don't pan out, and it's fun to have a light rod for fishing the small streams and pan-size trout that abound in much of the high country.

Four-piece travel rods are handy to backpack or lash to a horse, but two-piece rods pack well enough. I've done most of my hiking with 9-foot, two-piece rods, and I'd pack high-performance, two-piece rods over mediocre travel rods any day. A pair of graphite travel rods from the top makers can easily approach $1,000. St. Croix Legend Ultra travel rods are easily the most affordable, high-performance travel rods I've fished; I'm currently packing the 9-foot 6-weight and 8½-foot 4-weight.

Fly rods should be packed in a hard tube that won't bend or crush if you fall or drop the pack on it. Aluminum tubes are tough to beat for lightness and strength. A standard, 1½-inch-diameter aluminum tube will carry a pair of two-piece rods if you oppose the butt ends. Slip both rods into a single divided rod sock. I carry the rod I use most with the butt pointing up so I can remove it from the sock without removing the other butt section. If I'm packing two tip sections that are the same length and color, I color the tip guide of one with a permanent marker so I can identify either tip at a glance. Most aluminum tubes are plugged at the bottom with a cap that can work loose as the tube takes a pounding; secure the cap with tape. Duct and electrical tape are handy for making many temporary equipment repairs; I take a yard of each wrapped around my rod tube.

Travel rods can be carried in various ways, depending on your pack design, but a long tube must usually be lashed vertically to one side of the pack frame. Rig a pair of nylon straps to stay on the frame when you remove the tube. My last two packs have had tunnel side pockets, designed for carrying skis, that are ideal for carrying a rod tube. I just slide the tube into the tunnel, where it's held firmly in place by pressure from the pack contents. If I'm hiking in timber and the tube is catching on overhead branches, I reach back as I'm walking and pull it down for more clearance. I've also seen hikers use a rod tube as a walking stick, but I'm not into walking sticks of any kind; I think they upset the flow of hiking, divert attention from your footing on tricky terrain, and actually make you work harder. Also, tubes and rods can be damaged by repeated impact.

At night break your rods down and store them safely in the tube. Before I began following this advice, I had two cork rod handles gnawed by rodents. Deer and mountain goats are often bold enough to wander through camp at night, too, and could easily step on a rod propped against a rock or bush. Above timberline an assembled fly rod standing on its butt is also a potential lightning rod.

REELS

For my 4-weight rod, I carry a compact reel loaded with a weight-forward floating line and 75 yards of 20-pound backing. For my heavier rod, I carry a medium-size reel that holds a weight-forward line and 100 yards of backing, plus a spare spool loaded with a weight-forward line with a sinking tip.

For all practical purposes, a well-made cast reel with a smooth drag will perform as well as a much more expensive machined model. Still, reels machined from bar-stock aluminum are structurally stronger than cast reels. Twice I've struck cast reels on rocks with enough force to peen an exposed spool rim tight against the reel frame. I usually carry cast reels in the backcountry and leave my machined reels home, precisely because I tend to ding them pretty regularly while fishing rocky lake shores. Now that some good machined reels are available for a shade over $100, however, the niche for well-made cast reels is narrowing.

Good fly reels require very little maintenance, except for an occasional wiping and light lubricating of the gears, pawls, and spindles. Check all reel screws periodically to see that they're tight.

LINES AND LEADERS

Weight-forward lines are well suited for long casts and windy conditions. The long, thin belly of a weight-forward line has much less surface area than a double-taper and slices through water with less resistance, helping protect light tippets. This is especially important on lakes, where powerful, deep-running trout will tow an entire fly line in a big arc. The

vast majority of my high-country fishing, including most of my nymphing, is done with weight-forward floating lines. For streamer fishing on
rivers and for nymphing deep on lakes, I carry a weight-forward line
with a 13-foot sinking tip (Scientific Anglers Wet Tip III).

During a week of intensive fishing, you need to clean and lubricate
a fly line several times to keep it casting well. Scientific Anglers Fly Line
Cleaning Pad scours dirt and scum from a line with just a couple of
passes. Scientific Anglers Fly Line Dressing is an excellent line lubricant
that requires no drying time or buffing.

I hand-tie my own monofilament leaders from butt to tip; this allows
me to control the diameter, stiffness, length, and strength of every stage.
I know that every knot is carefully seated and that my leaders are fresh.
Because knotted leaders have visible stages, they can be quickly rebuilt to
their original dimensions without using a micrometer. I print the leader
formula on the back of a business card and carry it with my spare leaders.

My basic backcountry leader is 10 feet long with a 4X tippet. I can
easily tailor this leader back to 8 feet with a 3X tippet or extend it to 12
feet with a 5X tippet to cover most situations. For streamer fishing with
a sinking-tip line, I tie 5-foot 2X leaders.

SPLIT SHOT, STRIKE INDICATORS, AND RIGGING TECHNIQUES

Dead-drift nymphing, drifting a nymph at the same speed as the current, is a primary tactic on moving water, especially during nonhatch
periods. When fish aren't rising on streams or rivers, I'm quick to knot
on a nymph and probe the deep-refuge lies where inactive trout usually
retire to hide and conserve energy.

Sinking-tip lines are very useful for casting and actively retrieving
nymphs on stillwater. On moving water, however, where dead-drifting a
nymph is often the best presentation, you're almost always better off rigging with a floating fly line and adding split shot to the tippet to sink
the fly to the desired depth. In moving water, current speed is substantially slower near the bottom and banks because of hydraulic friction.
That's why resting fish seek these places. A monofilament leader is much
thinner than a sinking-tip fly line and slices through current with less
drag. Neutralizing drag allows you to drift a nymph naturally in the
productive bottom zone.

In most dead-drift nymphing, the cast is made directly upstream or
upstream and quartering across the current, and the nymph is allowed to

drift downstream at the same speed as the current. As you work your way through a series of runs, or even through a single large run, you'll encounter a variety of depths and current speeds. To sink your nymph quickly and keep it close to the bottom throughout the drift without constantly snagging the bottom, you have to continually fine-tune your split-shot arrangement. I carry split shot in a variety of sizes, but I usually rig with one or more small shot in #5 to #9. Adding or removing shot in small increments lets me precisely control the depth of my drifts.

Tiny, round shot aren't designed for easy removal from the line, as some larger, dog-eared shot are. But round shot can be opened readily with a little trick. To remove a small, round shot from a tippet, stretch the tippet and the shot over the tip of a finger, with the groove in the shot facing your finger. Use a forceps to gently squeeze the back half of the shot at a right angle to the groove. Do this precisely and the shot will open up; it may even be reusable. I carry several sizes of small shot mixed together in an empty pencil-lead vial. To fine-tune my rigging, I shake a half-dozen shot into my palm and quickly select those I want.

Casting with shot on the tippet is not the abomination that many anglers profess it to be. Simply slow down your backcast and let it extend completely, then throw a relaxed and open forward cast. When you're nymphing with a lot of weight to get down in very fast water, you can usually get away with working close to the fish and casting a very short line. In fast water I often flip the line downstream after a drift and let the current load the rod. Then I shoot the line upstream without making a backcast.

When trout are on their feeding stations but aren't rising regularly, I often use a technique I call long-line nymphing. I weight the tippet lightly to sink the nymph just a foot or two, and I fire medium- to long-range casts from concealed positions. In long-line nymphing forget the standard advice about lobbing your forward cast. Instead, accelerate crisply through the forward stroke—much the way you would to make a roll cast. Stop the rod sharply a bit above horizontal and shoot any additional line. For a bit of extra casting distance and for complete leader extension, drop the rod to horizontal and slide the elbow of your rod arm rearward as the cast is straightening. When long-line nymphing I often haul on my pickup and/or my forward cast to increase line speed and casting distance. With a little refinement in your casting stroke, you can present lightly or moderately weighted nymphs at medium to long ranges with tight loops and near dry-fly accuracy.

When nymphing you'll detect a lot more strikes if you use a strike indicator. That's true for veteran and novice anglers alike. A trout that inhales an artificial nymph will recognize it as a phony and reject it quickly. Usually you have only a second or two to detect a strike and set the hook. An indicator gives you a fixed, highly visible point on the leader that you can focus on throughout a drift. If the indicator darts upstream, pulls under suddenly, or does anything unnatural, set the hook.

For most of my nymphing, I use a putty-type strike indicator positioned 2 to 3 feet below the butt end of the leader. Putty can be pinched off in any quantity, molded to reduce wind resistance, and easily moved to any position on a knotted leader.

When I'm using an indicator to regulate the depth of a nymph, I use the pinch-on, adhesive, foam type. Foam indicators are very buoyant, sit high on the surface, and wobble to telegraph light strikes. I often use an indicator to regulate depth when I'm nymphing a very slow run for inactive but visible fish. I put just enough split shot on the leader to suspend the nymph vertically below the indicator. Then I position the buoyant indicator to keep the fly at the precise depth of the fish throughout the drift. When spooked or inactive trout are bunched up in a refuge lie, you can often have a field day by drifting a small nymph through the school repeatedly. Tiny nymphs don't alarm trout. After the trout become accustomed to your presence, which usually takes about ten minutes, you can often stand in plain sight of wild fish and proceed to mop up.

On lakes I sometimes use a buoyant foam indicator to suspend a small nymph or larval imitation at a desired depth. Then I subtly twitch the fly to attract the attention of cruising fish as they approach.

VESTS AND TACKLE PACKS

Because my tackle doesn't fit in a shirt pocket, I have to fish out of something else. I've tried fishing out of a fanny pack, and I've looked closely at specialized chest packs and day packs designed for fly fishing. But I haven't seen any that keep tackle and tools as organized and accessible as a fishing vest.

If you're worried about the weight of a vest, grab an empty one off a rack and compare it with any tackle pack that even approaches it in capacity. The vest will be as light or lighter, and when loaded it will distribute weight more comfortably. The rear pouch on a vest expands to hold the rain suit, food, and other gear you need to fish away from camp all day, eliminating the need for a separate gear pack.

Buy a vest that's oversize so it doesn't restrict your casting stroke when you wear it over a fleece jacket or down vest. If it's raining hard, I wear my raincoat over my fishing vest, so I also buy my raincoat oversize.

On travel days there's often time—or the irresistible temptation—to stop periodically and wet a line. I pack my fishing vest so I can quickly pull it from my backpack without removing any other gear. Vest pockets should be designed to hold tackle securely when the vest is turned upside down, as it frequently will be.

Accessories pinned or clipped to a vest have a way of snagging and pulling free as the vest is yanked from a pack. If you use a fly-drying patch, sew it on. Simms makes a virtually unbreakable retractor with a coiled, telephone-type cord. The cord has enough range and strength that I keep my forceps snapped to it even while unhooking fish—which has put an end to lost forceps. I use electrical tape to bind the retractor to a D-ring on my vest.

LANDING GEAR

Few backpack anglers carry a net, but in recent years I've found myself toting one on quite a few trips. A net weighs only ounces and is easily strapped to the outside of the pack. It helps land fish of all sizes more quickly. If you're photographing yourself with a fish, a net left in a quiet pocket in the shallows provides a secure place where the trout can begin to recover while you set up camera gear and compose the shot.

In bear country rinse a net bag thoroughly after use to eliminate as much of the fishy smell as possible, and hang it with your food at night.

When I'm not packing a net, I keep a spare bandanna strung through the D-ring on the back of my vest. To tail a big fish, I wrap the bandanna around my hand for traction. A big trout has a long tail shank that you can grab firmly without injuring the fish.

WADERS AND FLOAT TUBES

Too many trout anglers jump right into the water and end up wading when or where they shouldn't. Whether to wade should depend strictly on whether wading produces more or bigger fish.

As I'll discuss in detail later, high-altitude lakes tend to have limited shallows, which produce most of the trout forage. Fish normally invade these shallows to feed, and most shallows are within casting range of shore. Often you can spot and cast to cruising fish more effectively from elevated points on shore than by wading. This is particularly true of lakes above timberline, which tend to have excellent vantages and plenty of backcasting room. On meadow lakes or lakes above timber, more than 90 percent of my angling is from dry land. When I'm hiking to familiar lakes where I know waders aren't an advantage, I leave them behind.

On some lakes waders are an advantage, though. Wading along heavily timbered shores increases your backcasting room. Wading can occasionally put you within casting distance of a feeding flat that's not workable from shore. If I know waders are an advantage, or if I'm exploring lakes that are mostly in timber, I pack them.

For remote lakes I pack nylon stocking-foot chest waders that weigh under a pound and fold compactly. Saltwater-flats-style neoprene wading boots are lightweight, fast drying, and suitable for most lake wading. High lakes can stay cold right through summer, so when you're wearing lightweight waders, you may need to exit the water periodically to warm up.

For headwater rivers I pack lightweight hip boots. There are always deep runs and pools where chest waders would be an advantage, but hippers position me to cover most runs effectively. On backcountry rivers I usually fish several miles of water a day, and for extensive walking hippers are so much lighter, cooler, and less confining than chest waders that I'll gladly sacrifice a little wading capability.

On some backcountry lakes, a float tube is a distinct advantage, but on most trophy-trout lakes with low fish densities, you're far better off hunting for the widely scattered fish from high vantages than blind-casting from a tube.

If you pack a tube, you also need fins, an air pump, and waders for insulation. All of that gear is bulky and can total more than 10 pounds. If you plan to fish a specific lake where you know a tube will be a big advantage, though, the extra weight may be justified. A group of anglers can easily share a float tube and divide the weight of the equipment. For a solo hiker, hauling a tube all over the backcountry as standard practice is not worth the effort.

CHAPTER 12

Flies and Primary Fly Tactics for the Backcountry

From northern Montana southward through New Mexico, and from the front range of Colorado westward into Oregon, the Rocky Mountain backcountry spans a vast geographic area. And from the depths of Hells Canyon at barely 1,000 feet above sea level to Colorado lakes lapping the sky at 11,000 feet, the swing in elevation between fisheries is staggering. Within that vast three-dimensional zone, an array of trout species feeds on everything from meaty sculpins and clouds of freshwater shrimp to tiny zooplankton, terrestrial insects, and a smorgasbord of aquatic insects.

Major insect hatches have been charted for most of the West's premier roadside waters, but when it comes to buying or tying the right flies for the backcountry, you're pretty much on your own. So what flies should you pack?

Well, it's true of almost all trout waters that you can catch fish on a limited selection of workhorse fly patterns much of the time. It's equally true, however, that when trout become highly selective to a specific food form, both your imitation and your presentation had better be convincing if you want to hook more than the odd fish. In selecting my own flies, I encompass both philosophies. I go heavy on the flies I'm likely to fish the most, and I go light on a broad selection of patterns to approximate in silhouette, size, and color almost any significant insect or organism I might encounter.

My experiences at a favorite golden trout lake in the Wind River Range illustrate the advantages of packing a comprehensive fly selection. I've made the 35-mile trek in to the lake more than a half dozen times. The lake is larded with freshwater shrimp that the resident goldens routinely gorge on. My Fast-Sinking Scud is an effective shrimp imitation, and many days it's the only fly I need here. But the lake periodically hosts a variety of insect hatches that send the goldens into feeding frenzies and cause them to feed selectively.

One glass-calm August evening saw an incredible midge hatch that drew trout from all over the lake to feed on a rocky flat in as little as a foot of water. The hatch was so dense that the goldens didn't cruise between rises—they actually wallowed in fixed positions as they gorged. Big goldens midged so steadily that their backs were exposed for long intervals. It was an unforgettable experience to gaze across the flat into the low sun and see those broad, luminous dorsals carving the calm surface. My Topwater Midge with a pheasant tail body and two turns of grizzly hackle was a convincing imitation of the naturals. I'd drop the fly in a pod of boiling fish and watch for my leader to twitch in the glassy film. At the sting of the tiny hook, another in a long succession of thick, powerful goldens would porpoise through the air before diving for the rocks. It was the most volatile midge fishing I've seen in or out of the backcountry.

A September mayfly hatch on the lake was just as spectacular. Lakes above timberline aren't generally regarded as mayfly havens, but many high lakes host stillwater mayflies, and wavy, well-oxygenated shores can harbor excellent populations of current-loving species. This hatch blossomed two hours before dark. The rocky shallows suddenly teemed with wriggling nymphs. A stiff wind blowing from shore carried many emergers over deep water. Some goldens fed tight against the shoreline rocks, while others cruised offshore. In the cold, blustery conditions, the freshly emerged duns had trouble getting off the water, and the trout feasted on them. A #14 Blue Dun tied Catskill-style with wood-duck wings was a close match for the slate gray natural duns. I skated the hackled fly to simulate a dun struggling to get airborne and to attract the attention of cruising fish. Fortunately I had a half dozen Blue Duns with me, because the goldens shredded them all, and one of my last fish was a slab-sided male of 23 inches with flanks of brilliant, bloody crimson. He was the biggest golden trout I've taken on a dry fly.

Fishing a fly that imitates the prevailing food form is the very essence of fly fishing, and packing a fairly comprehensive fly selection is the only way I know to be prepared for an array of unanticipated hatches. There's nothing in fly fishing quite as satisfying as sticking trout steadily during a hatch—and nothing quite as frustrating as fumbling through a hatch without a convincing fly. Flies are light as feathers. I'd rather err on the side of excess any day.

I carry my backcountry fly selection in nine small to medium-size fly boxes and my hackled dry flies freestanding in compartmentalized boxes; everything else goes into boxes with flat foam inserts. A medium-size box with foam inserts will easily carry two or three hundred nymphs, emergers, or no-hackle drys, and the box is spillproof, windproof, and floats if dropped.

Six of my fly boxes go on every trip: one of nymphs and emergers, plus one box each of hackled mayfly duns, no-hackle mayfly duns and spinners, adult caddis and a few terrestrials, small streamer and baitfish imitations, and tiny midges and micronymphs.

Three fly boxes go only to certain waters. For high lakes I pack a box filled with scuds in a range of colors and sizes. On river trips I skip this box but still carry a couple dozen assorted scuds in my nymph box. For backcountry rivers I pack a box of Muddlers, Buggers, and big stonefly nymphs. For moving water I also pack a box that beefs up my selection of big drys, including stoneflies, hoppers, and large mayfly drakes.

Packing tools and materials to tie flies in the backcountry has never struck me as practical, but I stash a tying kit in my car for replenishing flies between trips. I do pack an aquarium dip net and a couple of vials of alcohol for collecting organisms for identification or as fly-tying models.

Tying flies cuts your cost per fly drastically, but more important, it also lets you create precisely the flies you need to solve the fishing challenges you encounter. Many of my most productive fly patterns for the backcountry are my own designs. For the benefit of readers who tie, I'll briefly discuss design and materials for some of my patterns below; if I've published an article on any of these patterns, I'll mention the publication and issue. I also tie flies commercially and market them directly to anglers. To request my free mail-order fly catalog, write to Rich Osthoff, N6868 Sandstone Drive, Mauston, WI 53948.

Fishing a fly right is just as important as fishing the right fly. For this reason I'll discuss primary tactics for presenting specific flies, too.

CADDISFLIES

Better than two hundred species of caddisflies occur in the Rockies. Some are well adapted to lakes, others to rivers, making caddis abundant throughout the backcountry.

Most caddis larvae build cases from bits of rock or vegetation. The next time you're on a high lake, take a good look in the shallows, where decaying plant debris collects. You'll likely see big caddis larvae with their heads and legs extending from their cases as they slowly clamber and feed along the bottom. Fat, chenille-bodied flies tied in brown or black with a couple of turns of soft hackle just behind the head are good imitations. These flies should be tied in #10 or #12 and retrieved very slowly right on lake bottoms with the aid of a sinking line.

Cased caddis larvae are easily observed in streams; just pick up a few rocks. In moving water cased caddis anchor to stones or sticks and aren't usually abundant in the drift. Free-living (uncased) larvae thrive in cold mountain streams and can be abundant in the drift, however, making imitations excellent flies for prospecting the water. Simple larval imitations can be tied with dubbed abdomens ribbed with copper wire, along with a fuzzy thorax of peacock, ostrich herl, or picked-out dubbing. I tie my imitations unweighted or lightly weighted in #12 through #18 and add split shot to the tippet as needed, or fish them on a sinking-tip line.

Following several stages of growth, caddis larvae enter the pupal stage and develop adult characteristics. At emergence the pupae swim rapidly toward the surface or are buoyed by gas bubbles. Emergence from the pupal shuck to the winged adult takes place in or just beneath the surface film. Freshly emerged caddis adults tend to get off the water quickly, so during hatches trout often feed selectively on the more vulnerable emerging pupae, making pupal imitations important to anglers.

Caddis emergers are tied in several styles. Traditional soft-hackle wet flies have floss or dubbed bodies and long, soft hackles that pulsate in the water to suggest the swept-back wings and antennae of caddis emergers. Because of their enticing movement, these flies also shine for fishing subsurface on lakes with various strip retrieves, even when there's no hatch. Gary LaFontaine's popular Emergent Sparkle Pupa uses an Antron sheath to imitate the shuck and trapped gas bubble of an emerging caddis. Emergers can also be tied with stubby wings and a trailing length of Antron to imitate an emerging pupa half out of its shuck. Small caddis pupae tied with bead heads and trailing wisps of soft hackle can be deadly when drifted just subsurface to rising fish.

Caddis adults usually get off the water quickly—but not always. During some hatches, especially in cool weather, throngs of adults ride the surface for a considerable distance, and fish take adult imitations greedily. These adult imitations are also important during egg-laying flights, when fertilized females return to the water. Some species lay their eggs by dipping onto the surface, while others crawl or dive underwater to deposit eggs on the bottom before swimming back to the surface. During egg laying, adult imitations skittered on the surface, or cast downstream and then pulled underwater (as appropriate), take fish. Soft-hackle wet flies also imitate adult caddis swimming underwater. On high lakes under dead-calm conditions, emerging or egg-laying adult caddis sometimes scamper over glassy surfaces for long distances, creating distinctive wakes that trout home in on like guided missiles; skating adult caddis imitations on calm water is thus a fundamental lake tactic. After egg laying, spent caddis sometimes fall to the water, and then flush-floating, spent-wing imitations will produce.

Adult caddis imitations should be carried in #12 through #18. Wing and body colors of the naturals run the gamut from cream to black; tan, olive, and gray are common. The wings of adult caddis fold tentlike over the back and can be uniform in shade or mottled. Imitations for fast water are often tied with elk- or deer-hair wings and palmered hackle, for durability and a high, dancing float. Imitations for slow water and lakes—where fish get a better look at the fly—often have quill-section wings for a more convincing profile.

My Upland Caddis is extremely lifelike in silhouette and color—probably why it's my most productive adult caddis imitation for wary fish on flat water. And considering its realism, the Upland Caddis is easy to tie. I use a simple technique for building a realistic, tent-style adult caddis wing from two game bird body feathers: I streamline these feathers with Flexament and bond them into a tent canopy before tying them atop a hackled body. The crisscrossed stem butts of the two feathers simulate the prominent antennae of caddis adults. Various upland game bird and waterfowl feathers can be used to precisely match the wing color and mottling of virtually any adult caddis. (See *Fly Tyer* magazine, Spring 1996, for tying details.) I tie all of my adult caddis with stiff hackle so they can be skated on the surface. If I want the fly to sit low on the surface, I trim the hackle. To imitate a spent caddis, I separate the wings on an Upland and trim its hackle flush with its body for a low float.

Because freshly emerged adult caddis often get off the water quickly, and emerging pupae are rarely observed, caddis hatches can be all but invisible. If you see rising fish but don't observe any insects on the surface or in the film, emerging caddis are likely suspects. Splashy rises with an occasional fish vaulting clear of the water also indicate a caddis hatch; the momentum of a trout chasing a swiftly ascending pupa can carry the fish right out of the water.

Adult caddis typically live for a couple of weeks, so fish get used to seeing them and will grab them opportunistically, even when there's no hatch. Adult caddis imitations also resemble small stoneflies, large midges, and small hoppers, which boosts their effectiveness as prospecting flies. On lakes and streams I catch more trout on adult caddis imitations during nonhatch periods than on any other type of dry fly.

MAYFLIES

Roughly two hundred mayfly species inhabit the Rockies, but only a fraction of them are important to anglers. In the backcountry mayfly hatches occur almost daily on streams and rivers and periodically on lakes, right up to the highest elevations that fish inhabit.

Mayflies spend the bulk of their lives as nymphs foraging beneath the surface on plants, algae, and decaying plant or animal matter (a few species are carnivorous). They can be grouped into four categories based on the physical shape and behavior of the nymphs: crawlers, clingers, swimmers, and burrowers.

Crawling and clinging nymphs have flattened profiles and are well adapted to foraging in the rocky, tumbling streams typical of the high country; crawlers can also occur in high-altitude lakes, along rocky shores that see frequent wave action. The flattened profile allows these nymphs to crawl along the bottom or cling to the substrate without being swept away in swift current (some nymphs also use suction). Crawlers and clingers are poor swimmers; if dislodged by the current, they drift or swim feebly near the bottom until they can reattach. Shortly before emergence, nymphs become active and more available to the fish. Some species migrate from fast water to smoother currents more suitable for emergence. The *Ephemerella* genus of crawling mayflies produces several famous and widespread Rocky Mountain hatches that go by the common names of western green drakes, small green drakes (also called flavs), and pale morning duns (PMDs). The March brown is the common name of the best-known clinging mayfly distributed throughout the Rockies.

Mayfly swimmers are agile, streamlined nymphs that dart and forage actively among plants or along the bottom. They're widely distributed in rivers and lakes, and are fairly available to trout during nonhatch periods. On lakes mayfly nymph imitations retrieved with erratic strips of line can be effective at any time. I tie my lake nymphs with slender bodies and soft-hackle tails and legs to better imitate the wriggling action of swimming nymphs. *Callibaetis* (commonly called speckle-wings) are the predominant mayflies on many Rocky Mountain lakes. Small *Baetis* mayflies (commonly called blue-winged olives) inhabit most moving water in the Rockies.

Burrowing nymphs tunnel into the silt bottoms of lakes and slow-moving rivers and are represented in the Rockies by just a couple of species, which occur infrequently. One, commonly known as the brown drake, is a large, burrowing mayfly that emerges near dark on a few gentle rivers in Yellowstone country.

During a hatch most mayfly nymphs swim or buoy to the surface, where they emerge from the nymphal shuck as winged duns. Early in a hatch, trout often feed primarily on these emerging nymphs, which out-number winged duns and are more vulnerable. If the duns lift off the surface quickly, trout may concentrate on emergers throughout a hatch. Typically, however, the duns of certain species ride the surface for some distance as their wings dry in preparation for flight; also, most duns drift longer in cool weather. When duns do ride the surface like this, trout often feed selectively on them. Drifting duns resemble sailboats as they float with their wings clasped above their backs, like butterflies at rest. Some hatches produce many crippled emergers, and trout may feed selectively on these.

When you encounter a mayfly hatch in the backcountry, note the weather, time, and type of water. If conditions are similar the following day, you can anticipate the same hatch at the same time. Head for the same type of water a couple of hours before the hatch and work nymph imitations near the bottom, where scores of natural nymphs are probably active.

To imitate mature clinging and crawling mayfly nymphs, I fish a modified Hare's Ear Nymph in #10 through #18. A high percentage of mature mayfly nymphs are dark olive to brown, and over a season a Chocolate Hare's Ear is my most productive variation. I blend hare's ear dubbing, using lots of stiff guard hairs and soft underbody fur, plus 25 percent finely chopped Antron. To tie a Hare's Ear with a flattened profile, I dub an oversize ball of fur at the thorax and brush the finished fly with a stiff nylon brush, raking from under the thorax up toward the edges of the wing case. Vigorous brushing flattens the thorax. Guard hairs and soft underfur projecting from the sides of a brushed nymph move in the current, simulating legs and gill filaments. (For various brushed nymph techniques, see *Fly Tyer* magazine, Summer 1997.) Brushed nymphs also capture and diffuse light throughout their soft margins; they simulate the translucency of living nymphs much better than smooth-bodied imitations, which simply reflect light. The wing pads on mature mayfly nymphs are usually dark gray and can be nicely imitated by quill sections from Canada goose wings. Viewed from above, clinging and crawling nymphs are broad in relation to their length; to get that robust look, tie the thorax and wing case about half the body length. For a more realistic Hare's Ear, tie a tail using just a few barbs of pheasant tail or wood-duck flank rather than a clump of fur, and rib with very fine wire rather than flat tinsel. For versatility I tie Hare's Ears with little or no weight on the hook shank. This way I can fish them anywhere, from just under the surface to right on the bottom, by adding split shot to the tippet or using a sinking line.

Once a hatch is under way, emerger imitations can shine. The rise-forms of trout telegraph the stage and depth of the hatch that the fish are working. Snouts breaking the surface indicate that trout are taking emergers in the surface film or drifting duns; in the latter case, you should be able to see winged flies riding the surface. If only the backs or tails of rising fish break the surface, they're taking emergers under the surface. During some hatches trout intercept ascending nymphs so deep that their feeding creates little or no surface disturbance. During *Baetis* hatches I often catch more and bigger fish by working a small Pheasant Tail Nymph just above the weeds or bottom.

My primary mayfly emerger imitation for fishing near the surface is the Floating Nymph, which I carry in #10 through #20. A brown Floating Nymph approximates the majority of emergers in color, but I also carry olive, cream, and sulfur versions. I tie this simple pattern with an exaggerated wing case of dark gray closed-cell foam to represent the unfurling wings of the emerging dun. The foam wing case also suspends the fly in the surface film. I dub Floating Nymphs with beaver fur mixed with 25 percent chopped Antron. For a flattened profile, and to simulate legs and soft gill structures, I lightly brush the finished fly from underneath up toward the sides. The Floating Nymph should be tied on a light-wire hook with sparse tails of split or splayed hackle barbs to help support it in the surface film.

I pack several styles of dun imitations. Even in the backcountry, no-hackle duns often fool more fish than traditional hackled duns, particularly on smooth water, where trout get a good look at the fly. My Duck Shoulder Dun (DSD) consistently takes selective trout, even on heavily fished catch-and-release water. I tie this no-hackle using duck shoulder feathers rather than quill sections for the wings. These shoulder feathers offer several advantages. They have a more realistic, rounded profile; and their center stems make them much tougher than quill wings. The stem butts of shoulder feathers make tying in the wings and manually adjusting their positions a snap. Various ducks produce opaque shoulder feathers in a range of subtle shades, from cream to light dun and slate gray, for matching any freshly emerged dun. In recent years I've been using cock pheasant shoulder feathers to imitate the mottled and speckled wings of some mayflies. The cupped shoulder feathers from the very leading edge of a bird wing are structurally strong and maintain their shape and fullness when wet. When mounted at a low angle, cupped feathers merge nicely over the top of the fly and flare outward along the bottom edges to stabilize it upright. DSDs are dubbed with beaver underfur and have splayed tails of stiff hackle fibers. (See *American Angler,* March/April 1994, for tying details.)

In most of my tying, I strive to create a convincing silhouette from lifelike materials. Once I have a proven design, I run it up and down the scale in size and color to imitate an array of naturals with the same configuration. Packing DSDs in the following sizes and shades gives me a workable imitation for most hatches: Blue-Winged Olive in #16 through #20, Pale Morning Dun in #14 and #16, Sulfur in #18 and #20, Blue Dun in #14 through #18, Callibaetis in #14 and #16, March Brown in #12 and #14, Green Drake in #10 and #12.

Traditional hackled duns still have their place. Some natural duns sit very high and skitter on the water before takeoff. On windy days when drifting duns are being buffeted about, hackled duns can be the best imitations, even on hard-fished waters. On lakes where trout normally cruise for their food, skating a hackled dun on a calm surface attracts fish from a wide radius. I carry five standard patterns—Light Cahill, Gray Fox, Blue-Winged Olive, Blue Dun, and Adams—in #12 through #18, providing a reasonable size and color match for most mayfly duns.

Humpies and Wulffs suggest large mayfly duns and are tied in a range of natural and attractor colors. My Industrial-Strength Dun combines the toughness and visibility of a Wulff with a more convincing mayfly wing silhouette—a pair of hen saddle hackle tips bonded with Flexament into a tough, upright wing. I-S Duns have sparse but stiff moose-hair tails and are well hackled for a high float. (See *Fly Tyer* magazine, Autumn 1995, for tying details.) I carry the I-S Adams in #12 and #14 for prospecting fast water and the I-S Green Drake in #10 and #12.

Within hours or days of emergence, mayfly duns molt into sexually mature spinners. After mating in midair, the females lay their eggs, usually by dipping onto the water. Spent females fall to the water with their wings extended to the sides, like planes, and heavy spinner falls generate frenzied and selective feeding by trout. Spinner falls occur at various hours, depending on the species. Cliff swallows feed voraciously on dancing swarms of mating spinners, so swallows wheeling high above the river often signal an approaching spinner fall.

Spinners have transparent wings and sleek bodies, usually in the olive-to-brown spectrum. As a general spinner imitation, I pack the Rusty Spinner in #12 through #20, tied with a reddish brown body, clear Antron wings, and split tails. I also carry a few spinners in light tan, plus black-bodied spinners in #22 for matching the occasional Trico spinner fall encountered in the backcountry.

STONEFLIES

Stoneflies are widely distributed throughout the Rockies. Huge *Pteronarcys* stoneflies (their common name is salmonflies) and the slightly smaller *Acroneuria* stoneflies (golden stones) garner most of the attention from trout and anglers, but there are numerous small species.

Stonefly nymphs live almost exclusively in rocky riffles, where they crawl along the substrate to forage. Some species are predatory; others eat decaying plant or animal matter. The nymphs swim poorly or not at all. When dislodged they drift near the bottom for a time and are often taken by trout. Dead-drifting a large stonefly nymph imitation near the bottom is among the most productive ways to fish major backcountry streams throughout the season.

Nymph imitations range from golden brown to black and are often tied heavily weighted on #4 through #8 long-shank hooks. There are scores of realistic stonefly nymph imitations that look great sitting on coffee tables, but most are tedious to tie and use stiff materials that don't look natural in the water. Softer, more impressionistic imitations account for more trout. Charles Brooks's series of simple stonefly nymphs tied with wool bodies and a couple of turns of hackle and ostrich herl over the thorax, to simulate legs and gills, are excellent producers. I often fish my Soft-Hackle Woolly Worm in #6 with a black body and hackle palmered over just the thorax.

The heaviest concentrations of big stonefly nymphs occur on large backcountry streams and rivers. Complete development of the nymphs takes two to four years, so there are always nymphs of various sizes present. Before emergence mature nymphs migrate toward shorelines, and big trout gorge on these migrations. Emergence is usually in the evening. The nymphs crawl out of the water onto rocks or vegetation, where the adults emerge. Many hatches occur in early summer, when rivers are high with runoff and passes are still blocked by snow. Even when I fish backcountry rivers early in the season, I often miss the peak of the stonefly emergence, as evidenced by the thousands of nymphal shucks I see littering the shorelines when I arrive.

In the week after emergence, adults mate on streamside foliage, and some fall or are blown onto the water. Females also fly over the water to oviposit eggs on the surface, and big adult stoneflies are clumsy fliers that often wind up in the drink. Adult stones represent such a substantial meal that big trout may rise to an imitation weeks after most of the naturals have died.

Adult stonefly imitations vary widely in design. Many are tied with flared hairwings and palmered hackle; perhaps trout take these bushy imitations for fluttering stoneflies. Other imitations incorporate realistic synthetic wings tied flat over the back. Still others have bullet-style deer-hair heads and resemble grasshopper patterns. Imitations of big stoneflies are tied on #4 through #8 hooks. Some of the smaller species, such as the little yellow stonefly, common around Yellowstone, can be imitated with adult caddis patterns.

MIDGES

Chironomid (commonly called midges) inhabit virtually all freshwater lakes and streams. Most species are small enough to be imitated with flies tied on #16 through #24 hooks. Various species emerge year-round on moving water. In late summer, when hatches of larger aquatic insects taper off, midges frequently provide surface action when little else is on the water. In the high country, more than half of the lake hatches I encounter are midges.

Midges have a larval, pupal, and adult stage. The slender larvae feed on the bottom and on plants; they're common items in both stream drift and trout diets. On rivers where resting trout can be readily spotted, drifting a larval imitation right to an inactive fish will often produce when nothing else does. On lakes I sometimes pinch a tiny split shot on my tippet and use a buoyant, foam strike indicator to suspend a larval imitation at the desired depth. I retrieve the fly in front of visible fish with slow, subtle strips of line.

My most productive larval imitation is my Pheasant-Tail Midge in #16 through #22. This simple pattern is tied without appendages. The elongated abdomen is wrapped with a few strands of pheasant tail and ribbed with copper wire. The thorax is two turns of the same pheasant tail used on the abdomen; the butts of the tail fibers produce a thorax that's fatter and darker than the abdomen. The Pheasant-Tail Midge is also a good imitation of many uncased caddis larvae, which could partially account for this fly's effectiveness.

Speaking of crossover imitation, most high-altitude lakes that support fat, healthy trout also teem with wriggling zooplankton, some of which exceed 2 millimeters in length. I frequently net plankton or see them suspended in the shallows. In summer, at the peak of their population cycles, plankton can number in the thousands per cubic meter of water; trout, particularly rainbows and goldens, gorge on them. As a practical matter, plankton are too small and numerous to imitate. Many plankton are reddish brown, however, and a #22 Pheasant-Tail Midge is in this ballpark in both size and color, so perhaps some fish take it for that reason.

Midge pupae have slender segmented abdomens; their compact thoraxes and heads are generally darker than the abdomens. At emergence pupae float to the surface and suspend in the film, where the two-winged adults escape the shuck and quickly take flight. During a hatch trout often feed mainly on the more vulnerable pupae.

Pupal imitations can be simple dubbed flies with slender segmented abdomens and picked-out thoraxes. I carry a range of colors, from cream to olive and black. Pupal imitations are usually fished dead-drift in the film on 6X or smaller tippets. On lakes I catch more fish if I cast my pupal imitation into the wind and let it drift toward me; casting with the wind puts the fly on a tight line and sinks it. In midge fishing such subtle differences in presentation can make all the difference.

Adult midges sometimes hatch in incredible numbers. I've seen shoreline boulders above timberline covered with freshly hatched adult *Chironomid* that resembled mosquitoes in size and appearance. Midges sometimes land on fly vests and swarm about (I've inhaled scores), but they don't bite.

My Topwater Midge does double duty as an emerging pupa and adult midge imitation. It's a simple fly that I tie in a range of colors. Bodies are dubbed with fur or wrapped with a few strands of pheasant tail. The thorax has two or three turns of very short, stiff, dry-fly hackle from the base of a genetic cock neck. The hackle is trimmed flush with the bottom of the body so the fly sits low on the surface. To enhance the emerging profile of the fly, I sometimes add a sparse trailing shuck of Antron. The Griffith's Gnat is also a good imitation of some large midges.

During a midge hatch, thousands of naturals pepper the water, so your tiny imitation faces stiff competition. Even if your fly and presentation are right, you may need to put that fly out over a midging fish repeatedly before it's selected. On lakes and river eddies where fish cruise as they midge, I like to cast from a high vantage so I can see individual fish and put my imitation right on their noses again and again.

Swarms of adult midges sometimes gather on the surface in mating clusters, and a few flies are tied to specifically imitate these. If you encounter clusters and lack a specialized pattern, the Griffith's Gnat in #18 or larger nicely imitates small midge clusters. A foam beetle is a workable cluster imitation, too.

Mosquitoes are from the same order (Diptera) as *Chironomid*. Mosquitoes boom in the backcountry, especially in wet years, but they tend to hatch from seeps and shallow ponds that don't support fish. I don't pack flies specifically to imitate mosquitoes, but a Pheasant-Tail Midge fished in the film serves as a good imitation of mosquito larvae and pupae.

DAMSELFLIES AND DRAGONFLIES

In the backcountry the heaviest populations of damselflies usually occur on lakes below timberline that support significant plant growth. On weed-free lakes near or above timberline, damselfly populations are usually spotty.

Damsel nymphs are much more available to trout than the winged adults and are the most important stage to imitate. These predatory nymphs are long and slender with large, protruding eyes; they stalk smaller organisms among submerged weeds. At emergence, usually in midsummer, the nymphs swim toward shore at various depths and crawl onto exposed vegetation, where the adults emerge. Nymphs swim slowly but with a lot of wiggle.

Nymph imitations are usually tied on long-shank hooks in #8 through #12 with soft materials, such as marabou and ostrich herl, that pulse at slow retrieve speeds. Some imitations are tied on jointed hooks for extra wiggle. Bodies run from green to olive to brown, with slightly darker wing cases. Dumbbell eyes of melted monofilament imitate the large, dark eyes of the naturals.

Adult damsels feed and rest around water. Fish take any that fall or are blown onto the surface. At rest adult damsels hold their wings over their bodies; dragonflies extend their wings to the sides. There are some elegant adult damsel patterns with parachute hackle and extended bodies of blue foam or other synthetics.

Dragonflies also prefer slow or standing water. The heaviest concentrations occur on lakes that are rather warm and weedy by mountain standards. Dragonfly nymphs are much stockier than damsel nymphs and are vicious predators. Some move in quick bursts by expelling water from their gills. Soft-Hackle Woolly Worms in olive or black retrieved with abrupt strips are good imitations. On lakes I often fish Woollies with strip retrieves as general attractor flies, and their resemblance to dragonfly nymphs is probably a factor in their excellent productivity. Adult dragonflies are swift, strong fliers, and I suppose trout ambush a few, but I don't carry an adult imitation.

TERRESTRIALS

Land-based insects can be surprisingly available to trout. I once cleaned a 12-inch brown trout that had ingested thirteen adult hoppers, and it was still before noon! Imagine how many hoppers that trout might have ingested when the afternoon heat and wind got these bugs moving. Indeed, all types of terrestrials wind up on the water more frequently on windy days. Whenever wind gusts spur an increase in the tempo of rising activity, be quick to suspect some form of terrestrial as the main trout entrée.

I see scattered grasshoppers above timberline, but they're more important on the meadow sections of moderate-elevation streams and rivers. Hoppers mature by late summer, and populations can stay strong well into autumn. There are many good hopper patterns; I always carry a few crickets, too.

Ants seem to thrive everywhere, and trout relish them. I pack black ant imitations in #12 and #16, plus red ants in #18 and #22. I once found myself in the midst of an amazing flying ant hatch without a convincing imitation. It was on Slough Creek in Yellowstone on an August afternoon. Tiny red ants with clear wings blanketed the water, and the big cutthroats were feeding selectively. Reddish midge imitations took some fish, but I saw mostly refusals. Since that day I've always carried flying ant imitations.

Terrestrial beetles are abundant in forests and grasslands. The hundreds of species vary widely in size and color, but trout feeding opportunistically will usually take a black beetle imitation in #14 or #16. The standard closed-cell foam pattern is a good one, although I replace the fragile deer-hair legs with unbreakable strands of monocord. On smooth water trout that approach but refuse a hopper imitation will often sip a beetle. Beetle imitations also seem to click in late evening, after natural hopper activity has ebbed for the day.

Various species of aquatic beetles inhabit most streams and lakes. The larvae and adults live underwater and aren't commonly seen by anglers, but the adults do surface to breathe. On high lakes with little vegetation to harbor terrestrial beetles, I've had big trout take beetle imitations very purposefully after ignoring other drys, so maybe fish see significant numbers of aquatic beetles. Water boatmen and back swimmers are predatory insects that live mainly along weedy lakeshores, and a slender beetle in brown or dark tan is a workable imitation for the adult form of either.

PROSPECTING NYMPHS

Over a season and on a variety of waters, probing near the bottom with nymphs will produce more and larger fish than skimming the surface with drys. This is true of both lakes and moving water. I like to catch trout on dry flies as much as anyone, but when there's not a significant hatch and fish have shifted from shallow feeding stations to deeper resting lies, I'm one of the first to go deep. There's no question that a skilled nympher is a more versatile angler than a dry-fly purist, and in backcountry fishing, versatility is the name of the game. You're constantly fishing waters that you've never seen before and that you'll probably never return to unless you can quickly pound up some representative fish. Often that means nymphing.

Some of the best nymphs for prospecting subsurface during non-hatch periods are impressionistic types that don't imitate a specific aquatic organism but approximate many. The Woolly Worm is the classic example of a nymph (or wet fly) that just looks buggy. In my first few seasons of fly fishing, I caught more trout on Woolly Worms than on any other subsurface fly. As I began tying my own flies and looking at materials critically, I realized that the buggy silhouette of the Woolly Worm had to be the huge drawing card, because the standard materials—saddle hackle, a chenille body, and a scrap of wool for the tail—are nothing special.

The Woolly Worm still flourishes in my fly boxes, but I tie it now with soft, buggy materials to help the fly fish to its true potential. I use a pair of soft, webby hen hackles (short hackle palmered over the rear of the fly and longer hackle palmered over the front), a dubbed rabbit fur body, and a tuft of rabbit fur for the tail. The finished fly is raked from all sides with a nylon brush to sweep back and distribute the hackle and to fuzz the dubbed body so that it blends with the hackle. (See *American Angler,* November/December 1993, for tying details.)

The resulting Soft-Hackle Woolly Worm is a super-buggy fly that moves and pulsates seductively. It's effective when dead-drifted in current like a standard nymph; it can also be pumped or stripped like a wet fly to make its hackles pulse enticingly. As an all-around prospecting fly that produces on all types of water, the Soft-Hackle Woolly Worm has a reserved parking space in my nymph box.

My bread-and-butter version of the Soft-Hackle Woolly Worm has a black body and tail with grizzly hackle. Olive and grizzly, and all black with a hot orange tail, are also excellent versions. Black maintains a bold silhouette in deep or discolored water and in low light—situations in which I'm apt to reach for a prospecting fly. I carry the black-and-grizzly Woolly in #6, #12, and #16. The #6 is a valuable prospecting fly on big rivers and swift pocket waters that harbor an abundance of big stonefly nymphs. The #12 is my standard prospecting Woolly for lakes and streams. The #16 is perfect for light rods, small streams, and skittish fish. I tie all my Woollies lightly weighted so they punch through the surface. If I need to get deep, I add split shot to the tippet or use a sinking line.

SCUDS

If I were limited to a single fly pattern for fishing backcountry lakes, it would not be an insect imitation. It would be a scud or shrimp imitation. Most high-altitude lakes that support fat, healthy fish have a forage base of scuds or shrimp, and the importance of packing effective imitations can't be overstated.

The relatively small scuds of the *Hyalella* genus are able to thrive in fairly acid lakes, with little or no weed growth, right up to extreme elevations. These shrimplike crustaceans have jointed shells and numerous legs and are quick, darting swimmers. The naturals are primarily #12 through #16 and range from light to dark olive.

In small, cold lakes at extreme elevations, freshwater shrimp, commonly called fairy shrimp, are even more abundant than scuds. Shrimp are easily recognized—they swim on their backs with their feet and gills rippling upward from the sides of their bodies. Shrimp also have long, slender tails and are so transparent you can see their dark digestive tract. Light tan or light olive with amber highlights are common colors. Most naturals are #12, but they can range as large as #8. I commonly scout shoreline pockets along high lakes to confirm the presence of shrimp. As lake levels recede following spring runoff, shrimp become trapped in pockets. In summer, when their populations boom, clouds of shrimp are readily observed in these pockets.

I tie a fly I call the Fast-Sinking Scud to imitate scuds and shrimp. On lakes above 9,000 feet, this fly has taken more big trout for me than all other flies combined. It has both scud and shrimp characteristics, and as its name implies, it sinks quickly to the level of cruising fish.

The body of the Fast-Sinking Scud is dubbed from equal parts rabbit and finely chopped Antron. The back is clear elastic pulled forward and ribbed with 5X tippet material. For the slender body-length tail, use soft hackle from a grouse or hen pheasant. Rake the finished fly with a nylon brush from under the belly up toward the edges of the shellback to project soft rabbit fur and translucent Antron right from the edges of the shell. (See *American Angler,* January/February 1995, for tying details.)

In silhouette and opacity, the Fast-Sinking Scud closely resembles a scud, but the fuzzy underbody and the smooth elastic shellback cause the fly to flip onto its back and swim like a shrimp, and the body-length tail also suggests a shrimp. There's a secondary advantage to the Fast-Sinking Scud swimming on its back—virtually all fish are solidly hooked in the upper snout.

I tie the pattern on the Tiemco 3761 hook, which has a straight shank and a Sproat bend to suggest a little curvature. Shrimp are quite straight while swimming, and scuds in water are not as radically curved as most scud imitations.

The fact that the Fast-Sinking Scud flips onto its smooth elastic back and sinks quickly with only moderate weight wrapped on the hook shank is an important design element. Big goldens and brook trout cruise fast and deep much of the time. On lakes with just a few big fish, opportunities at visible cruisers can be fleeting. A fly that is a convincing imitation of the primary forage, casts like a bullet, and quickly drops to the level of cruising fish is invaluable. I often fish the Fast-Sinking Scud on a 12-foot leader with 5 feet of 4X tippet to enhance its sink rate.

An olive-and-gray Fast-Sinking Scud in #12 is my standard version, but #16 performs noticeably better on lakes loaded with small scuds. I also carry a heavily weighted #8 version that I call the Mega Scud. It's a big, flashy attractor scud tied with an orange body and a flashback of peacock herl and silver Flashabou pulled under its shellback. The Mega Scud shines for working deep or roiled water and is often the difference between boom and bust when lake conditions are tough.

BAITFISH IMITATIONS AND STREAMERS

The vast majority of high-altitude lakes scattered across the Rockies were barren of trout until humans intervened. Lakes that were naturally inaccessible to trout were also inaccessible to baitfish, and minnows have never been introduced to most high lakes. Trout may strike baitfish imitations out of instinct, hunger, or aggression, but—with the exception of trout fry—there are usually no small fish in high lakes for anglers to imitate.

The reaction of high-lake trout to baitfish imitations seems to vary by species. Golden trout show little interest. Cutthroats and rainbows are more aggressive. Nice brookies positively savage a realistic baitfish imitation I call the Bobbing Baitfish.

The Bobbing Baitfish is tied with a buoyant closed-cell foam underbody beneath gold or silver mylar tubing. It also has a short marabou tail and a pair of buoyant doll eyes. The dorsal surface of the fly is tinted with black and olive markers before the tubing is coated with five-minute epoxy. The doll eyes are mounted when the epoxy is tacky. For high lakes I tie the pattern on #6 and #10 long-shank hooks. I often bump the fly off the bottom with a sinking-tip line. With each strip the fly dives, following the path of the line, and with each pause the buoyant fly rises—an erratic action that really triggers strikes. Because the fly rises at each pause, it's relatively snag-free on rock bottoms.

The Bobbing Baitfish provided the most memorable evening I've ever enjoyed with a baitfish imitation on a high lake. The scene was in mid-August on a sizable lake above timberline in the Beartooths of Montana. It was a gusty evening with a chop on the water. Schools of fat brook trout were cruising well out from shore. There was an occasional strong surface swirl in the chop, but casting dry flies to widely scattered risers was not producing. A Bobbing Baitfish retrieved near the bottom had taken fish that afternoon, so I knotted the fly on again, but this time I stayed with a floating line. When a school of brookies swung within casting range, I fired the baitfish in their midst and began stripping it across the surface. The results were heart stopping. Even with the chop on the water, I could see multiple wakes as fish raced for the fly. In the last two hours of light, I landed one hefty brook trout after another. Several fish topped 17 inches, and I've never taken heavier trout of that length from any water at any elevation.

Woolly Buggers also produce on lakes for all trout species. Buggers, especially in small sizes, are more suggestive of leeches and large nymphs than baitfish, and that's probably a factor in their effectiveness. On lakes Buggers are worked with enticing strip retrieves, and at various times trout take them anywhere from just under the surface to right on the bottom. I tie Buggers in the same style as I do Soft-Hackle Woolly Worms—with soft hen hackles and dubbed fur bodies that I brush vigorously. On Buggers I retain the standard marabou tail and mix in a few strands of flash material. An all-black Soft-Hackle Bugger in #8 or #12 is my primary lake streamer.

In the backcountry baitfish imitations shine on the larger streams and rivers, which often teem with sculpins. Sculpins are well camouflaged and are shaped for hugging the bottom in swift current. The Muddler Minnow and its many variations are excellent sculpin imitations. For much of my streamer fishing, I still prefer a fairly standard Muddler. I dress mine with wing and tail slips of bronze turkey, an underwing of gray or red squirrel tail, a short but well-defined collar of stacked and flared elk hair to simulate the prominent pectoral fins of a sculpin, and a substantial head of clipped deer hair in natural or dyed olive. I don't weight my Muddlers, but I do wrap a stout, slightly oval body from gold metallic embroidery thread. Even though healthy sculpins are bottom huggers, I often fish a Muddler at medium depths or just under the surface to imitate an injured sculpin caught up in the current. A buoyant

Muddler with a full, tightly packed deer-hair head flutters and swings more enticingly than heavily weighted or wool-head versions. I carry Muddlers in #6 and #12.

For highly predacious bull trout, which are primarily encountered in western Montana and Idaho, I pack a few Marabou Muddlers in #4. Natural brown marabou from the butt of a wild turkey or a pheasant imitates the coloration of a sculpin nicely. I supplement the marabou wing with gold flash material and add some red marabou tips to the collar to simulate the flared gills of a wounded baitfish. Bull trout often hold in deep pools, so I weight these Muddlers for fishing deep.

Muddlers can be fished on floating or sinking-tip lines, depending on the desired depth. On tumbling streams and brawling rivers, Muddlers tend to fish best when cast directly across stream or quartering down and across, then worked back across the current on a fixed length of line. As the fly swings back across the current, pump your rod tip and actively probe with the fly around boulders and other likely holding lies. It's always a thrill to see a big trout launch from a hidden lair and chase a swinging fly. Trout often follow and strike a Muddler at the end of the drift, as the fly is hanging downstream, so always let the fly hang for a bit, and make a few short strips before picking it up. The Muddler is also an excellent locator fly; even when large fish are not in the mood to strike, they often flash at a Muddler and reveal their holding lies. It can pay to carefully mark such fish and return when they're feeding more actively.

Soft-Hackle Buggers are superb streamers on moving water, because they're effective on a dead drift or when actively pumped. My primary Bugger for moving water is my Soft-Hackle Bi-Bugger. The rear half of this fly is grizzly hackle palmered over olive rabbit, and the front half is black hackle palmered over black rabbit. The tail is black marabou over olive marabou with gold flash. The multitone color scheme suggests both sculpins and crayfish, and is superb wherever these food forms flourish. I pack Bi-Buggers in #4, #8, and #12.

CHAPTER 13

Speed-Scouting for Trout in Backcountry Lakes

When I began fishing the high country, I was in the same boat as most trout anglers—virtually all of my fishing had been on moving water. Through years of observation, I'd learned to read moving water—to look at a stream and identify the areas where trout were likely to feed and hold. Then I began fishing high lakes and had to learn to read water all over again.

Without question, learning to quickly locate fish in unfamiliar lakes is an essential skill for high-country anglers. Nothing accelerates the learning curve like fishing lakes on a regular basis. One of the best ways to learn to read lakes is to pick a range that's loaded with lakes and go exploring. In some ranges you can easily visit several lakes in a day and upward of two dozen lakes in a week. After a few trips like this, you'll be able to blow onto a strange lake and home in on fish like an osprey.

Speaking of ospreys, watching birds fish can teach you a lot about how to attack a high lake. Most high lakes are small, covering from 20 to 100 acres. The water is usually clear enough that fish and shallow structure can be seen, especially from high vantages on sunny days. Given these conditions, I rarely scout a lake by fishing. Instead, I circle it and scan the water through polarized sunglasses.

Getting above a lake greatly increases your ability to see beneath the surface. I frequently scout from ledges and slopes that are much too high to cast from. From a sharply elevated vantage, the profile of a lake snaps into focus. You can readily distinguish shallows from deep water. You can see trout cruising very deep or well out from shore—fish that would be nearly impossible to spot from a low angle. On some cross-country approaches, you get your first look at a lake from several hundred feet above it. Take full advantage of this bird's-eye view before descending. Note the locations of all shallows, and scan for cruising fish.

Cruising trout may or may not be easy to spot, depending on the lighting, backdrop, and water clarity. Trout viewed from above against a shallow backdrop are generally darker than the bottom and thus easy to spot. If a fish is exceptionally light in color, the dark shadow it casts on the bottom in bright sunlight may be more apparent than the fish itself. Trout viewed against a backdrop of deep water, however, often appear as fleeting, aqua-green reflections and can be tough to spot, especially if it's choppy or overcast, or if the fish are cruising well beneath the surface. Lakes that are normally clear can also be clouded by sediments carried by melting snow. Big waves can stir bottom sediments, making fish and structure difficult to see for a period. Inlet streams can deposit fine glacial sediments that suspend in the water almost indefinitely; some glacial flours are ground so fine that they suspend in a cup of water overnight. Lakes that are permanently clouded with heavy loads of glacial flour are usually sterile—sunlight penetration and photosynthesis are largely blocked, fish eggs are suffocated on the redds, and even stocked fish are stressed to survive.

You can see more subsurface detail when it's sunny and calm. Mountain mornings are often clear with light winds; they're excellent times to scout. When the water is glassy, even distant riseforms are very noticeable. On lakes with few fish, a single rise can be a valuable clue to fish location.

When scouting in blustery, overcast weather, you have to be patient and linger at a good vantage until there's a lull in the wind and the sun peeks through—then a lake bottom can light up, revealing fish and features that were invisible moments earlier. Even when spotting conditions are poor, it can be worth waiting for brief periods of illumination. Fish often cruise established routes; once you determine those routes, you know where to work your flies when spotting conditions deteriorate.

Trout aren't distributed evenly throughout a lake. You'll locate them faster if you concentrate your scouting on areas that consistently attract fish. On high lakes most trout forage is produced in shallow water, where sunlight penetration is high and summer water temperatures are moderate. Wind can carry hatching or mating insects over deep water, and at times trout forage on the bottom at considerable depths, but feeding trout usually invade water that's less than 15 feet deep. If you locate the primary feeding flats and watch them at the right times, you'll find fish.

From a distance shallow flats usually appear lighter than deep water. Most flats are adjacent to shore, but some are isolated by deep troughs, and a shorebound angler may not be able to reach them. A flat doesn't have to be large to be a hot spot. I've seen fish swarm over small flats while ignoring extensive ones.

Rocky flats provide stable, year-round habitat for a wide range of aquatic organisms and almost always attract fish. Sandy flats are unstable and support very little fish forage. Silty flats with a high soil content are more fertile and may even support weed growth. Weedy flats are relatively rare on high lakes, but when they occur, they're almost always loaded with scuds, damsel nymphs, or swimming mayfly nymphs. In high lakes weed growth may amount to no more than a short nap along the bottom, and you may have to look carefully or drag a fly right along the bottom to discover these weeds.

Some good lakes lack significant flats but are almost completely rimmed by shallow shelves that extend 5 to 15 yards from shore before dropping off abruptly. Shelves offer cruising trout the best of both worlds—the abundant food of the shallows and quick access to the security of deep water. As you scout, watch for trout cruising parallel to shore over the outside edges of shelves. On lakes that have both shelves and flats, trout often use the shelves as travel routes to the flats. Where a shelf starts to veer away from shore and widen into a significant flat is often a major trout crossing.

Some high lakes have several miles of shoreline, and you may not have time to scout it all. By studying the surrounding terrain, though, you can often project where shallows extend into a lake, saving yourself time and legwork. A steep slope or hanging wall dropping right to the water's edge usually indicates deep water near shore. A low, level shore often indicates shallow flats extending into a lake.

Few high-country lakes are landlocked; most are connected to neighboring lakes by tumbling streams. Large inlet streams deposit shallow deltas off their mouths and extend their current well into a lake, distributing nutrients and oxygen. A strong inlet flow provides substantial habitat for current-dwelling aquatic insects and transports drifting forage to trout, which abandon their lake-cruising habits and establish feeding stations in the flow, just as river fish do. The mouths of major inlets usually attract some trout throughout the day, and large numbers of fish may stack up in the current at peak feeding times.

Inlet streams also provide gravel and well-oxygenated water for spawning. Most trout in high-country lakes spawn at the mouths of inlet streams or run upstream as far as they can navigate. Cutthroats, in particular, tackle some surprisingly steep slopes. The timing of spring spawning varies with elevation and the severity of the previous winter and can vary by several weeks from one year to the next on a given lake. Cutthroats, rainbows, and goldens spawn shortly after ice-out, but at elevations of 8,000 to nearly 11,000 feet, all of these species may spawn as early as June or as late as early August. Brook trout spawn in fall or early winter, but at high elevations they often adopt their brilliant spawning hues and begin staging off inlets by September.

Hitting a lake at the peak of spawning reveals volumes about the size and numbers of its adult fish. But you shouldn't severely disrupt spawning activity or kill significant numbers of trophy fish, which are particularly vulnerable at this time. Pinch down your hook barbs, and play and release spawning fish quickly without removing them from the water. After you've caught some representative fish, move on. When fish are spawning and highly visible throughout an area, it's a good time to limit your actual fishing and visit as many lakes as possible, just to check out the sizes and numbers of fish. In a week or two of hustling, you can go to school on a lot of lakes.

Some lakes have several inlet streams. Streams that descend from neighboring lakes are usually larger and more productive than inlets fed primarily by melting snow or spring seepages. Snow-fed inlets and small seepages often dry up in late summer or freeze solid in winter, limiting their ability to support insect life. Lake-fed inlets usually flow year-round and reach more moderate summer temperatures, which increases their value to trout as feeding and spawning sites.

Lake outlets are usually worth checking out for fish activity. Golden trout are particularly fond of spawning in outlets. On some lakes goldens spawn successfully on rocky, wavy shoals adjacent to outlets rather than in the stream itself. An outlet stream with significant depth and flow will attract feeding fish throughout summer. The best lake I know of for big goldens has an outlet flow that tapers to a deep channel for 30 yards before cascading downhill toward the next lake in the chain. During summer evenings big goldens sometimes establish feeding stations deep in the outlet channel; the most productive angling is river-style, dead-drift nymphing with a strike indicator, split shot, and a scud imitation.

If you're new to high-lake fishing, you may have to revise your understanding of how sunlight and heat affect trout activity. On low-elevation lakes hot, bright weather normally sends trout into the cool depths for much of the day; fish invade the shallows to feed mainly at the margins of daylight or on overcast days when these shallows are coolest. Lakes near or above timberline tend to remain so cold in their upper levels throughout the brief summer that trout often stay fairly shallow all day. Both insect and fish activity often surges as the bright midday sun heats frigid shallows to moderate temperatures. On very high lakes I catch many of my best trout during sunny afternoons, when good numbers of fish are active in the shallows and spotting conditions are ideal. Midday fishing is particularly productive from early to midsummer. During calm evenings the lack of wave action allows the shallows to retain their warmth longer, and this can trigger fast evening fishing.

By mid-August in an unusually warm summer, high-altitude trout may vanish to the depths for much of the day, but soon after the sun leaves the water, some fish usually start patrolling the flats. If a lake has a prominent peak or ridge immediately to its west, evening shade will hit part of the lake with several hours of daylight remaining. By late summer fish on some lakes clearly adjust their feeding routines to forage during the prolonged evenings. In this scenario you want to finish your dinner early and be on the water when the shade hits.

High lakes are at their coldest at dawn, which makes daybreak angling comparatively slow for much of the summer. On travel days I usually hike and establish my new camp in the morning so I'll be set to fish by afternoon, when trout become more active. Daybreak fishing can suddenly pick up toward the end of a hot, dry summer, though, especially on lakes below timberline.

Trout are easier to locate on lakes with high fish densities, not just because there are more fish, but also because intense competition for food forces them to cruise the shallows almost continuously regardless of food availability, water temperature, and weather conditions. On lakes where trout are in balance with the food supply, the fish are more selective about their feeding times—they'll gorge for brief periods when conditions are favorable, then vanish to deep water for much of the day.

Large lakes that hold just a few big fish are the toughest to pattern, but even here the fish are usually concentrated. On a lake with 2 miles of shoreline, several good fish might be feeding for just a few hours a day on a flat that's only 50 yards wide—and the rest of the lake will be dead. On this type of lake, I scout a lot and angle very little until I locate fish, because an hour of angling at the right time and place will yield more hookups than days of random casting.

Once you discover a high lake with big trout, you'll invariably itch to go back. On a return trip, immediately scout the areas where you took fish in the past. If conditions are similar, the fish will likely be in the same areas. If conditions are radically different, however, there's a good chance you'll have to relocate the fish. On some lakes that I visit repeatedly, the bulk of the trout shift their feeding preferences among four or five sites. On other lakes, I consistently catch most of my fish on a single flat.

Large lakes with just a few big fish are always risky destinations. If the fish aren't keying on an observable area, they may be scattered and virtually impossible to pattern. Those are the lakes that treat you royally on one trip, then shut you out on the next. When you do hit the jackpot on such a lake, jot a few notes right on your map about the time of year and the type of summer it is. The lake could get stingy on subsequent trips, and you may need to precisely duplicate the conditions of your successful trip to hit the lake when it's on again.

CHAPTER 14

Determining the Trophy
Potential of High Lakes

The majority of high lakes have two of the three ingredients needed to produce trophy trout: dependable supplies of cold, clean water and fishing pressure light enough that most trout reach maturity. Yet perhaps 10 percent of high lakes produce fat, healthy trout, and roughly half produce skinny or stunted fish.

Population density is the factor that separates most trophy lakes from the kind that produce only average or small fish. Where the trout population is in balance with the food supply, individual fish can exhibit good to excellent growth rates, even in high lakes that are covered with ice eight months a year.

Few high lakes have indigenous trout, but most lakes capable of supporting trout have been stocked at some time. In many lakes introduced trout have reproduced so successfully that they've depleted their food supply, and individual fish are small. Too much spawning habitat in the form of cold, clean feeder streams has been the downfall of many a high lake. In reality, many high lakes have a fish surplus, not a food shortage.

Other lakes, particularly seep lakes, which lack permanent inlet and outlet streams, have no spawning habitat and require periodic stocking to maintain a fishery. Stocked lakes can produce nice trout, especially if fish are stocked in fairly low densities and the waters are rested between stocking rotations so that the forage base can rebuild. A lake planted at eight-year intervals, however, holds older fish in only its third through perhaps sixth year after stocking. After that, it has no adult fish until its next class of stocked fingerlings matures, which can take years. Most high lakes that are planted at frequent intervals are accessible by day hikers and are managed as put-and-take fisheries. They're seeded with high densities of small fish, and heavy angling pressure tends to remove these fish before they mature.

As you scour the high country for lakes that continuously produce fat, healthy trout, you're basically looking for lakes that are at least slightly alkaline and have successful but limited natural reproduction. Such lakes, unless they're discovered by too many catch-and-kill anglers, can indefinitely support a relatively limited but stable population of trout, most of which eventually grow large. These lakes tend to be quite remote or at least off maintained trails, although there are exceptions.

Not surprisingly, my largest high-country trout have consistently come from lakes that hold relatively few fish. Since 1985 I've made six treks to a particular golden trout lake that lies nearly 30 miles from the nearest trailhead. In those six trips, I've landed less than twenty fish on the lake, but most of them have been bruisers of 20 to nearly 25 inches.

This lake covers about 70 acres, has roughly a mile of shoreline, and is the largest of four golden trout lakes in a chain. All four lakes lie within 2 miles of each other and range from about 9,500 to 10,000 feet in elevation, which is not particularly high by golden standards. The tumbling creek that connects them is too steep to allow significant passage of fish upstream from lake to lake, although some downstream movement occurs. The lakes have similar water chemistry and contain pure-strain goldens probably descended from the same stock, but fish size varies from lake to lake according to population density.

At only 10 acres, the highest trout lake in the chain is also the smallest. I've taken as many as a dozen goldens here in an hour, but few have been over a foot long; the biggest was 15 inches. Although this lake isn't severely overpopulated, competition for food is clearly sufficient to curb the growth of individual fish.

From the outlet of the small lake, the stream cascades some 250 feet in ¼ mile to the large, 70-acre lake I described earlier. Few trout journeying downstream from the small lake would survive the tumble. This helps limit the trout population of the big lake, which has the lowest population density and the biggest fish in the chain. Another factor may also help limit the population of the big lake: Spawning occurs in a swift outlet chute that flows level for only 30 yards before plunging toward the next lake in the chain, and it's likely that some newly hatched fry are swept downstream by the powerful current. Most of these fish probably never return to the parent lake, although I believe some adults make the climb at high flows.

The third lake in the chain covers 20 acres; it lies just 200 yards downstream and 50 feet lower than the big lake. Since this third lake produces its own fish and receives fry from the big lake, it's not surprising that it has a higher population. In an afternoon I've caught as many as eight goldens ranging from 14 to 18 inches here. The fish are solidly built but lack the truly impressive girth of the fish in the big lake, and I've yet to take a 20-incher from the third lake.

After exiting the third lake, the stream drops another 150 feet in ½ mile. Several falls are high enough to block any upstream movement of fish, although some downstream movement probably occurs. Wherever the stream flattens for a bit, there are pods of hungry little goldens that spend their lives scraping out a meager existence in the stream. In addition to competing for limited food, these stream fish must constantly expend energy to feed and hold in the current. The stream goldens are brilliantly marked and have the same growth potential as the big trout in the lakes, but even the adults rarely reach 10 inches. When I'm hungry for a meal of golden trout, I head for the stream and thin the population a bit.

The fourth and lowest golden lake in the chain covers about 30 acres and sits just below a smaller lake that's too shallow to sustain trout in winter. With plenty of small fish living upstream, you might expect the fourth lake to have a high fish density, but it doesn't. Perhaps the freeze-out lake detains the bulk of the fish that drop down from the stream, and they perish in winter. In any case, the fourth lake falls between the second and third lakes in both fish size and density. In an afternoon I typically land three to six goldens ranging from 17 to 21 inches. This is the only lake in the chain with significant weed growth, and its goldens grow fat gorging on small scuds. When the big lake is dead in the afternoon, I often drop down to this lake and sight-fish for goldens cruising over the weedy flats.

The drainage I've just described is exceptional in that naturally reproducing trout have been present for several decades, yet fish populations are relatively low and stable. Most drainages aren't so fortunate.

Because high lakes tend to be small, with excellent spawning habitat and very little angling pressure or natural predation, they're particularly prone to population explosions. Throughout the Rockies I've seen scores of high lakes that were reputed to be fine fisheries for a few decades after trout were introduced, but that are now drastically overpopulated.

Where a trout population has far outstripped its food supply, the situation is apparent at a glance. Gaunt fish with disproportionately large heads and emaciated bodies cruise listlessly but relentlessly, expending more energy than they consume. Unfortunately, when the population spirals out of control, stunted or snaky fish can occur in high lakes that have good water chemistry and fertility. I know lakes that support a tremendous biomass of trout—all in 8-inch increments. On the other end of the spectrum, a low trout population is not a guarantee of fat, healthy fish. Some high lakes have such poor fertility that trout are stressed to survive even though the population is sparse.

Many high lakes have a trout surplus that's not overt. Although the trout aren't malnourished to the point of deformity, they lack the physique, wariness, and vitality to furnish interesting sport for an experienced angler. The black-spotted cutthroat native to some eastward-flowing drainages, including Yellowstone Lake, the Yellowstone River, and the upper Missouri, has been widely transplanted to high lakes throughout the Rockies. It's typically a long, slender ecotype that often exceeds 15 inches even in nutrient-poor waters. In some high lakes, Yellowstone cutts run 18 inches but weigh barely a pound. When hooked they writhe snakelike for about ten seconds, then turn over. This is not an indictment of the fighting ability of cutthroats; I'll discuss many fine cutthroat fisheries later. I mention it to point out that a food shortage or abundance affects various species of trout differently. Eighteen-inch cutthroats aren't necessarily worth catching, and 14-inch brook trout can be a blast if they've been chowing down.

Of course, along with population density, the productivity of any trout lake is influenced by its water chemistry and the extent of its shallows. Shallows are important because they produce the bulk of the trout forage. A lake needs a deep, well-oxygenated bowl to sustain its trout through the long alpine winters, but beyond that, the more extensive its shallows are, the better. It's possible for a lake with very limited shallows to produce big trout, but only in low numbers. High lakes that support good numbers of healthy trout invariably have extensive shallows.

Two lakes with similar structures can vary widely in their productivity, depending on water chemistry. Hard, alkaline water with a high lime content supports a richer food chain than soft, acid water. In the high Rockies, where topsoil is thin and many drainages are primarily composed of gneiss, schist, and granite, most lakes are slightly acid to slightly alkaline. But localized rock and soil conditions vary. Springs seeping from sedimentary sandstone or limestone, or organically enriched soils, boost the alkalinity of some high lakes substantially. Lakes containing marl or phosphate deposits laid down in old seabeds are also quite alkaline.

There are high lakes fertile enough to sustain large populations of big, fat trout, but such lakes are so rare that I'm always surprised to encounter them. At one of my favorite golden trout lakes in the Wind River Range, I've caught as many as four dozen hefty goldens in a day ranging from 15 to 18 inches, plus an occasional brute to 23 inches. For a golden lake that supports some true trophies, this lake has by far the highest fish densities I've encountered. I've visited it seven times since 1978, and in twenty years the size of its top-end fish has not diminished. In fact, I landed the largest golden I've taken in this lake on my most recent trip.

At a favorite brook trout lake above timberline in the Beartooths of Montana, I've taken over fifty squaretails in a day ranging from 13 to 18 inches—fish built so much like footballs I was surprised they didn't have seams and laces. The fish in this lake are obscenely fat by any standards. Although the last 3 miles are off trail, the lake is only 13 miles from a trailhead, so I pop in frequently. In the early 1990s I visited the lake for five consecutive summers, and if anything, both the population and the size of the top-end fish appear to be increasing.

With so many lakes of varying productivity to explore, backcountry anglers have to be able to move onto an unfamiliar lake and determine its trophy potential quickly. The easiest way to do this is to catch a fish and examine it. In small mountain lakes, cruising fish have equal access to food, so body type tends to cut across an entire population. If the first fish you catch has a skinny or average build, the rest of the population will likely follow suit. Even if it's only a 10-incher, if that first fish has a relatively small head, thick back, and deep belly, the lake probably has trophy potential.

So much of the history and mystique of fly fishing for trout revolves around moving water that many anglers neglect lakes. That's a shame, because the best high lakes are enchanted places with moods, allures, and rhythms of their own. Sublime in sunshine, menacing in storm, frequently stingy but occasionally benevolent—you'll never forget it when such a lake smiles on you. Even as you walk away, you'll be plotting your return—and this, more than the size of the fish, is the real yardstick of any fishery.

CHAPTER 15

Trekking for Trophy Goldens

Golden trout are widely considered the most brilliantly colored trout in the world. After two decades of chasing goldens, I wouldn't contest that view. Yet when I think of goldens, most of the superlatives that spring to mind revolve around their sporting qualities. Aside from their physical radiance and the matchless beauty of their alpine habitat, big, healthy goldens are superb game fish. Elusive, wary, acrobatic, powerful—they are, pound for pound, a match for any trout that swims at any elevation.

The golden trout found in the Rockies are native to the Kern River system of the Sierra Nevadas of California. Several subspecies of goldens evolved there in isolated headwater streams at around 10,000 feet. It's unclear whether goldens descend from rainbows or cutthroats, although anyone who has watched a big golden repeatedly go airborne would probably guess at a rainbow lineage.

Goldens have been transplanted to high-altitude waters throughout the West. In the Rockies minor populations exist in Colorado, Utah, and Idaho, and I've caught goldens in all three of these states. But the best populations are found in Montana and Wyoming, particularly in the Beartooth Mountains and the Wind River Range.

In the tumbling streams of their native Sierras, goldens seldom exceed a foot in length, but when transplanted to lakes they grow larger. In some Sierra lakes, goldens achieve weights of 3 pounds or more. Currently the largest golden trout in the world are probably swimming in the Rockies. The Wind River Range produced at least two goldens of over

11 pounds in the 1940s, shortly after fish were introduced into its virgin lakes with untapped food supplies. Such conditions have largely vanished, and it's doubtful that many goldens of this size are alive today. I'd estimate that three dozen lakes in the Winds hold goldens of 20 inches. I've landed a half dozen goldens in the 23- to 25-inch range that unofficially weighed 5 to 6 pounds. As many as a dozen lakes in the Winds may hold a few goldens of this size or larger, although I've never seen or tangled with a golden that was clearly larger than those I've landed. At Lightning Lake in the Beartooths, where 4-pounders are caught every year, a 10-pound golden was reportedly gillnetted and released by fisheries personnel around 1990. That's easily the biggest pure-strain fish I've heard of since I began fishing goldens.

As with all trout, the coloration of goldens varies considerably from water to water and even among fish from the same population. Spotting is similar to the cutthroat's, with large, dark spots clustered on and near the tail, and sparse spotting over the dorsal surfaces and head. Dorsal surfaces are typically olive with a bluish tint, but some goldens are a striking, dark ebony across the back. Small goldens have nine or more distinct crimson parr markings, but these vertical markings are usually absent or indistinct on fish that weigh over a pound. In adult goldens the coloration of the lateral surfaces varies considerably with the sex of a fish and with the season. Spawning males are the most vividly colored; their sides are stained a brilliant, bloody scarlet that can wrap completely under the belly. The jaws of mature males are more angular than those of females, with some males displaying a pronounced, ball-like tip on the lower jaw. In postspawn males the sides usually fade to yellowish gold with a dark, rosy strip along the lateral line. Mature females tend to be silver sided with a rosy tint and are shaded much lighter overall than males. Bellies of both sexes range from white with scarlet stains to muted yellow. Heads are two toned, with the olive shading of the dorsal surfaces dominating the upper head and the vivid colors of the lateral surfaces layered below. Ventral and anal fins, and often the dorsal fin, are tipped with white. Scales are small and fine, giving goldens a glossy sheen. Goldens are also the most radiant of the trouts internally—their flesh is the deep, fiery orange of fresh salmon steaks.

To sustain pure goldens, a lake must be protected from invasion by other trout species. For this reason golden lakes are typically the highest fisheries in a drainage and must be separated from lower lakes by impassable waterfalls that block upstream migration of other trout species. Goldens, cutthroats, and rainbows are all spring spawners, and wherever two of these species inhabit the same water, they'll cross to produce hybrids that display mixed characteristics from both parent strains. I've caught golden-rainbow hybrids in several western ranges, including the Wind Rivers, where colorful goldbows of 3 pounds and larger provide some hot action. A few lakes are actually managed for these hybrids. In the Absaroka-Beartooth Wilderness of Montana, many pure-golden populations have been lost through hybridization with rainbows or cutthroats. Brook trout are fall spawners and will not hybridize with goldens, but brookies are notorious for invading and overpopulating high-country lakes, crowding out existing trout species. Brook trout have largely usurped goldens in what were historically some of the best golden waters in the Winds, including Washakie and Cook Lakes.

I caught my first goldens in 1977, fittingly enough at Golden Lakes below Hay Pass in the Wind River Range. It was a July afternoon, but the sky was low and spitting snow, and gusty winds pounded waves against the shoreline rocks, christening me with cold spray. Goldens are typically described in gemlike terms, and that day I witnessed why. In contrast to the bleak sky and the brooding rock faces hemming the lakes, the trout were as resplendent as jewels. Like all of the goldens I'd seen pictured, however, they were small.

The following summer, if it could be called a summer, my golden trout fishing was largely derailed by heavy snowpack. On a sunny morning in mid-June, I hiked out of Sinks Canyon above Lander, Wyoming, bound for some high-lake fishing in the Winds. By early afternoon I was into deep snow at 9,000 feet in the timber around Three Forks Park. I should have turned back right there and headed for some low-slung mountains, but I was able to convince myself that I'd find bare ground and open lakes in the unshaded basins above timberline. That proved a serious delusion. Except for exposed rocks, I did not step on bare ground again for five gut-busting days.

The snowpack was still 3 feet deep on the level. The nights were cold enough to harden the snow, so I usually made decent headway in the mornings, but the shirt-sleeve days brought blinding sunshine that softened the crust, and without snowshoes I was usually floundering by noon. In places I punched thigh deep on every step; covering 100 yards was a dogfight. Once, without warning, I plunged into a buried deadfall, somehow wedging a foot into the twisted limbs so that I couldn't extract it. After shedding my pack, I managed to untie my boot, snake my foot out, and wrench the boot free with my hands. By the time I clawed my way out and reassembled, I'd fired off every four-letter word in my arsenal.

After fording the screaming-cold North Fork of the Popo Agie, I continued up the river to the Cirque of the Towers, then veered north to Valentine Lake, pushing to nearly 12,000 feet. Above timber the rock cairns were buried and there was no trace of the trail. I was on my own, navigating in unfamiliar country without topo maps. At Valentine, where I'd planned to wet a line for goldens, I had a tough time finding the lake. Finally I determined that I was standing on it. Covered with deep snow, the lake was barely distinguishable from the surrounding basin.

From Valentine I pushed north to Grave Lake, still hoping to find a spit of open water and maybe a big mackinaw trout cruising the ice-out shallows, but Grave was locked up tight. That pretty much doused any hopes of finding open lakes up high, but I stuck to my route, crossing the Continental Divide at Hailey Pass and descending toward the Big Sandy Openings. Just below Dads Lake, at 9,500 feet, I forded a small stream and stepped onto a patch of winter-killed grass. After five days of bucking snow without cutting a human track, I'll never forget how fine that soggy little spit of sun-kissed earth felt under my bare feet.

After that I wandered west to Idaho. By the time I drifted back into Wyoming and golden trout country, it was late August and summer was winding down. From Dubois I headed back into the Winds, making my inaugural march into a remote drainage that I was later to fish many times. As I moved up the drainage, I was detained by excellent cutthroat fishing at several lakes, and by the time I reached golden water, I was rationing my food. I did hang around long enough to hook what I would later appreciate was a truly big golden—a fish of about 6 pounds. At the sting of the hook, that powerful trout shot across a rocky flat, porpoising a half dozen times before diving for the rocks and leaving my leader in shambles.

The following August I returned to the same drainage with my dad and my brother Eric. We bypassed most of the cutthroat fishing, hoarding our time for the golden lakes. That turned out to be the right approach, because it took us three days to really crack the smaller and better of the two golden lakes.

The first day my dad and brother landed a golden each—their very first. Eric's fish was an eyeful—a bloodred male with a wicked kype and humped back. He looked like a sockeye salmon in spawning garb. At 17 inches that golden must have weighed over 3 pounds, and he had the deepest body I'd ever seen on a trout of that length. One glance was enough to keep us pounding the water between downpours.

On the second day rain and lightning pinned us in our tents until late afternoon. When the storm slackened, I finally landed my first sizable goldens, on back-to-back casts from atop the same boulder. Both fish nailed a black-and-grizzly Woolly Worm retrieved just under the surface in a strong chop.

On the third day the bad weather broke and the lake turned generous. After a slow morning, we hit a hatch of big mayflies at the head of the lake and enjoyed an unforgettable afternoon. Under a bright sun, we could see cruising fish clearly and drop our dry flies right in their paths. For several hours big goldens prowled the shoreline, inhaling our Wulffs and Humpies voraciously before zipping away on wild, cartwheeling runs. That evening we took more good fish along the shore near camp, primarily on Woolly Worms stripped just under the surface. On that third day we landed better than three dozen goldens that probably averaged 17 inches, with several nosing the 20-inch mark. Those goldens were gorgeous—and not just in color. They were superbly built with small heads, broad backs, and deep bellies. For the first time I saw that in the right lake, goldens could attain a large average size and provide superb sport.

That trip was to loom even larger in retrospect, because the three of us never made it back to the lake as a group. Although I've made the long trek alone six times in the ensuing twenty years, I still consider it our lake. The goldens are still there. The same funnel-shaped snowfield perches above the lake. And I can still see Dad in his crusher hat and hiking boots, battling a big golden in the evening sun.

After that I began to target larger goldens. As it turned out, the bulk of the premier golden lakes in the Rockies are in the Winds. Although I wish goldens were more prevalent in the high Rockies, there are enough good lakes in the Winds alone to keep an angler scrambling for a lifetime of summers.

Most lakes that hold large goldens (or large trout of any species) are sparsely populated, and you can't bank on seeing significant insect hatches or pods of rising fish. Day in and day out, fishing for big goldens often boils down to hunting for individual fish. Solitary goldens usually cruise fast and deep, and just spotting several fish a day requires effective scouting and long hours on the water. Hooking fish before they vanish is another challenge. Usually you have a single cast to do everything right. In this kind of fishing, you can't be groping for an effective fly. You need one that's proven so you can concentrate on spotting fish and putting your fly in front of them.

The Fast-Sinking Scud was the breakthrough fly that let me consistently hook deep-cruising goldens. Since scuds and shrimp are important forage in most of the better high lakes, fish are naturally receptive to imitations. As I fished various scud patterns, I noticed that those tied with smooth shellbacks tended to flip onto their backs and sink quickly. With a few modifications to enhance turnover and sink rate, it didn't take long to design a scud that sank quickly yet was lightly weighted for firing long casts.

When casting to visible cruisers, I usually rig with a #12 olive-and-gray Fast-Sinking Scud, a 12-foot leader with a 5-foot section of 4X tippet, and a floating line. The exceptionally long tippet allows a lightly weighted scud to quickly drop to depths of 10 feet and has significantly more stretch and strength than a short tippet. A floating line makes it easier to track the location of the scud and allows long pickups, which can mean an extra shot at a cruising fish before it vanishes.

If a golden is 10 feet down and really moving, you may need to lead it by 20 yards to sink the fly right in its path. After the cast, track the position of your fly, but also watch the trout for a reaction. A slight veer in course or a sudden acceleration is an indication that the fish has seen the fly and is interested. Goldens often take the Fast-Sinking Scud in a very unnerving manner—they rush the dropping fly but slam on the brakes when they reach it. The take by a stationary fish is imperceptible, unless viewing conditions are so good that you can see the fish's mouth flash open. Whenever a charging golden stops in the vicinity of a dropping scud, I hesitate for a moment, then set the hook. More often than not, the fish has the fly.

As in most fly fishing, the first presentation to a given fish is the one that's most likely to fool it. If an approaching golden doesn't react to a dropping scud, or if you think the fish hasn't seen it, strip the fly to draw attention. Some goldens prefer a moving scud. At times the right retrieve is surprisingly fast, with the scud skipping along in rapid bursts. When stripping, keep your rod tip low and slack out of the line, so that you'll feel a take immediately.

The tendency to cruise fast and deep gives goldens an elusive, ghosting quality that's reinforced by the constantly shifting light of the high country. One moment the water in front of you appears barren. The next moment the sun breaks through or the wind subsides, and you find yourself casting frantically to get a fly in front of a fleeting apparition. As you hunt for visible fish, it can pay to keep the fly pinched in your line hand and some loose coils of line in your rod hand so that you can get into action quickly. One windy afternoon I was handcuffed by a dandy golden cruising right along shore. The fish came in under the chop and was less than 5 yards away and closing when I spotted it. I froze, fully expecting the trout to spot me and bolt, but the choppy surface must have distorted my image, because the big golden cruised right by me. I had the fly pinched in my left hand, and as the fish passed, I flicked a little bow-and-arrow cast that required only slight movement. Before I could exhale, the fish was into my backing. It turned out to be a robust 22-inch golden—the best of the trip.

Some feeding flats are overlooked by handy observation and casting towers. I've spent many afternoons lounging atop house-size boulders and ledges 20 to 30 feet above the water. From this angle you can see a fish coming at 50 yards. I strip out half the fly line and coil it loosely on the rock so I can make a long cast quickly. When you're casting from high vantages, the fly should land well beyond the path of the fish, because as the line settles and sags, the fly will slide back toward the rod.

In poor light or roiled water, it's tough to see fish—and it's tough for fish to see the fly, too. When visibility is nil I head for a flat where fish should be present and probe deliberately near the bottom with a #8 orange-flashback Mega Scud. This fly is highly visible to fish and can be worked as deep as 10 feet with a floating line or much deeper with a sinking-tip. The Mega Scud consistently produces on high lakes when nothing else is really clicking, and I wish I'd tied this fly ten years earlier.

Bad weather and fishing blind often go together. It's enthralling to stand on a wind-whipped shore with low clouds swirling like smoke and obscuring everything much beyond the rod tip. It's a world of buttoned-up collars, snugged-down hat brims, numb hands, and narrow focus. When you feel the living jolt of a powerful take and line peels from your reel at an alarming rate, you're warmed—instantly.

The Fast-Sinking Scud is so effective on deep-cruising goldens that I now fish it almost exclusively during nonhatch periods. Goldens will rocket off the bottom from considerable depths, however, to hit a fly on or near the surface. Before I added the Fast-Sinking Scud to my fly boxes, I often stripped Soft-Hackle Woolly Worms from just subsurface to a few feet down, and many times I saw fish launch from as deep as 10 feet to nail the fly. When visibility is good, you can clearly see a big golden as it torpedoes upward, and the overwhelming temptation is to take the fly away by setting the hook too early. This reflex can be especially tough to tame in crystalline water, because a brilliant, hard-charging golden often appears to be closer to the surface than it is.

The best time to prospect with a dry fly during nonhatch periods is when the surface is glassy. In summer winds tend to lessen in the evening as the sinking sun stops fueling rising thermals. When a lake is absolutely flat, skating a dry fly on the surface creates a wake that deep-cruising goldens can detect from afar. For prospecting with a dry fly, I usually choose a #16 adult caddis pattern. Caddis are the most prevalent sizable insect on lakes, and the adults are relatively long lived, so fish get used to seeing them. On flat water, where fish get an undistorted look at the fly, a realistic adult caddis pattern—like my Upland Caddis—often takes fish that eyeball and refuse less convincing hairwing patterns.

During significant insect hatches, goldens rise as freely as any other trout. Unlike stream fish, which rise repeatedly from a fixed station in the current, trout in lakes cruise between rises. To catch a specific fish, you have to observe its last rise, gauge the speed and direction of the fish, and put the fly in its path at a comfortable rising interval. Hatches occur under all types of lighting. During sunny afternoons, you can see the fish clearly. During choppy, overcast evenings, you may have to guess the direction and speed a fish is traveling from its last riseform.

During a sporadic hatch, goldens tend to cruise fast and fairly deep. After rising, they slant quickly back to a cruising depth of 5 feet or more so they can survey a large surface area. By the time you spot a riseform and react, a fish may have traveled 5 yards, and your cast may need to be a good 10 yards ahead of the last rise to put the fly ahead of the fish. As a hatch increases in intensity, goldens cruise shallower and slower, with more frequent rises, and don't have to be led as far. At the peak of a heavy hatch, goldens will actually wallow at the surface, and the fly should be placed just a few feet in front of them.

On moving water, dry flies are usually drifted drag-free and motion-less in the feeding lane of a waiting trout. During a heavy hatch, this feeding lane may narrow to several inches. In the interest of feeding efficiently, a trout is unlikely to pursue a fly that's outside of its lane or that's moving erratically. Stillwater trout do patrol large areas of surface, however, as they actively cruise for winged insects, and skating a dry fly definitely catches the attention of fish. On lakes I routinely skate a dry fly with a series of short strips, then pause before moving it again. When rising activity is sporadic, I strip the fly vigorously to cover more water and create a more noticeable wake. As rising activity increases, I skate the fly more subtly and let it sit longer. When fish are wallowing, I move the fly just a little to help fish spot it.

If the surface is calm during a hatch, most feeding activity will be close to shore. I've draped casts across grass and rocks to take fish rising within inches of shore. If an offshore wind is pushing emerging insects over deep water, trout will be fanned out, some patrolling the shoreline and others working well out from it.

Once you hook a big golden, the real fun begins. That superb body type—the small head, broad back, and deep belly—translates into wonderful fighting ability. For covering the spectrum of fighting antics, from aerial acrobatics to bulldogging for the bottom, big goldens are the hottest trout I've hooked in high lakes.

Most big goldens are hooked over shallow flats, and at the sting of the hook, they bolt for the security of deeper water. Many fish string together several porpoiselike jumps before boring deep along the bottom as they vacate the shallows. The bottoms of most flats are rock-studded places that can grab fly lines and devour leaders. During the initial run, your main worry is keeping your line off the rocks. Hold the rod high to angle the line over as many near-shore rocks as possible, but keep it almost parallel to the water so the fish strips line under safe, consistent drag pressure. Hopping up on a boulder or quickly moving a few yards down the shore can angle your line away from trouble.

Goldens of better than 4 pounds almost always run into the backing before slowing over deep water. Open water away from the jagged rocks and tight quarters of the shallows is exactly where you want a big golden to spend itself, so let it stay there until you can control it.

After the initial run, a big golden will often turn and zip parallel to shore, towing the line in a big arc. Towing an entire fly line at high speed can generate enough drag to pop a 4X tippet, even if pressure from the rod and reel is minimal. Fight from an elevated position and hold as much line as possible off the water to reduce line drag at this stage of the battle.

As a fish begins to tire, move to a point where the shallows drop off close to shore. Keep the fish over deep water until you can keep it from diving. A golden that's led into the shallows before it's whipped may bore into a rocky crevice. If this happens, attempting to force it out on a tight line is likely to snap or cut your leader. Completely relaxing line pressure can confuse a fish and cause it to swim out of a rock cavity on its own.

I love just roaming the mountains, but it's the thrill of catching big trout in improbable lakes among the peaks that lures me back so religiously. And the allure of trophy goldens is the strongest of all. When you get right down to it, you can catch every other trout that swims the high country at sea level as well. But to pursue goldens, you have to travel high into their rarefied realm of enveloping clouds, booming thunder, and dazzling light. Cradled briefly in disbelieving hands, a big, radiant golden is a fitting culmination to such a journey. May the golden ones continue to grace the roof of the Rockies.

CHAPTER 16

Hunting Big Brookies

Over time most high-country brook trout lakes with good spawning habitat tend to become overpopulated with stunted fish. I can count on one hand the number of high lakes I know that have supported good numbers of large, wild brook trout over a period of a decade or more—and I've seen hundreds of brook trout lakes. That's a shame, because where brook trout grow well, they provide great sport. In my eyes nice brook trout are also the most beautiful fish in the mountains. Golden trout are more brilliant, but brookies display an unmatched palette of bold and subtle hues.

Once established in a drainage, brook trout tend to infiltrate both downstream and up as far as they can navigate. They fan out to inhabit every accessible niche in a drainage, and a few wind up in lonely places with little to do but eat. Where brook trout get plenty of forage, they can balloon in a couple of years. Other trout have to be well built and top 20 inches before I consider them big, even by high-country standards. But I've caught 17-inch brookies so deep bodied they knocked my eyes out.

Often the conditions that create big brook trout in high mountains are temporary. A newly impounded beaver pond is a classic example. In the first season or two, a pond is usually quite fertile, and the resident fish grow fast. But in time rotting wood leaches acid into the water, and unless the water is quite alkaline to begin with, the pond loses much of its fertility.

There are beaver ponds above 10,000 feet, but a lot of the best beaver habitat is in the more verdant aspen and willow country in the lush lower valleys of wilderness areas, or lower yet where ranch country abuts the mountains. Backcountry anglers bound for the high elevations often blow right by most beaver ponds.

Beavers continually build new ponds to take advantage of fresh food supplies. A drainage can have a maze of ponds in various stages of construction or abandonment. As you hike by ponds, watch for fresh stumps or cuttings close to the water and dams built of green sticks—signs that a pond is still young and fertile.

Beaver ponds, with their willow-lined banks, boggy edges, and soft bottoms, are not easy places to fish, especially in hiking boots. Wading in the muck or walking the soft banks sends shock waves that scatter the trout. One of the best approaches is from directly below the dam. You can cast undetected from behind the dam and use the stream channel for unobstructed backcasting.

When beaver-pond trout aren't actively feeding, they often lie in the submerged stream channel. Presenting a nymph or wet fly deep will usually produce. Actively feeding trout scatter through the upper levels of a pond and may respond well to dry flies.

Ironically, a lake that's prone to periodic winterkill can produce big brook trout. During a hard winter, fish may completely die out of a shallow lake. In spring trout from a feeder stream will repopulate the lake, but they, too, perish if the next winter is harsh. Over a series of hard winters, like those in the mid-1990s, a lake may be virtually devoid of fish for several years. During that time plankton, scuds, and insect life have an opportunity to build. Then comes a series of mild winters, and the fish that trickle into the lake survive for two or three years and grow fat gorging on the abundant food. In the late 1980s I was taking dozens of fat brook trout to 18 inches from a shallow, dishpan lake high atop the Flat Tops Plateau in Colorado—a lake that has since winter-killed regularly.

Some drainages have small lakes that are almost, but not completely, isolated by falls. During high flows a few trout manage to climb or wash into the lake, where they gorge and grow in seclusion. If such a lake lacks spawning habitat and never develops its own fish population, it may remain a recruitment lake indefinitely, periodically kicking out an exceptional brookie or two for the observant angler who happens to hit it right.

Large brook trout tend to be very bottom oriented in their feeding. They rise on occasion, but during nonhatch periods they tend to cruise right on the lake bed. If I'm not seeing rising fish, I work visible flies close to the bottom with a sinking-tip line in water as deep as 20 feet. An orange Mega Scud with a silver flashback has been my most consistent producer of nice brook trout since I began fishing the pattern.

Brook trout also tend to hit baitfish imitations more aggressively than other high-lake trout. Flashy streamers, Muddlers, and mylar-bodied minnows are exciting flies to work when big brookies are in the mood to chase.

By the time you hear of big brook trout through the grapevine, the conditions that created them are often gone. More than any other trout, catching good brookies in the high country requires keeping an eye peeled for short-term bonanzas and making the effort to check out those out-of-the-way spots that most anglers bypass. The payoff can be eye popping in more ways than one.

CHAPTER 17

Fishing Headwater Streams

The summer was winding down fast. By the time I reached Mountain Sheep Lake, high above Lander, Wyoming, I had just two days left to fish. On Saturday morning I'd have to hike out to my car at the Worthen Meadow Trailhead, drive 1,300 miles home, and be at work on Monday morning.

Rumors of big brook trout had lured me to Mountain Sheep. A 4-pound brookie sounded like a nice way to cap the summer. The lake looked to have potential. I quickly caught a fat brook trout of 14 inches, but in more than a day of prowling the shoreline I never saw or caught another. Not wanting to end the summer on a hollow note, I broke camp at noon on Friday and went looking for some fish. As I dropped down to Tayo Creek, I wasn't even sure where to head. There was a golden trout lake 5 miles away that rated a look, but by the time I got there I'd have only a few hours to fish, and the trip would leave me with a longer exit hike the next day.

At Tayo Creek I dropped my pack, broke out the maps, and mulled my options. Sitting there in the August sun, I was already missing the mountains. I listened to the breeze toss the overhead boughs. I watched the clarion light bounce off the sparkling waters of Tayo Creek. The longer I lingered, the less I felt like turning that final afternoon into a mad scramble.

Then, as I gazed at the creek, a blur of quicksilver shot from beneath a willow to intercept something in the drift. When the disturbance settled, I could see the dark, mottled back and white-gilded fins of a small brook trout hovering over a patch of clean gravel. Suddenly everything snapped into focus. There wasn't much time left, but there *was* time to savor this little stream.

I broke out my 4-weight rod, tied on an Elk Hair Caddis, flattened the barb, and put the sneak on the brookie. On my first cast, the fish smashed the fly with a predatory zeal that belied its modest size. And size was its only evident shortcoming: Cupped in my palm, that little trout seemed perfectly formed, perfectly imbued, perfectly created.

I moved up the shimmering creek with a lightness in my step, flicking the fly ahead, watching the line unfurl, enjoying the sun on my shoulders. There were brazen little trout in every pocket—dusky brookies, coppery cutts, and even a chrome-bright 'bow. All were small, but each was exquisite. For a while I was totally absorbed in the rhythm of casting, in reading the water, and in the antics of the trout. By the time I packed my little rod away, I was content to head home.

The backcountry is laced with sparkling little freestone streams—like this one—spilling from the highlands. Many are unnamed. Most rarely see an angler. On the whole they're taken for granted, but given a chance to reveal themselves, each is a gem.

Some headwater streams flow in and out of sister lakes. Some glide, and tumble, and free-fall for miles. Some stretches of stream are quite accessible; others snake through tangled blowdowns and labyrinth canyons. As headwater streams drop, they gather tiny feeders and grow steadily. Eventually these larger streams merge into major forks that transcend wilderness boundaries.

Where high-gradient streams flatten a bit, they become little Shangri-las. Sometimes you can look down from a barren escarpment on a pocket meadow—an oasis of green in a sea of rock. Where a few acres of topsoil have been detained, there are clumps of willows, stands of shallow-rooted firs, and just enough grass to interest a reclusive mule deer buck. Meandering through the meadow are a couple hundred yards of glistening stream full of gullible trout. From above, a meadow like this can look tantalizingly close, but getting there can be an adventure.

In summer headwater streams may look like storybook trout habitat, but for their year-round residents, it's a hardscrabble existence. From November to May trout are sandwiched between the anchor ice of the stream bottom and snow bridges that blot the sky. Even summer doesn't bring easy living. Finning against the tireless current as they patrol the meager drift, few trout in these cascading streams attain much size, but they exude a hammered beauty.

I've noticed something else about small trout: In lakes they no longer hold my attention, but in streams they still captivate me. When a trophy-trout lake doesn't pan out, or when I just want a break from stillwater, a headwater stream is a welcome respite. It's easy to while away an afternoon on such a stream, probing crystalline pockets where the trout have never seen an artificial fly. There's an undercurrent of discovery and anticipation as you stair-step upward over moss-covered boulders with shafts of golden sunlight streaming through the trees. A day like this always ends too soon.

Over its course a headwater stream has many personalities, depending on elevation and topography. In tumbling pocket water, the trout are usually small and quick to pounce. Where a stream meanders through a meadow, the fish are likely to be a bit larger and more leader-shy. Selectivity is rarely pronounced; these trout must take what they can get or go hungry.

Trout lakes high in a watershed just about guarantee a population of trout downstream. Where streams meet with lakes, your chances of taking a big trout jump markedly. Large trout may enter tiny streams to spawn. At high altitudes most spawning runs are short, but sometimes trout climb a surprising distance up steep mountainsides. Trout also drop downstream from lakes to spawn. If water levels drop, they may have trouble getting back to the lake. Sometimes fish simply elect to linger and feed in a stream. The biggest trout I've caught in a stream above timberline was a 5-pound golden still hanging out in a nice plunge pool in early September, weeks after spawning was completed. I scope out that pool every time I go by, but I've never seen another big fish there.

Topo maps are indispensable for exploring headwater streams. They show the easiest access routes as well as stream gradients. For good fishing, look for remote areas with a relatively low gradient. Also look for spots where streams meander, especially through meadows—this often signals slower, deeper runs and relatively large trout.

As a class, headwater streams are the most underutilized water in the backcountry, but to ignore them in single-minded pursuit of the larger trout in lakes and rivers is to miss much of what the mountains have to offer.

CHAPTER 18

Spin-Fishing the Backcountry

Most of us fly-fish because it matters how we catch fish. To many anglers, however, simply catching fish is more important than the method, and that's fine: Catching fish is what hooks most anglers on the sport and leads to refinement in technique. Like a lot of fly fishers, I came to fly fishing from spinning. If truth be known, I packed spinning tackle during my first two summers of fishing the backcountry, and I didn't make the transition to full-time fly fishing until my third summer. In those first two summers, I ran up some staggering fish counts, primarily on small brook trout and cutthroats, and proudly recorded some triple-digit catches in my journals. Not coincidentally, I stopped counting my catch and started targeting more interesting backcountry waters the very same summer I made the switch to fly fishing.

I've included this brief chapter on spin fishing in a fly-fishing book for several reasons. First, much of the information in this book is equally pertinent to spin fishers, who still outnumber fly fishers in the backcountry (although fly fishers are definitely increasing). Also, the fly fisher who has a basic grasp of spinning techniques can help novice anglers in his party quickly catch some fish. Finally, it's important to recognize that the Rocky Mountain backcountry is a big chunk of public land with elbow room for all types of ethical anglers. Anyone who eats primarily small fish from overpopulated waters, and carefully releases both young and mature fish on trophy-producing waters, is an ethical angler in my book.

Besides being a simpler method of fishing to learn, spinning has at least three distinct advantages over fly fishing. It requires no back-casting room, so it's easier to cast from wooded shores. Spinning tackle also casts fairly well into the screaming winds that hamper fly casting. And spinning tackle allows you to work very deep or distant water more efficiently.

Ultralight and light spinning rods are suitable for most backcountry waters. For versatility, and to have a backup, all anglers should carry two rods. An ultralight rod for $1/32$- to $3/16$-ounce lures plus a light rod for $1/16$- to $3/8$-ounce lures make a versatile combination. Spinning reels are prone to mechanical problems, and spinning lines are prone to twisting, so pack two reels, along with a spare spool (preloaded with line) for each reel. Four- and 6-pound lines are strong enough for most applications, and these light lines provide better casting range and accuracy with light lures.

Spinners are widely effective on lakes and streams. An 001 or 002 Mepps spinner with a gold blade and a tail dressed with fox squirrel was my pet spinner on my home streams in southwestern Wisconsin, and it quickly proved to be a winner in the Rockies. In fact, on my very first evening alone in the mountains, at Sherd Lake in the Bighorns, a Mepps produced several fat cutthroats just shy of 20 inches.

On lakes vary the retrieve speed and depth of a spinner to see what excites trout. The blades on Panther Martin spinners revolve nicely at very slow speeds and emit a lot of vibration, making them good for fishing slow and deep along lake bottoms.

On streams trout normally face into the current, so spinners should be cast upstream and retrieved down. Hold your rod tip high and retrieve the spinner with just enough speed to keep it off the bottom. Drop the rod tip, or slow your retrieve momentarily, to let a spinner work near the bottom in slower pockets. To keep a spinner near the bottom in heavy current, or to increase casting distance, pinch split shot on the line a few inches above the lure. A small snap swivel reduces line twist.

Trout tend to hit spinners reflexively. If they don't strike on the first presentation, they often won't strike at all. Spinning, particularly on streams, is generally more productive if you make a cast or two to each promising piece of water and then move on. By covering a lot of water, you'll show a spinner to a lot more trout in the course of a day, and that usually translates into more strikes.

Spoons, such as Little Cleos, cast like bullets and sink like rocks. They allow spin fishers to probe deep or distant lake waters that fly fishers can't reach from shore—just the type of water in which trout often seek refuge in hot weather or when they're not actively feeding. Spoons in basic colors such as gold and silver produce well.

Small minnow-imitating crankbaits such as Rapalas and Rebels take lots of big, predatory trout. Floating crankbaits cover the upper levels of streams and lakes, whereas sinking models can go deep.

A few wilderness waters with special regulations allow only a single, barbless hook. For these waters the treble hooks on spinning lures need to be replaced. The hooks on most lures are woefully dull right out of the package, anyway, and they get duller with use. Touch up new hook points with a hone or, better yet, replace the standard treble hooks on lures with a single high-quality hook. A single hook with a long shank and a large gap hooks as many fish as a small, stubby treble hook and is much easier to extract from fish. Chemically sharpened fly-tying hooks have extremely sharp points, small barbs, and excellent temper, and are available in a wide range of styles, including straight-eye streamer hooks that trail nicely behind lures.

Marabou jigs of ⅛ ounce and smaller can be worked with slow, tantalizing retrieves, which frequently appeal to trout that ignore faster, flashier lures. Black, olive, white, and chartreuse jigs are all good at times. Pack plenty of jigs—they're inexpensive, and rocky bottoms can gobble them up.

A plastic bubble provides the weight to cast flies with spinning tackle. True fly fishers may snicker at this concept, but I've seen it work extremely well on various trout, including big, difficult goldens. In fact, presenting flies behind a bubble was probably what propelled me into fly fishing, because it showed me just how effective flies could be when trout weren't responding aggressively to hardware.

The fly-and-bubble technique is better suited to lakes than to moving water. Actively pumping a wet fly or skating a dry fly behind a bubble on a lake can attract cruising fish from a distance. Woolly Worms, scuds, and soft-hackle wet flies will trail a bubble at various depths, from just under the surface to several feet down (if a split shot is used to sink the fly). For fishing dry flies behind a bubble, choose heavily hackled or palmered flies with excellent skating properties—Wulffs, Humpies, and Elk Hair Caddis are good.

Casting with a bubble requires a sidearm lob. Accelerating too quickly during the forward cast causes the bubble to shoot ahead of the fly and usually results in a tangle. Some bubbles can be filled with water to increase their weight; these can be lobbed quite a distance. Bubbles are made in clear or colored plastic. Colored ones are easier to see but may spook more fish. Bubbles are made in several styles; the easiest ones to rig have a core of surgical tubing that twists to grip the line. No knots are required, and the bubble can be quickly repositioned.

From casting flies with a bubble to presenting them with fly tackle is not a huge leap. Basic fly-fishing instruction is offered by many fishing clubs and fly shops, and most people can learn to fly-cast moderate distances in a couple of hours. After that, fly fishing is like everything else—if you really delve into the sport, you can advance pretty quickly. There may not be a better place to make the transition from spinning to fly fishing than in the backcountry, where relatively gullible trout still abound on many waters, and a novice fly fisher can catch plenty of them while honing fly-fishing skills. Why bother making this transition? Simply put, fly fishing is an infinitely fascinating way to fish and takes you to beautiful places. That's a pretty compelling combination.

CHAPTER 19

Photographing the Fish

The first half dozen summers I fished the backcountry, I didn't carry a camera. My reasons were mostly philosophical: I felt that constantly stopping to photograph fish or scenery detracted from the experience. To some extent I still feel this way, but there are overriding practical reasons to pack a camera, and I eventually came around to them. Most anglers want a photographic record of their fishing, and in the Rockies both the trout and the scenery are particularly stunning. If you write about fishing, good photos help sell your writing. And if you speak to angling groups, slide shows greatly increase the entertainment and informational value of your presentations.

For photos that are suitable for publication, or simply for high-quality shots, go to the 35-millimeter format. Fortunately, backpack anglers can now pick from dozens of 35-millimeter compact cameras that weigh under a pound and take excellent photos. Most anglers who shoot a modest amount of film will get better results with a compact camera than with a heavier single-lens reflex type, and simplifying angling photography without sacrificing much in results is the focus of this chapter.

Compacts with zoom lenses are quite versatile, although they don't accept interchangeable lenses as SLR cameras do. A compact with a 38- through 110-millimeter zoom lens takes wide-angle scenic shots (at the 38-millimeter setting) or zooms in fairly tight for close-up fish photos (at the 110-millimeter setting). Zooming up or down in lens length also lets you bracket a shot to include just the elements you want without changing your distance from subjects.

For detailed fish photography with an autofocus compact camera, minimum focusing distance is a critical variable. I like an autofocus camera that's capable of focusing on subjects as close as 2 feet; by comparison, a 3-foot minimum focusing distance results in a 33 percent loss in size and detail. Two-foot focusing capability combined with a lens that zooms to 100 millimeters or longer lets you fill the entire frame with a good fish, or just a portion of a fish. For the most detailed close-ups, work with large fish.

When shooting close-ups of fish with an autofocus camera, it's easy to inadvertently get too close for the camera to focus. In this event some cameras simply take an out-of-focus shot, and you don't discover the error until you see the photo. An autofocus indicator, however, warns if the subject is too close for proper focus; with the shutter depressed halfway, this indicator is visible in the viewfinder. The real value of the autofocus indicator is that it lets you pinpoint the minimum camera distance from fish so you can consistently achieve the greatest possible detail on close-ups.

For most autofocus cameras, the infinity focus setting kicks in at fairly short range. For all subjects more than 8 to 10 feet from the lens, the focus setting is the same. As I'll discuss a bit later, knowing the distance at which infinity focus begins for your camera is an advantage when shooting self-photos.

Big trout are often caught in low-light conditions that require a flash. My current camera has four flash modes, and I find myself using them all: the auto mode, which automatically fires the flash in low light; the fill-in mode, which fires the flash on every shot regardless of light; the red-eye reduction mode, which dilates a subject's pupils; and off. When it's questionable whether flash is needed, take a shot with and without. Flash provides no benefits beyond about 20 feet, so for scenic shots, turn off the flash to conserve battery power. Recycling time between flashes varies depending on temperature and battery condition, but a flash indicator will tell you when the flash is charged.

In low light autoexposure cameras automatically select a slow shutter speed. Since the best films for general outdoor photography are slow to begin with, a tripod is almost mandatory for sharp photos in low light. Most compact 35-millimeter cameras have a standard tripod socket. Finding a suitable tripod that isn't heavier and bulkier than a compact camera is another matter. For years I got by with a 6-inch-tall plastic tripod that weighed about an ounce and was pretty usable as long as there were rocks around to stand it on. Along grassy shorelines the short tripod was a disadvantage, though. And because I was unable to buy a truly light tripod that suited my needs, I made a unipod from an arrow shaft. It works well and is feather light.

To make a unipod, take an aluminum arrow shaft of average diameter (I used a 2017) and pull the plastic nock off. The pointed aluminum cone under the nock becomes the tip of the unipod, which will be jammed into the ground. Saw through the shaft a foot from the nock position, and then saw another foot-long section (the unipod packs in two foot-long sections). To join the two sections, epoxy a short spigot-type ferrule between them (a section of wooden dowel works fine). For attaching the camera, buy a ¼-inch-diameter nylon bolt to fit a standard tripod socket. Cut the head off the bolt, and epoxy the bolt into the top section of the unipod, leaving a ½-inch section of threads exposed. You're done. In use the unipod is surprisingly slick—it can be driven into the ground or into a lake or streambed and is stout enough to steady a compact camera.

If you have a partner along when you land a particularly large or photogenic fish, you're in luck. Photographing and releasing fish when you're alone is infinitely more difficult. I don't even attempt to take a photo of myself holding a fish unless there's a good chance that it's the biggest I'll catch on a given trip. Even then my main concern is releasing the fish unharmed. I work quickly and keep the fish in the water for all but a few seconds. Often I don't get the shot I want, but over time I get some good photos.

To photograph yourself with a fish, you need a place to park the fish in the water while you set up the camera. If you have a net, leave the fish inside it in the shallows. Otherwise, find or build a rocky pocket alongshore to corral the fish; you can often fashion a secure cavity quickly by adding a few small rocks to an existing pocket. Leave the fish hooked; this eliminates preliminary handling of the fish and keeps it on the line in case it escapes from the holding pen.

With practice you can set up a camera for a self-photo in thirty seconds. Screw the camera onto the tripod, or unipod. Select for the flash, self-timer mode, and other desired options. Keep the camera on a wide-angle lens setting, and position it so that you can pose at least 8 feet from the lens. This puts you into the infinity range of most autofocus cameras and avoids out-of-focus self-photos. Be aware that in self-timer mode, most autofocus cameras set the focus when the shutter button is pushed. Since you're not yet in the frame, the camera usually sets the focus at infinity based on a distant background. If you step into the frame within a few feet of the lens, you'll be out of focus.

Framing a self-photo is guesswork at best. Posing about 10 feet from the camera decreases the chance that you'll crop part of your head or the fish. At this distance, too, a wide-angle lens setting will give you a shot that includes peaks, sky, and water in the background. To my taste, a scenic shot like this has more atmosphere than a tight shot of an angler and fish. Self-timers give you about ten seconds to retrieve the fish and pose— which can be a scramble if the fish doesn't cooperate. With most cameras you'll have to manually depress the shutter button and repose for each shot.

My current camera has a remote-control shutter release, which is far superior to a self-timer for fish photos. A remote release coupled with automatic film advance lets me get into position with the fish and stay there for as many successive shots as I wish. I loop the remote release to a D-ring on my vest and simply drop it once the camera is activated. The cordless release activates the camera at ranges to 16 feet via an infrared beam, and the camera fires after a three-second delay.

When posing with a trout, I usually wrap a wet bandanna around the fish's tail section. The cloth provides a secure grip on the tail that won't injure internal organs. I can keep the fish in the water and under control with one hand while I operate the remote release with the other. After dropping the release, I slip my free hand under the trout's belly and gently lift it from the water. Over the course of several shots, the fish is out of the water only for very short intervals, and I never touch the fragile gills.

If a fish is particularly striking and I want a detailed photo, I beach it on its side in shallow water, lay the rod butt and reel next to it for perspective, and snap several quick shots without ever touching the fish. Smooth rock or gravel is a better beaching site than silt, which is easily roiled. Automatic film advance lets me work quickly. For maximum detail, I zoom to my longest lens setting and work as close to the fish as focus will allow. I snap a few shots with flash and a few without, then release the fish. If you vary the camera angle, you can get an assortment of interesting perspectives. Remember, though, that grit easily filters into a fly reel laid in the shallows; before you resume fishing, pull your spool partially out of the frame and thoroughly rinse the reel.

The hardest photos for a lone angler to get are action shots. When I do travel with a partner, I concentrate on taking casting and fish-fighting photos. In the backcountry the water is so clear that you can often photograph spawning, cruising, or rising fish in their natural movements. Lenses on SLR cameras can be topped with polarizing filters to reduce surface glare, but often you can get good results from a compact camera without a filter by shooting from a high angle.

Few cameras are submersible, but fishing cameras should be weatherproof to withstand rain and spray. A weatherproof camera will operate if water pools on its shutter-release button—a common occurrence when you're handling fish.

Automatic film loading, rewinding, and indexing are all convenient features. Of course, when most operations on a camera are electronic, the batteries can wear down quickly. Always carry a fresh set of spare batteries. In cold weather warming drained batteries with body heat will usually revive them for at least a while.

Compact cameras have advanced by leaps and bounds in the last twenty years. Who knows what capabilities they'll eventually have? For my money, Olympus is the reigning master at packing a lot of performance into an extremely compact design. All three of my backcountry cameras have been made by Olympus. My current model is the Super-Zoom 3000 with optional remote-control shutter release.

If you even suspect that you might try to sell photos for publication, use 35-millimeter color slide film (in their guidelines, most publications refer to slides as color transparencies). Most magazines have a vertical format, so shoot plenty of photos with the camera held vertically. Slides also give you the flexibility to build a slide presentation, and fishing clubs and shops are always looking for interesting programs. If you want to make prints from some of your better slides, it can be done easily and inexpensively.

For pictures of fish and of anglers posing with fish, stick to film speeds of 50 to 100. These low-speed films are fine grained, so they capture more detail and produce sharp enlargements. Faster film speeds of 200 to 400 are better for low-light conditions and action photography (such as freezing a fly line in the air), but enlargements exhibit more grain.

Kodak and Fuji make the most popular slide films. Kodak film is known for excellent color saturation in skin tones and warm colors such as red and orange, and nicely captures the warm hues of trout. Fuji film tends to be strong in the blue-to-green spectrum and produces vibrant scenic shots of the green meadows and cobalt blue skies typical of sunny weather in the high country. I shoot a mix of Kodak and Fuji film.

Buy film in rolls of thirty-six exposures so you have fewer rolls to pack. For a weeklong trip, I usually pack five rolls (180 exposures), but I rarely shoot more than 100 frames. That's peanuts compared with the amount of film real photographers burn up, but it's more than enough to get some good shots if I land the right fish. Keep a spare roll of film in your camera case so you'll have it when you leave camp.

Film should be stored at cool temperatures and developed promptly. If I leave film in a vehicle while I'm in the backcountry, I wrap it in a blanket and store it low in the front portion of the trunk. (Most of the heat that builds up in a car trunk is absorbed by the top layer of cargo.)

Beyond a good camera and film, use sound technique. Hold the camera steady, keep fingers and straps from blocking lenses or meters, work with a clean lens, and keep grit out of the camera body. Look at your photos critically to see what's working and what's not, and to determine what types of photos you need.

Destinations

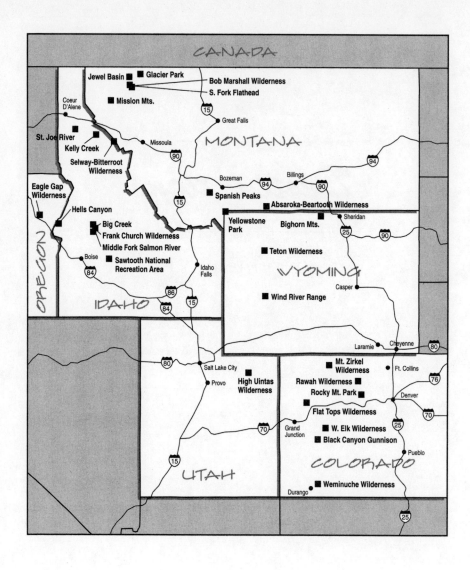

PART FOUR

Backcountry Waters— A Perspective

CHAPTER 20

Backcountry Fish Management— Past, Present, and Future

Wind River Trails, by Finis Mitchell, is a compact and entertaining guidebook to hiking the Wind River Range. Sprinkled throughout the book are interesting notes on the recent history of the range. Finis moved to the Wind River country as a boy with his family in 1906, and he never left. By the time his guidebook was first published, in 1975, Mitchell had devoted much of his long, active life to hiking, climbing, and photographing the Winds. He also played a pivotal role in establishing trout populations.

In his guidebook Mitchell recounts that the high-altitude lakes of the range were not a natural trout paradise. Prior to 1930 only a few lakes on the southwestern slope of the range held cutthroat trout. The vast majority of lakes were in glacial cirques above impassable falls and had never been stocked.

The Great Depression cost Mitchell his steady job with the railroad. In 1930 Finis and his wife, Emma, pitched a tent and opened a fishing camp in the Big Sandy Openings on the southwestern slope of the Winds. They borrowed old horses and saddles from local ranchers. The horses were rented to anglers at a dollar and a half a day (the camp kept the dollar, the ranchers got the change). Emma served meals for fifty cents. Finis rode out with the anglers to make sure they caught fish, but his guide services were on the house. That first summer the camp grossed

$300. The fact that only three lakes in the immediate vicinity had good fishing limited the potential of the business.

In the summer of 1931 Finis, along with his brother and father, began packing fingerling trout into the surrounding mountains and releasing them in virgin lakes. A state fish hatchery provided the trout, and the Mitchells packed them in for free—they were just happy to improve the fishing around their camp.

The trout were delivered to the Mitchells' camp in 5-gallon milk cans, a dozen cans at a crack, up to a thousand inch-long trout in each. The cans were covered with burlap and strapped two to a horse for a hurried trip into the mountains. The horses had to be kept moving to replenish oxygen in the cans or the fish would die. Water that splashed out was replaced at stream crossings. Before the decade was over, the Mitchells stocked some three hundred Wind River lakes with two and a half million cutthroat, brook, rainbow, brown, and golden trout. These fish or their progeny eventually migrated by stream to hundreds of additional lakes. Many lakes in the range are still populated with trout descended from the original stockings.

The two decades following the introduction of trout were truly the golden years of fishing in the Wind River Range. How I'd love to make a summerlong trek into that era. Many of the virgin lakes were packed with forage, and trout exhibited phenomenal growth rates in their adopted homes. Mitchell's guidebook is sprinkled with photos and accounts of impressive trout from that time. Brookies frequently weighed 3 pounds in their third year. Cutts quickly achieved weights of 5 pounds and more. One day in 1945 Finis hiked in to Washakie Lake to try his luck and landed a 31-inch golden trout that weighed over 11 pounds. Had this fish been certified, it might have gone into the books ahead of the long-standing world-record golden of 11 pounds, 4 ounces, taken in 1948 by Charles Reed at Cook Lake in the Winds.

Like so many other western booms, the trophy-trout boom in the high-lake country was destined to fade. The days of hauling lunker trout from scores of trailside lakes would not endure. As naturally reproducing populations took hold, fish densities soared in many lakes. Increased competition for food caused an inevitable decline in fish size. By 1975, when I began making regular trips to the Winds, some trophy fisheries remained, but the majority of lakes no longer produced the behemoths they once had.

The introduction of trout followed a similar pattern in mountain ranges throughout the West. Many suitable lakes were planted prior to 1950 by outfitters or individuals working in cooperation with hatcheries, or by the states themselves. Once trout were established in a few lakes in a drainage, they often migrated to others.

Anglers have assisted in the spread of trout by releasing some of their catch in fishless lakes. In his book Mitchell mentions that prior to stocking trout for the state, he and his father caught seventeen cutthroat trout to 10 inches in Big Sandy Lake and released them in a nearby lake that was barren. Two years later, when they returned to check on their handiwork, Finis promptly caught a 5-pound cutt that looked like it had been blown up with a pump. Opportunities for anglers to transport trout to virgin lakes are rare today, and of course, the practice is now illegal.

In retrospect, the introduction of trout throughout the high Rockies was haphazard. Trout were often stocked without assessing the forage base or spawning potential of a lake. Different trout species were stocked in connected lakes, resulting in hybrid populations or intense competition. The impact of exotic trout on native species was rarely considered. By and large, a potpourri of species was simply dumped.

Unquestionably, the single biggest mistake was the liberal stocking of brook trout from hatchery strains. The brookies introduced throughout the Rockies were early-maturing, short-lived strains developed to prop up collapsing eastern brook trout fisheries. The life span of these char rarely exceeds four years, making it difficult for individuals to grow large, even in fertile lakes. These same brook trout become sexually mature at only 6 inches, giving them the ability to swiftly overpopulate remote, lightly fished waters wherever they have access to good spawning habitat. Once in a drainage, brook trout tend to infiltrate and eventually dominate any lakes they can navigate to. Unfortunately, domesticated brookies were widely introduced before these pitfalls became apparent.

The bull trout, a native char of the Rockies, was originally found in some Pacific-flowing drainages in western Montana, Idaho, and eastern Oregon. The best populations are now in large lakes and reservoirs outside wilderness areas. Bull trout prey mainly on baitfish and small trout. Where forage is plentiful, they attain double-digit weights and can exceed 20 pounds. Most river populations have dwindled dangerously. Idaho and Montana now prohibit the harvest of bull trout on most rivers. Some of the best backcountry populations are in the Salmon drainage of Idaho and the Flathead drainage of Montana. Check current regulations before pursuing bull trout.

Montana grayling were originally common in the upper Missouri and its major tributaries but have disappeared from most of their range. Montana's Big Hole River has the last significant fluvial population. I recently caught a half dozen of these sublimely beautiful fish on a cold little tributary to that river. Grayling have been transplanted to a number of wilderness lakes, primarily in Montana and Wyoming, and backcountry anglers have some excellent opportunities to catch them.

Cutthroats are relatively easy to catch, are susceptible to hybridization with rainbows, and require cold, pristine water. Following the widespread introduction of rainbows and browns, and the degradation of most main-stem rivers in the Rockies, cutts retreated to remote headwater streams. The backcountry is the final stronghold of most surviving subspecies. Various strains of cutts have been widely transplanted to high-elevation lakes; as the native trout of the Rockies, cutthroats are increasingly favored in backcountry management strategies. They are replacing other species in many lakes that require periodic stocking.

Considering the immense popularity of rainbow trout and the successful transplantation of California strains throughout the lower elevations of the Rockies, it's surprising that rainbows aren't established in more alpine lakes. There are local exceptions, but in lakes across the backcountry, brook trout and cutthroats are far more common. Rainbows tend to be travelers and readily cross with cutthroats and goldens, resulting in hybrid populations wherever these species mingle. Otherwise, rainbows are well suited for high-lake survival. For dazzling leaps and sustained runs, they're the only high-lake fish that can rival goldens. It's unfortunate that rainbows aren't established in lieu of brook trout in many waters.

Small numbers of sea-run rainbows and chinook salmon still run the gauntlet of dams on the Columbia and Snake Rivers to spawn in the Clearwater and Salmon drainages of central Idaho, some 700 miles inland. Some fish ascend wilderness tributaries, like the Middle Fork of the Salmon, but there are few legal angling opportunities for anadromous species in true backcountry.

The export of golden trout from California ended more than twenty years ago. Wyoming and Montana strip eggs for limited operations from their own established stocks. Attempts to establish new populations of goldens are ongoing in several selected drainages in the Beartooths of Montana; the hope is that a few more first-rate golden fisheries, like Lightning Lake, can be established there. In the Wind River Range goldens are established in more than a hundred lakes, but that number is probably at its peak. Idaho and Colorado have established a few new golden populations in the last decade. As a nonnative species, however, goldens aren't likely to be established in many more lakes in the Rockies. That's unfortunate, because they're uniquely suited to thrive at high elevations and are a superb sport fish.

On the one hand, the introduction of trout throughout the backcountry was helter-skelter. On the other, we're probably fortunate to have the fisheries that we do. The bulk of the backcountry waters in the Rockies now lie within classified wilderness areas; such areas are increasingly being managed to minimize human impact and to preserve natural ecosystems.

There's a remote region in the Wind River Range known as the Brown Cliffs. It's the most pristine area left in the range. There are no official trails and no plans to build any. About a dozen sizable lakes have never had fish, and there are no plans to introduce any. I once spent several days roaming around up there, looking at the lakes and salivating. To me the area represents a rare opportunity to introduce trout (my choice would be goldens) strategically into a handful of virgin lakes. To a growing number of people, however, the area represents a rare opportunity to leave a corner of the wilderness largely undisturbed, and there's value in that, too.

Here and there a few new lake fisheries are being developed. And stocking, mostly done now by aircraft, is continuing on many existing wilderness fisheries that are dependent on it. But the era of wholesale trout introduction into the backcountry is over. There aren't that many fishless waters left.

In the future, creating outstanding angling opportunities, particularly for large trout, will require more effective management of existing fisheries. The backcountry is large and budgets are limited, but a restructuring of fishing regulations and stocking policies could create a significant number of trophy fisheries at very little expense.

Even in wilderness areas, cutthroats are susceptible to overfishing, especially on sizable streams and rivers that attract a lot of anglers. Since the 1980s catch-and-release and slot-size regulations have dramatically boosted cutthroat densities and sizes on several wild rivers. These special regulations should be extended to all cutthroat rivers on which liberal harvest is clearly depressing fish numbers or sizes.

Ironically, wilderness lakes that can't sustain wild trout may offer the best opportunities to create additional trophy-trout fisheries. Any sizable lake that has abundant food and limited or no wild trout production can be made to produce larger trout by manipulating stocking rotations and densities, and by restricting harvest so that fish reach maturity. This is being done with impressive results on private ponds all over the West. Without a doubt, we could create significant numbers of trophy-trout lakes in wilderness areas, including some very accessible lakes. For this to become a priority with management agencies, however, more anglers have to request such opportunities.

Fisheries managers should take the lead in applying special regulations to backcountry lakes that produce large, wild trout but are either so well known or so accessible that angling pressure is clearly depressing fish populations. I could cite many examples. Elbow Lake lies right on the heavily traveled Highline Trail on the west slope of the Wind River Range; it's the best-known golden trout lake in the range that regularly produces trophy fish. Unfortunately, anglers are killing most trout before they mature. Elbow is potentially a very special golden lake, and is an obvious candidate for catch-and-release regulations or a delayed opening date to protect spawning fish. Special-regulation lakes do have the potential to draw increased human traffic, of course, which could damage shorelines. Where this is a concern, prohibiting camping within ¼ mile of the lake would greatly reduce human impact.

As a group, backcountry anglers need to adopt a much stronger catch-and-release attitude toward trophy-producing waters. Since the pan-size trout that abound in the backcountry taste great and are easy to cook, it's particularly senseless to kill large fish or fish that have the potential to become large. Eat fish from overcrowded waters. Let 'em go where they're destined to grow. This approach will benefit all fisheries and anglers. I'd like to see fishing regulations restructured to promote the release of large fish and the harvest of small fish on all wilderness waters so that this practice eventually becomes ingrained in anglers.

Under current management policies, little is being done to reduce populations of stunted trout. Given the numbers and remoteness of many afflicted waters, it's a tough problem. Use of poisons is against policy in wilderness areas, although rotenone has recently been used to eradicate brook trout from a few waters in national parks. Some new strategies need to be explored, perhaps on backcountry lakes that aren't subject to wilderness restrictions. On many lakes physically blocking fish access to a single spawning stream would cut reproduction significantly.

Overgrazing by domestic livestock continues to damage fish and wildlife habitat on public lands throughout the West; I've seen some incredible abuses even in classified wilderness areas. Some backcountry rivers are also being damaged or threatened by logging and mining in watersheds above wilderness and park boundaries. Often private industries are paying far less than market rates to extract resources from public lands and are severely degrading those lands in the process. The upside of increased angling pressure is that more anglers translates into increased economic and political clout. As the long-term value of healthy fisheries to local economies and the public is recognized, private interests will have a tougher time exploiting valuable recreational lands.

Whirling disease is popping up throughout the Rockies. Nobody knows where it will end or which waters will eventually be hardest hit. Isolated wilderness waters are probably at the lowest risk. So far the biggest fish kills have been on lower-elevation rivers, but the disease may yet ascend wilderness tributaries, and native cutthroats appear to have little resistance.

Another threat to high-country fisheries is in the wind. The acidity of precipitation in the Rockies is now about ten times higher than it was in preindustrial times. So far, acidification has not killed lakes in the Rockies as it has in the East and Europe. But many alpine lakes have limited buffering capacity and are clearly susceptible to acidification.

Across the West the best streams and rivers on private land are being converted to fee fishing or are being closed to the public, at an alarming rate. At the same time, the fly-fishing boom has fueled severe crowding on the premier public rivers. These trends are only likely to accelerate. Inevitably, more and more fly fishers will turn to the backcountry as a place to fish for wild trout in solitude.

I'd like to see more big-fish opportunities in the backcountry, and I believe we can create some, but ultimately, the real value of this fishery lies in its sheer abundance of wild trout waters, including the wealth of sparkling lakes and streams that produce pan-size trout. There are bigger trout elsewhere. But there is not much finer or bigger country to roam and fish in. To future anglers of modest means and an independent bent, such a vast, public fishery will be invaluable.

To some, it already is.

CHAPTER 21

Spilling the Beans

Anyone who writes about fishing destinations should anticipate the wrath of anglers already in the know. Backcountry fishing is by its nature a secretive pursuit, so there are fellow backcountry anglers who will wish a double hex on me for mentioning certain wilderness waters in print. Because I know I won't get a better opportunity, let me offer the following observations on why and how I've chosen to write about Rocky Mountain backcountry angling destinations.

First, many backcountry waters could be more effectively managed—but before that's likely to happen, the fishery as a whole needs more advocates. My hope is that writing about the broad spectrum of fly-fishing opportunities in the backcountry will help gain the fishery the recognition and support it needs to become a higher management priority.

As the human population spirals upward and access to private land plummets, recreationists will descend on public lands in unprecedented numbers. The population of the United States is projected to double, to more than five hundred million, by 2050. Wilderness fisheries will attract increasing numbers of anglers, and backcountry waters will be written about—these are givens. So I might as well use what I've learned in a fashion that fosters respect for the resource.

The current vogue for castigating angling writers who publicize uncrowded destinations is largely unwarranted. The phenomenal growth in fly fishing is being fueled from many angles. The equipment industry, conservation and fly-fishing organizations, guides and outfitters, and the sporting press all promote fly fishing effectively. And as blood sports go, catch-and-release fly fishing is uniquely suited to our times and is highly promotable. Well, legions of new fly fishers are hungry for new angling horizons. I believe that the writers who publicize alternative destinations are feeding that demand more than creating it. On balance, I'd even argue that writers who promote alternative destinations and forms of fly fishing are dispersing fishing pressure—witness the tremendous growth in warm-water, saltwater, and international fly fishing. The Rocky Mountain backcountry certainly has the potential to deflect significant angling pressure from traditional western fly-fishing waters.

Rather than hot-spotting a handful of premier backcountry waters, I cover a large number and variety of destinations over the length and breadth of the Rockies within the United States. I'm comfortable that any additional fishing pressure generated solely by this book will be widely distributed.

I have few qualms about naming and discussing the major back-country streams and rivers. Most have significant mileage and are under special regulations. Most are not huge secrets; it's the difficulty of access-ing them that holds pressure down. That last point applies to many back-country waters—knowing of them is one thing, fishing them another.

Still, some trophy-trout lakes with low fish densities can be hurt even by light angling pressure. Many of these lakes are fairly small, and removing even a dozen good fish a year could send big-fish numbers into a nosedive. Directing scores of anglers to my favorite lakes of this type would damage my own fishing, and within a few years everyone else who visited these lakes would be disappointed, too. At some points in this book I describe some of my very favorite lakes and mention their general locations to highlight the angling potential of various areas. But I do not name a lake if I feel that doing so would damage its fishing.

I do name good lakes that for various reasons can absorb more fish-ing pressure. Many of the lakes that fall into this category provide faster, more dependable action than low-density trophy waters and are well worth fishing. For anglers who are looking primarily for action or fish to fry, I name quite a few lakes that produce mostly small or average fish. A big part of finding trophy trout is eliminating the many lakes that don't hold big fish, so there's value in knowing the status of any lake.

For each area covered, I attempt to convey the character of the country and the fishing, as well as the size of the fish, because these are important aspects of any angling experience. I've visited all of the areas and the vast majority of the waters that I describe. In my research I've identified some waters I'd like to fish that I simply haven't gotten to yet. If these waters are close to others I have visited and could easily be fished on the same trip, I mention them, but I note those destinations I haven't personally fished. I do not attempt to expand the coverage area of the book by describing waters based on information gleaned from state wildlife agencies or other secondhand sources.

Any firsthand account of a resource this vast is going to have holes in it. If I compared notes with another angler who had fished the backcountry for twenty summers, I'd be surprised if we'd visited many of the same waters, particularly lakes. And of the waters we'd both visited, I'm sure we'd have some differing impressions, depending on when we were there and how they were fishing at the time. Wilderness waters turn on and off and see peaks and valleys in productivity, just like other waters. Over several visits you can get a pretty good handle on a given water. But an impression based on a single visit can be off the mark.

In many ways I'm attempting to provide the kind of information that I would have welcomed twenty years ago, when I knew little about the character and fishing potential of many backcountry areas. There's considerable detail on major backcountry areas that are liberally laced with trout water and a broader overview of many smaller areas. This book should provide a framework that will help you identify areas you'd like to explore further on your own.

Few of the lakes and rivers I discuss are household names. If you're intrigued by the description of an area, obtain a map with a scale of ½ inch to the mile, or larger. When you have a reasonably detailed map in hand, the lay of the land and locations of specific waters will become clear. Such a map will also show access roads, maintained trails, and other vital information you'll need for trip planning. See chapter 9 for more information.

Do I spill all the beans about backcountry fly fishing in the Rockies? I don't believe any one person could even come close to doing so. That's the magic of this fishery. From neglected lakes to phenomenal river runs, there are still plenty of secrets in these mountains. And most will be ferreted out only by an ambitious few.

PART FIVE

Major Mountain Ranges and Wilderness Areas

CHAPTER 22

Bigger Is Often Better

If I could design a wilderness area from scratch, I'd give it two things—a big, rugged interior and a maze of trout water. All of the areas covered in this part of the book possess these two attributes in varying degrees, and not surprisingly, they all have exceptional fishing.

Large, famous wilderness areas attract more than their share of back-country anglers, but most of us have quite limited time or range; thus the bulk of the fishing pressure ends up concentrated in relatively accessible country. I'm not bothered by hiking out of a trailhead with fifty parked cars if my destination is 35 miles and an off-trail pass away. Distance and rugged terrain are great dispersers of fishing pressure.

The best backcountry rivers are found almost exclusively in large wilderness areas that cover hundreds of square miles. In such expansive areas rivers have a chance to gather dozens of feeders and grow to significant size before crossing wilderness boundaries. Many tributaries to the larger backcountry rivers are in themselves sizable streams that add many miles of productive water to the system.

Big mountain ranges with hundreds of lakes also provide the best lake fishing. It's a simple numbers game. The more remote lakes there are in a range, the better the odds are that a few of those neglected lakes will have the right conditions to grow exceptional trout.

Even for anglers who do their homework and legwork, big areas with hundreds of lakes tend to reveal their secrets slowly, in increments. It can take several trips to an area before you're ready to bypass an abundance of good lakes and hunt for a truly exceptional one. And even after you start to explore the hinterlands, you may need a few trips to locate such a lake. Once you've zeroed in on it, you might then require a few more trips to learn how to fish it, or to hit it when it's really on. There is an appropriate payoff for all of this effort: Discover an exceptional lake in very remote country, and you can usually count on great angling for years to come.

I always enjoy hiking and fishing new country. That goes for small and large areas alike. But I tend to have my very best backcountry fishing in large wilderness areas or ranges that I've visited many times. That's a point worth noting.

If you're looking for a big chunk of backcountry to really delve into and get to know well over several years, the areas in the following pages merit special consideration.

CHAPTER 23

Wind River Range (Wyoming)

Even though I live a thousand miles away, I consider the Winds my home range. I made my first western backpacking trip to this range, in 1973, and I've made far more trips here than in any other area—thirty-three to date. Most lasted seven to nine days and covered routes of 50 to 80 miles with the pack. Yet in hiking an estimated 2,500 miles—a distance longer than the Appalachian Trail—I've visited less than half of the estimated seven hundred trout lakes in the Winds. So it's a big range with a lot of water.

For sheer numbers of trout lakes, this range stands head and shoulders above any other in the West. The majority of these lakes have self-sustaining populations. Species are varied. There are good cutthroat lakes galore. Hundreds abound with brook trout. There are fine rainbow lakes. Grayling, brown trout, and lake trout swim in a smattering of waters. Even if the Winds had no golden trout, the range would be a high-lake shrine. But the Winds do have goldens, in more than a hundred lakes, including a couple dozen trophy fisheries. Of the top two dozen golden lakes in the Rockies, as many as twenty may be in the Winds.

The range sprawls across western Wyoming, from east of Jackson Hole all the way down to South Pass, where the Oregon Trail crossed the Continental Divide. The divide runs along the spine of the range for 100 miles and is crowned with numerous 13,000-foot peaks, including Gannett—at 13,804 feet, the highest in Wyoming. Grinding away at the massive peaks are several of the largest glaciers in the lower forty-eight. Glaciers and snowfields are the source of two major rivers. The Green

River (or the Seedskadee, as it was known to the mountain men who rendezvoused on its banks) is the largest tributary to the Colorado and is born on the west slope. The Green becomes a great trout river shortly after it leaves the Winds. The Wind River, which is renamed the Bighorn as it swings north toward Montana, drains the east slope. From Bridger, Colter, Ashley, and Astor to Sacajawea, Fremont, Sublette, and De Smet, there was scarcely a major player in the opening of the West who did not sleep in the shadow of the Winds and leave his or her name on the landscape.

No roads cross over the top of the Winds in the heart of the range. To visit the spectacular country along the divide, you have to hike or ride a horse. The range is as popular with climbers, trekkers, and outdoor schools as with anglers, which says a lot about its size and ruggedness. Many of the lakes are in rock and ice country above timberline, where opportunities for cross-country travel are frequent, especially as you get to know the lay of the land.

The Bridger Wilderness of the Bridger-Teton National Forest covers most of the west slope of the Winds. This 428,000-acre wilderness is 75 miles long and about 15 miles wide at most points. Access is good along the entire west slope, so backcountry use is higher here than on the east. Still, with some three hundred trout lakes, the Bridger Wilderness provides plenty of lonely destinations for ambitious anglers. One biologist I talked to estimated that 95 percent of the west-slope lakes capable of supporting trout have trout.

The east slope is roughly the same length and width as the west but is divided into three areas. The Fitzpatrick Wilderness of the Shoshone National Forest comprises the northern one-third. The roadless area of the Wind River Indian Reservation is in the center. And the Popo Agie Wilderness of the Shoshone National Forest is in the south. Public access to portions of the east slope is thwarted by the reservation. Persons who are not tribal members must purchase a fishing permit to hike, fish, or drive the access roads on the reservation—and even with a permit, they must hire an outfitter to drive them over certain access roads. Because of the layout of the reservation, reaching some lakes in the southern portion of the Fitzpatrick Wilderness from a national forest trailhead requires hiking 30 miles or more—which is not necessarily bad for the fishing. A biologist from the east slope estimated that 60 percent of the suitable lakes have trout. There are definitely more fishless lakes east of the divide, but nearly all existing fisheries have wild fish.

In the course of a trip, I often cross the divide, but to get a handle on the hundreds of lakes in the Winds, it's easier to discuss the west and east slopes separately.

THE WEST SLOPE—NORTHERN REGION

The major trailheads for accessing the northern one-third of the Bridger Wilderness are at Green River Lakes and Elkhart Park.

Green River Lakes sit at the northern end of the wilderness at 8,000 feet. To reach the trailhead, which has a forest service campground, drive 6 miles west of Pinedale on U.S. 191 and turn north on Wyoming 352, which runs 20 miles up the Green River and ends right at the lakes (the last half of the road is improved dirt).

Elkhart Park, some 20 miles south of Green River Lakes, is well positioned for reaching scores of destinations in the heart of the Bridger Wilderness. Elkhart sits at the end of a paved road about 15 miles east of Pinedale. The trailhead is at 9,200 feet, so it's a mellow climb to timberline. Elkhart and Big Sandy (see page 151, 153) are the two most popular trailheads on the west slope. In August, at the height of the summer backpacking season, I've counted nearly two hundred cars parked at Elkhart. On weekends the forest service campground is often full, and the first 5 miles of trail can look like a block party. I use this trailhead but I don't fish in the immediate vicinity anymore. These days when I hike out of Elkhart, I usually beeline through Angel Pass (an off-trail pass) to reach waters high on the eastern side of the divide.

If you wanted to hike the entire length of the Bridger Wilderness, you could jump on the Highline Trail at Green River Lakes and take it all the way to the Big Sandy Openings, about 80 trail miles to the south. The Highline Trail stays mostly above timber and below the rugged peaks as it parallels the divide.

The best angling near Green River Lakes is about 6 miles east at the head of the Clear Creek drainage. **Faler Lake** (13 acres, 10,175 feet) has nice golden trout. **Bear Lake** (107 acres, 10,548 feet) is a big lake a couple of miles southeast of Faler that has a history of kicking out a few big rainbows. **Daphne Lake,** another big lake a mile north of Bear, reportedly has rainbows. I haven't fished Daphne, but its elevation of 11,202 feet pushes the upper limits of trout habitat for this range, so I'd be surprised if the fish were big.

The most direct route to Faler Lake runs right up Clear Creek to **Clear Lake,** which has small goldens. From Green River Lakes to Clear

Lake, you gain 900 feet in 5 miles. From Clear Lake it's only a mile cross-country to Faler—but 1,300 feet uphill. Faler can also be reached by trail from Green River Lakes, though this requires a 15-mile swing through the Roaring Fork Basin. This trail runs by **Native Lake,** a small lake just north of Faler that's listed as holding rainbows and goldens, but I haven't checked it. From a base camp on Faler, you can day hike cross-country to Bear and Daphne. The Faler area is a good, low-mileage trip off the beaten path. Five days should be enough to check out all these lakes, and you won't see crowds.

To reach the first major concentrations of lakes from the Green River Trailhead, you have to buzz 15 miles south on the Highline Trail—which runs right past scenic Squaretop Mountain and on to the very headwaters of the Green River. The rest of the lakes discussed in this section are as close, or closer, to Elkhart Park. **Peak** and **Stonehammer** are two small lakes that sit above timber just east of the trail at the very head of the Green. I've taken pan-size goldens in both.

Elbow Lake, a couple of miles straight south of Peak Lake, has long produced trophy goldens of more than 4 pounds, despite the fact that it sits just west of the Highline Trail and is heavily fished. I've been to Elbow four times. The second time was in 1980 with my dad and my brother Eric. We caught goldens to 18 inches but failed to convert on some much better fish we saw. I had some maddening refusals to dry flies and nymphs that several very big goldens swarmed all over without taking. At the time, I was still pretty green at fly-fishing for goldens, and I didn't have the Fast-Sinking Scud in my fly boxes. I'd like to have that trip back. I've returned to Elbow a couple of times since then, looking to even the score, and I've taken a few good fish, but I haven't hit it red hot again.

At 80 acres and 10,777 feet, Elbow is a large golden lake that has held up remarkably well considering that it's fished almost daily in summer. Elbow has rare potential. If I could slap catch-and-release regulations on just one lake in the Winds, this would be it; I think the results would be impressive. Best of all, anglers with fairly limited time or range (a group most of us are in at one time or another) could enjoy first-rate fishing for trophy goldens. Meanwhile, you should voluntarily release everything on Elbow. If you want to dine on trout, **Upper Elbow Lake** (12 acres, 10,810 feet), just to the north, has small goldens, and there are plenty of cutthroat lakes in the vicinity.

From the Elkhart Park Trailhead to Elbow via Seneca Lake is an easy, scenic hike of 17 miles past some of the most heavily fished lakes in the range. **Miller Lake** (21 acres, 9,860 feet) has small brook trout. **Hobbs Lake** (20 acres, 10,075 feet), **Ecklund Lake** (9 acres, 10,275 feet), and **Seneca Lake** (159 acres, 10,270 feet) yield some rainbows of over a pound, but look for plenty of company. **Lower Jean Lake** (57 acres, 10,651 feet) and **Upper Jean Lake** (17 acres, 10,799 feet) are not far from Elbow. Both have cutthroats to 16 inches, although the average is smaller. I wouldn't target either lake, but Upper Jean is worth wetting a line in; I've had good action skating drys here. One year when Upper Jean was still iced over, I had fun on nice cutts stacked in the outlet stream. From Upper Jean it's just 2 miles to Elbow.

A second trail out of Elkhart Park, the Pine Creek Trail, drops 1,500 feet right out of the gate and bottoms out on Fremont Creek. There's no maintained trail up Fremont Creek, but you can hike and fish your way up the creek canyon through a series of four good-size lakes that all hold a mix of brook, rainbow, and cutthroat trout. Going up the canyon, the lakes are **Long** (126 acres, 7,875 feet), **Upper Long** (35 acres, 7,945 feet), **Gorge** (66 acres, 8,870 feet), and **Lost** (52 acres, 9,755 feet). If you make it all the way to Lost Lake, which is 8 miles above Long, it's a short cross-country hike to hit the Highline Trail just south of Lower Jean. If you want a route out of Elkhart with some lightly fished lakes along the way, this canyon rates a look.

A half mile due north of Long Lake are **Triangle Lake** (55 acres, 8,895 feet) and **Upper Triangle** (35 acres, 8,995 feet). The shortest route in is a mile-long 1,000-foot climb up the outlet stream of Triangle, which dumps into Fremont Creek. These may be the lowest lakes in the range from which you can nail a big golden, but the catching is slow.

If you stay on the Pine Creek Trail coming out of Elkhart, rather than bushwhacking up Fremont Creek, you'll climb to **Trapper Lake** (58 acres, 9,682 feet) in 7 miles. Trapper has average cutthroats. North of it is a cluster of lakes that are popular with horse outfitters. On a couple of tours of the area I've had good action at many lakes for small to average fish. **Trail** (20 acres, 9,753 feet) and **Coyote** (10 acres, 9,678 feet) have grayling. **Gotfried** (3 acres, 9,880 feet) and the two **Neil Lakes** (about 10 acres, 9,700 feet) have cutthroats and a smattering of rainbows. **Heart** (23 acres, 10,014 feet) and **Borum** (35 acres, 10,145 feet) have rainbows. Just northwest of this group are three lakes with pan-size brook trout: **Round** (22 acres, 9,952 feet), **Dean** (11 acres, 10,165 feet), and **Palmer** (19 acres, 10,165 feet).

Four miles north of Trapper, you break out of the timber near **Cutthroat Lakes** and **No Name Lakes,** a cluster of small lakes (all under 25 acres) loaded with foot-long cutts. These lakes are all just 4 easy miles west of Elbow.

Thompson Lakes and **Hidden Lakes** are just north of No Name. There are a half dozen brook trout lakes in this group, all under 30 acres and at about 11,000 feet. You have to hike cross-country to reach these lakes, but it's rolling, grassy terrain and easy going from several trails that get you close. One of my fly customers reported fat brook trout, including some over 14 inches, from a couple of these lakes. **Lozier Lake** (14 acres, 10,590 feet), north of Hidden Lakes, also has brookies.

All of these lakes, from Lozier south to Trapper, can also be reached from the New Fork Lakes Trailhead to the west. To reach this trailhead, drive about halfway up Wyoming 352—the same road that goes to Green River Lakes. Watch for a right turn that heads to New Fork Lakes. They're big lakes with several campgrounds, so you can't miss them. I've hiked out of this trailhead only once. From 7,800 feet the Double Top Mountain Trail climbs steeply to **Rainbow Lake** (8 acres, 10,190 feet) in 5 miles. Rainbow has small rainbows and brook trout. The trail continues right past Cutthroat and No Name Lakes to hit the Highline Trail within 3 miles of Elbow.

Just west of Elbow, a dead-end trail takes off south through Gunsight Pass. It's a short hop over to the two **Sauerkraut Lakes** (about 15 acres each, 10,150 feet), where I've taken a few cutthroats to 16 inches. The trail continues south for 2 miles before ending at **W3** (30 acres, 10,220 feet), which is one of the **Bridger Lakes.** I caught a 2-pound golden in a brief fling at W3. There are six other small off-trail lakes in the Bridger Lakes group that hold brook trout, goldens, or a combination of the two. You can't just swing by these lakes on the way to somewhere else—you have to come here on purpose, and few people do, so they're worth exploring.

Four miles due east of Elbow, there are golden trout in the Titcomb Basin. This basin is on the route to many big peaks and glaciers along the divide, so a lot of mountaineers and general trekkers pass through. I haven't fished these lakes, but they're rumored to produce goldens that occasionally reach 2 pounds. **Upper** and **Lower Titcomb Lakes** are both at 10,575 feet and cover 106 acres each. There's no route from Elbow directly to Titcomb Lakes, but from Seneca Lake a trail runs north right into the basin. The total distance from Elkhart Park via Seneca is about 15 miles.

If you head southeast from Seneca Lake on the Highline Trail, it's just 3 miles to **Cook Lakes.** These used to have big golden trout, but brook trout have infiltrated. Upper Cook (163 acres, 10,170 feet) is the larger of the two and still has some goldens, although I haven't seen any big ones. **Wall Lake** (105 acres, 10,450 feet), another big water, is just north of Upper Cook and produces an occasional large golden. I talked to a fisheries biologist who had flown over the lake on a calm day and seen several big fish from the air. Following that chat I spent a couple of days on Wall, but the wind was screaming. I took plenty of spray, but no fish. I haven't been back, but I haven't written off Wall. **Nelson Lake** (20 acres, 10,820 feet) is just west of Cook Lakes. If you come up empty on Wall and want some golden trout action, check out Nelson.

THE WEST SLOPE—CENTRAL REGION
Elkhart Park is the most popular trailhead for fishing the central third of the Bridger Wilderness. The Boulder Lake Trailhead, 20 miles to the southeast, is closer to lakes in the southern portion of this region, but it's almost 2,000 feet lower than Elkhart, so it's not used as heavily. To reach the Boulder Lake Trailhead and forest service campground, take the main highway (U.S. 191) south from Pinedale for 12 miles. Turn left on Wyoming 353. Watch the signs for a left turn onto a good dirt road that runs 8 miles to the trailhead and a forest service campground at the head of Boulder Lake. The trailhead is at 7,300 feet, so it's a long, steady 3,200-foot climb to timberline.

Heading east out of Elkhart Park, you'll hit **Pole Creek** in 9 miles. Several lakes along Pole have mostly small brook trout, with a few goldens and cutthroats. At Pole Creek you can swing south on the Highline Trail; this runs right by **Chain Lakes,** where I've taken some nice cutthroats to 17 inches. The three Chain Lakes, along with nearby **Spruce, Junction,** and **Barnes,** are all sizable waters that range from 20 to 100 acres and are at about 9,800 feet. All see a lot of traffic but offer good fishing for nice cutts, rainbows, and hybrids.

East of Chain Lakes are numerous brook trout lakes. I've caught solid brook trout of better than a foot in some of the small lakes scattered throughout the drainage.

From Chain Lakes you can continue south on either the Highline or Fremont Trail. The Fremont stays higher, but either trail takes you to North Fork Lake in less than 10 miles. **North Fork** (163 acres, 9,754 feet) was the first lake in the region to be stocked: It received cutthroats in 1907. North Fork is a big lake in the timber, but much of the shoreline is meadow and very fishable. Both North Fork and **Victor Lake** (139 acres, 9,834 feet) just to the north are loaded with cutthroats. I've taken a few trout to 19 inches in North Fork, but the average fish in both lakes is about a foot long.

From Victor a trail runs north to cross the divide at Hay Pass before descending to a flock of golden lakes (which I'll describe with the east-slope waters). The trail over Hay Pass follows the North Fork of Boulder Creek, which is large enough to be fun fishing when spawning cut-throats run up it from Victor. Several small lakes in the upper drainage just shy of the pass have good action for small cutts.

A few miles northwest of Victor are **Long Lake** (55 acres, 10,683 feet) and several more cutthroat lakes above timber in Europe Canyon. There aren't loads of fish in these lakes, but there are some nice ones. The trail up Europe Canyon passes right by **Prue Lake** (38 acres, 10,157 feet). Way back, Finis Mitchell reported 8-pound cutthroats from Prue. I checked this lake out in the late 1970s and caught some 20-inch fish, but they lacked heft.

South of Prue and in the timber is a swarm of midsize cutthroat lakes, including **Lower Pipestone** (21 acres, 10,125 feet), **Isabella** (51 acres, 9,719 feet), **Howard** (45 acres, 10,013 feet), and the three **Firehole Lakes,** which range from 23 to 30 acres and are all at about 9,600 feet. I once caught a 4-pound cutt at Firehole Lakes. I've taken small cutts from the others.

The rest of the lakes described in this region are as close, or closer, to the Boulder Lake Trailhead as they are to Elkhart Park. Hiking out of Boulder, you reach **Lake Ethel** (27 acres, 8,660 feet) in 6 miles. At Ethel, which has small cutts, the trail forks. Either fork takes you to North Fork Lake. Veer right to swing by Firehole, Isabella, and Pipe-stone Lakes (already described). Veer left to go by **Christina** (27 acres, 9,255 feet) and **Perry** (9 acres, 9,382 feet), both stacked with small brookies. **Eds** (4 acres, 9,025 feet) and **Norman** (16 acres, 9,386 feet), just north of Ethel, have small goldens.

A few miles west of North Fork and Victor, at the headwaters of the Middle Fork of Boulder Creek, are some good brook trout lakes. **Halls** and **Middle Fork** are the best and the biggest. Both lakes exceed 200 acres and have better than 2 miles of wide-open shoreline. I didn't fish Halls (10,262 feet) until recently, after I received a tip from a backpack angler whom I'd pointed toward some golden lakes. Halls has good num-bers of brookies from 14 to 18 inches. They're not footballs, but they're decently built. I kick myself for not checking this lake out twenty years ago when the fish were probably heavier, but it's still pretty good (release the better fish). Middle Fork (10,252) is east of Halls. I go way back on this lake. In the early 1980s I took some well-built 16-inch brookies here. The trout are smaller now, but they're still some of the prettiest brookies I've photographed. From Middle Fork you can pop over the divide at Kagevah Pass and drop into the Wind River Indian Reservation for some excellent fishing (see page 161).

Just south of Middle Fork at **Rainbow Lake** (76 acres, 10,341 feet), I've had a couple of fun evenings skating dry flies for rainbows up to a couple of pounds. From Middle Fork I usually head south along the eastern side of **Lee Lake** (about 80 acres, 10,305 feet), which has average brookies, and shoot through a little notch between Sentry and Nylon Peaks. There's no trail; it's a 1,300-foot climb to 11,600 feet, then a steep drop to small Sheila Lake, where I've seen no fish. **Jim Harrower Lake** (35 acres, 10,828 feet) is just downstream from Sheila and is a fine golden lake; on some maps it's simply identified as one of the Bonneville Lakes. I've taken a few goldens to 18 inches from Harrower, but nice, solid fish from 12 to 15 inches are the norm. I release everything here. **Bonneville Lake** (16 acres, 10,521 feet), immediately downstream, has smaller goldens.

THE WEST SLOPE—SOUTHERN REGION

The Big Sandy Trailhead is the main entrance to the southern third of the Bridger Wilderness. This trailhead is at 9,200 feet, almost 2,000 feet higher than Boulder Lake, so you might want to use it to reach some of the lakes I discussed above, which are closer to the Boulder Trailhead. To reach the Big Sandy Trailhead, follow Wyoming 353 as if you were going to Boulder Lake, but continue 20 miles to the end of the pavement. From there signs will direct you another 20 miles over improved dirt roads to the trailhead.

Lots of locals come up to the Big Sandy Openings on summer weekends to escape the heat of the outlying basins and to camp in the pleasant meadows along the Big Sandy River. There are also summer homes and a forest service campground near the trailhead, so the clump of lakes 5 miles northeast of the trailhead sees heavy use. **Black Joe Lake** (76 acres, 10,250 feet), just east of **Big Sandy Lake** (57 acres, 9,690 feet), has nice cutthroats and is the best lake within day-hiking range of the trailhead. The trail that goes by Big Sandy Lake pops over the divide at Jackass Pass and drops to Lonesome Lake in the spectacular Cirque of the Towers at the 10-mile mark. Lakes in this vicinity are described with the east-slope waters, but the hike from Big Sandy to lakes just east of the divide in the Popo Agie Wilderness is shorter than from any trailhead on the east slope.

The Highline and Fremont Trails also run out of Big Sandy. If you jump on the Fremont Trail heading north, you hit **Dads Lake** (53 acres, 9,741 feet) and **Marms Lake** (33 acres, 9,879 feet) in 6 miles. Both have small brook trout. At Marms a trail splits off to cross the divide at Hailey Pass 6 miles to the north. Two miles shy of the pass is **Maes Lake** (26 acres, 10,343 feet), which I haven't fished but officially has rainbows, plus a few browns and lake trout. A side trail skirts the west shore of Maes and ends at Pyramid Lake in a mile. **Pyramid** (55 acres, 10,570 feet) has respectable goldens, including an occasional fish of better than 2 pounds. For action I rate Pyramid a notch below Jim Harrower, but still pretty fair. Nice goldens taken in lakes this accessible should be released.

From Pyramid you can cross-country west for 2 miles to **East Fork Lake** (44 acres, 10,566 feet), which offers an outside chance at a big golden. Action for pan-size goldens can be good at the next lake downstream, **East Fork #6** (11 acres, 10,360 feet).

Back at Marms Lake, if you stay with the Fremont Trail, rather than heading for Hailey Pass, you'll continue northeast and hook up with the Highline Trail in a few miles. About 7 miles from Marms is **Cross Lake** (83 acres, 10,087 feet). In the next couple of miles you also pass **Raid Lake** (131 acres, 9,946 feet) and **Dream Lake** (63 acres, 9,842 feet). All three are big meadow lakes that have historically been used for grazing sheep. All have pan-size brook trout; Dream also has cutts. Since they're right on the Highline Trail, a lot of people naturally stop to wet a line.

Divide Lake (134 acres, 9,668 feet) is in the timber 5 miles due west of Cross. Divide has several species of trout and is reputed to yield a few big rainbows, but I haven't been there.

MAPS, GUIDEBOOKS, AND SERVICES—WEST SLOPE

The map of the Bridger-Teton National Forest (Pinedale Ranger District) shows the entire Bridger Wilderness, plus access roads to the trailheads; a waterproof version is available. Most of the range east of the divide is also shown. Scale is ½ inch to the mile, and contours are shown in intervals of 50 meters. You'll want more detailed topo maps for off-trail travel.

Earthwalk Press publishes a superb two-map series—"Northern Wind River Range" and "Southern Wind River Range"—which covers the entire range, except for a few fringe areas. These maps are printed on both front and back and cover the same area as thirty-three USGS 7.5-minute quadrangles. Scale is 1¼ inches to the mile. The contour interval is 40 feet. I own many USGS maps of the range, but I find the Earthwalk maps suitable for cross-country travel and much easier to read and pack than a bundle of topos. They're available in waterproof versions to withstand extensive use.

The Bridger Wilderness has seven special management areas where camping within 200 feet of lakes or trails is prohibited from July through Labor Day (ask for a map of these areas). Also contact the Bridger-Teton Forest for a booklet titled *A Guide to Bridger Wilderness Fishing Lakes.* This handy booklet shows the size, elevation, location, and resident fish species for most trout lakes in the wilderness.

The Most Complete Guide to Wyoming Fishing, by John Baughman, is primarily compiled from wildlife agency data. The book lists location, fish species, common fish sizes, and productivity (poor, fair, good, or excellent) for most lakes and streams in Wyoming. The book wasn't intended to hot-spot trophy waters, so bigger fish than are indicated swim in some waters. Still, this is a useful reference. Comparing the data from waters I know with that from waters I haven't visited has pointed me toward some interesting spots.

Wind River Trails, by Finis Mitchell, is a pocket-size trail and route guide that's spiced with entertaining personal and historical notes on the range. Unfortunately, the fishing has changed quite a bit since Mitchell's day—those 5-pound brookies, 8-pound cutts, and 11-pound goldens are a little harder to come by.

Pinedale is the major town on the west slope and has all services. The Great Outdoor Shop (just across Main Street from the post office) has fly-fishing gear, plus a full line of backpacking and mountaineering gear.

THE EAST SLOPE—FITZPATRICK WILDERNESS

The Fitzpatrick Wilderness (formerly the Glacier Primitive Area) covers 200,000 acres on the northern end of the east slope. This area has special significance for me. I made my first mountain hike here with my dad and my two brothers, and over the years I've taken many of my best golden trout here.

The Glacier Trailhead is the main entrance to the wilderness. To reach the trailhead, drive south from Dubois on U.S. 287. In 4 miles take a right on a dirt road that runs into Whiskey Basin. At the first fork, stay to the left (the right fork goes to a state fish hatchery). The road runs 8 miles past a series of lakes before ending above Trail Lake Ranch, a university facility. The trailhead is right on Torrey Creek at 7,500 feet. You can take a small car up this road, but go slow, because you'll probably bottom out on rocks a few times.

A couple of trails run out of this trailhead. The Whiskey Mountain Trail bears west. Eat your Wheaties—this trail climbs to almost 11,000 feet in 5 miles before dropping a bit to the Simpson Lake Trail, which continues west to Soapstone Lake at the 10-mile mark. **Soapstone** (10 acres, 10,000 feet) has lots of pan-size brook trout.

Simpson (170 acres, 9,730 feet) is a long, skinny lake 2 miles west of Soapstone. I've caught brookies and a few cutts to 14 inches here, but the lake has better potential. **Blanket Lakes** (9,670 feet), just to the north of Simpson, and **Long Lake** and **Dead Horse Lake,** just to the east, are small waters that have good fishing for average brook trout. **Pinto** and **Sandra,** a pair of 10-acre cutthroat lakes at 10,350 feet 2 miles south of Simpson, have cutthroats ranging to 18 inches.

For me the main local attraction is **Lost Lake** (16 acres, 10,361 feet), which sits in a pretty little cirque just a mile southeast of Simpson. The last time I fished Lost, I took a dandy golden of 20 inches and another of 17. After that, the fish size fell off the table. There were pods of plump 10-inch goldens all around the shore, so maybe a tremendous year class was in the making. I've always intended to go back to check on the progress of those little butterballs, but I haven't made it. The goldens in Lost are a rosy silver, and some of the palest I've seen.

Dyke Lake (32 acres, 10,265 feet) and small **Peat Lake** (both a mile west of Simpson) are supposed to have golden-rainbow hybrids. In an evening of fishing at nearby **Marion Lake** (20 acres, 10,410 feet), I caught several goldens not much bigger than tie tacks before sticking a lone 16-incher, so this lake probably merits a further look. I remember that it was 1988 when I was last in here, because the smoke from the Yellowstone fires made it look like dusk all day long.

If you have a four-wheel-drive vehicle, you can drive close to all of the lakes in the Simpson area, because they sit just inside the wilderness boundary. The Union Pass Road departs U.S. 287 north of Dubois and crosses the northern flank of the Winds. From the pass you can head east on unimproved ruts that run right to the wilderness boundary in 10 miles.

From the Glacier Trailhead, if you start up the Whiskey Mountain Trail but bear left at the first fork, you'll reach **Ross Lake** (474 acres, 9,675 feet) and **Upper Ross** (173 acres, 9,738 feet). The trail ends right at these lakes, which are 6 miles from the trailhead in a big, rocky cirque where good campsites are in short supply. Both lakes produce some nice rainbows, but local anglers hit them hard right after ice-out.

The Glacier Trail is used by the majority of climbing parties going to Gannett Peak. The trail heads south up Torrey Creek Canyon for a few miles and then switchbacks to timberline. Once on top, you continue to climb gradually through open meadows to 10,900 feet before descending to Burro Flat and **Double Lake** (30 acres, 10,000 feet) at the 10-mile mark. I've taken a few nice cutthroats to 18 inches and a few brook trout to 14, but loads of people fish here in passing. Nearby **Golden Lake** (19 acres, about 10,600 feet) requires a little off-trail footwork to reach, but the lake can be fun if you hit it right. As its name implies, it has golden trout.

Two miles south of Double Lake, the trail passes above **Honeymoon Lake** (18 acres, 9,838 feet). On that first family backpacking trip, my dad and brothers and I had a riot at Honeymoon catching and consuming vast quantities of rather skinny cutthroats to 15 inches. The fishing is still about the same, but these days I bypass Honeymoon to conserve fishing time. As I pass the lake, I always scan for rises and tip my cap to that long-ago trip. Dad is gone. Eric and his wife, Neysa, fly-fish Wisconsin and the West. Stu and his wife, Michelle, live near Ely, Minnesota, and publish *The Boundary Waters Journal,* a quarterly magazine that covers the Quetico-Superior canoe country. Stu has always been more a hunter than an angler, but he was the motivating force behind that family trip. He picked the Winds as our destination based on a story he'd read in *Outdoor Life.* I really just tagged along, but I came away from that trip with an itch I'm still scratching. Strangely enough, I've ended up hiking the Glacier Trail more than any other route in the Rockies.

Honeymoon is the final lake directly along the Glacier Trail, which ends 25 miles from the trailhead at the base of Gannett Peak. I use this route mainly to access the upper Dry Creek drainage, which is nearly 40 miles by trail from Trail Lake. From Honeymoon the trail descends to **Dinwoody Creek**—a large stream that's clouded with glacial flour and is basically fishless, except for just below the mouths of clear tributaries. At Downs Fork Meadows, a dead-end trail branches up the **Downs**

Fork, another milky, glacial stream. On the trip with my dad and brothers, this was our deepest penetration into the area. We found cutthroats in a couple of small lakes just north of the Downs Fork. Downs Lake, the big lake at the head of the drainage, has no fish. We did see an interesting phenomenon where a clear stream emptied into the Downs Fork: Casting into the milky current of the Downs Fork, we caught pale, silvery cutthroats devoid of color. Casting into the clear portion of the very same pool, where the tributary entered, we caught brilliantly colored cutts. Those trout were living within feet of each other and were probably related, yet they looked like different species.

The Glacier Trail crosses the Downs Fork and continues up Dinwoody Creek through a series of scenic, sandy outwash meadows below the big glaciers. The long, massive ridge to the east is Horse Ridge. The Dry Creek drainage is on the other side. The good news is that there's fine fishing over there; the bad news is that you're not there yet. About 5 miles below Gannett, the Ink Wells Trail cuts to the northeast to ascend Horse Ridge. Coming out of Trail Lake, I usually camp near this trail junction on my first evening so I can tackle Horse Ridge in the morning, while I'm fresh and before daily storm activity builds.

Lower Echo and **Upper Echo** are a pair of small brook trout lakes 2 miles up the Ink Wells Trail. The **Ink Wells,** a series of small brook trout lakes, are 2 more miles. From the Ink Wells, the trail continues northeast and climbs Horse Ridge to Scenic Pass at 11,400 feet. If you want to feel inconsequential, peer to the north and a bit to the west as you climb Horse Ridge. That high grassy country just 4 transparent, air miles away is Burro Flat, where the Glacier Trail dips down to Double Lake. If you've been making decent time, you were hiking across Burro Flat about the same time yesterday (it's about 15 zigzagging miles by trail).

From Scenic Pass the trail drops to Hays Park to meet the Dry Creek Trail; a four-wheel-drive road across Indian land ends within a mile of Hays Park. In the past anyone could use this road simply by buying a permit, so I've walked it several times; it's 13 miles from Hays Park to U.S. 287 near Burris, a one-house town. Now, however, persons who are not tribal members must hire an Indian outfitter to drive them up and down the road. For a group of three or four anglers who can split the cost of a jeep ride, the price is pretty reasonable, and eliminating the 60-mile round-trip hike from the Glacier Trailhead to Hays Park obviously saves fishing time. I'm still in the income bracket where I'll walk a couple of extra days to save nearly $400.

From Hays Park the trail drops to Dry Creek. In 4 miles you reach **Phillips Lake** (8 acres); **Grassy Lake** (23 acres) and **Native Lake** (52 acres) are just beyond. All three are just over 9,600 feet and have a smorgasbord of rainbow, cutthroat, and brook trout. Most of the fish are pan size, but some nice ones are around.

From Native the main trail climbs along a branch of Dry Creek. It's 2 miles to **Moose Lake** (13 acres, 10,000 feet). Moose has nice cutthroats and some brook trout. **Cub Lake** (43 acres, 10,380 feet) is 2 more miles upstream and has nice cutts, too. Just above Cub is **Don Lake** (38 acres, 10,475 feet), which has good fishing for cutts that can exceed 20 inches. I've also taken a few goldens, including one real beauty, here. The occasional golden in Don washes down from **Golden Lake** (40 acres, 10,530 feet) and can't make the climb back upstream. Golden Lake has only goldens, including some big ones, but they vanish for long periods. Above Golden Lake are several small cirque lakes tucked up against the towering walls of Horse Ridge; most are too cold and silty for fish.

From Echo Lakes on the Ink Wells Trail to Don Lake, via Scenic Pass, is 15 miles. I shave 10 miles by hiking cross-country over Horse Ridge from Echo to Don. It's steep, but you can get on or off Horse Ridge just north of Echo Lakes and just north of Don. Once you're on top, it's clear sailing at elevations to 12,000 feet—though I've been on top when the wind was strong enough to stagger me, and I wouldn't attempt this crossing in an electrical storm or dense clouds. You need a three-hour window of clear weather to pop over the ridge. Morning is usually your best bet. Using this shortcut, I can hit Golden Lake from the Glacier Trailhead by midafternoon on my second day.

There's more good fishing in this drainage. A couple of miles south of Cub Lake, at the head of the main stem of Dry Creek, are **Norman Lake** (58 acres, 10,500 feet) and **Rock Lake** (90 acres, 10,725 feet). Both are managed for golden-rainbow hybrids (goldbows) that can grow large. I've taken fish to 20 inches, and I've glimpsed a couple that were considerably larger. The outlet stream below Norman can be fun to fish for quite some distance, wherever there is holding water. Just west of the creek are several brook trout lakes; one of these, a recruitment lake, periodically yields a few nice squaretails.

There are a dozen more golden lakes in the far southern portion of the Fitzpatrick Wilderness. I've hiked cross-country to those lakes from the Dry Creek drainage, but they're easier to reach from trailheads on the west slope. From the Boulder Lake Trailhead on the west slope, you can cross the divide by trail at Hay Pass above Lake Victor. From Elkhart Park on the west slope, you can cross the divide at Angel Pass (no trail) above Cook Lakes. From either pass you drop to a string of three golden trout lakes, **Golden, Louise,** and **Upper Golden,** which are all about 20 acres and sit just under 10,200 feet. I caught my first golden trout here. The lower lake (Golden) produces an occasional fish over 15 inches, but most of the trout in this trio of lakes are smaller. **Dennis Lake** (69 acres, 10,630 feet), just below Hay Pass, also has goldens, but I haven't found any in passing. All of these lakes are on the Middle Fork of Bull Lake Creek, which drops into the reservation in a few miles.

If you follow the Middle Fork downstream from Golden Lake (there's no maintained trail), you'll come to an unnamed golden lake of about 60 acres at 9,434 feet. Milky Creek also enters this lake. Bushwhack southeast up Milky Creek for a mile and you'll hit the first of the **Milky Lakes,** more than a half dozen lakes that hold pure goldens of various sizes. A couple of these are in the Fitzpatrick Wilderness. **Milky Lake** (55 acres, 10,540 feet) is the highest in the group and is entirely on the Wind River Indian Reservation—you need a permit to go there. Two lakes of about 60 acres straddle the boundary.

Marked Tree Lake (65 acres, 9,318 feet) is on the Middle Fork of Bull Lake Creek just above the reservation boundary. At Marked Tree I've taken a few hefty golden-cutthroat hybrids to 20 inches (the cutts navigate upstream from Alpine Lake on the reservation—see next page). I've also had fun fishing for distinctively marked hybrids on the Middle Fork of Bull Lake Creek between Marked Tree and Alpine.

Bull Lake Creek is a bit north of the Middle Fork of Bull Lake Creek and also drains into Alpine Lake. Cutthroats haven't climbed above the reservation boundary in this drainage, so you'll find pure goldens in several unnamed lakes of various sizes. There's no maintained trail in here. The lakes are in the timber, so it's tight casting from shore.

A number of my favorite golden lakes, which I won't pinpoint here, are high on the east slope of the Winds in the Fitzpatrick Wilderness. If you're looking for lakes that consistently produce a few big goldens or lakes that have fast action for nice goldens, you'd be hard-pressed to find a better area to explore. When you hit the jackpot, just remember that big golden trout are a scarce resource. Treat them accordingly.

wind river range (wyoming)

THE EAST SLOPE—WIND RIVER INDIAN RESERVATION ROADLESS AREA

The roadless area of the Wind River Indian Reservation covers 180,000 acres smack in the center of the east slope and contains around a hundred trout lakes. I've spent only about three weeks hiking the reservation, so this is not the part of the range I know best. The reservation does not distribute detailed maps or any literature concerning fish species, size, or abundance for specific lakes; hiring an Indian guide or exploring extensively on your own are the primary ways to find the better waters. To complicate matters, many lakes are nameless on the USGS topos and forest service maps that cover portions of the area, so it's hard to pin down rumors. Fishing pressure is light. Trails are few and rugged, and there are many off-trail lakes, so carry detailed topo maps.

The Milky Lakes (previously described) along the Middle Fork of Bull Lake Creek are the only concentration of golden lakes I've fished on the reservation. **Alpine Lake** (170 acres, 8,957 feet), on Bull Lake Creek, reportedly has goldens. I've fished this big lake twice and have caught plenty of cutthroats averaging 16 inches, but no goldens. Goldens could drop down to Alpine from higher lakes, but with so many cutthroats present, I doubt Alpine actually produces many pure-strain goldens. I have leads on a few more golden lakes on the reservation, but I haven't seen them.

The reservation does have the best cutthroat fishing in the Winds. **Deadman Lake** (50 acres, 9,257 feet) is 2 air miles southeast of Alpine and can be approached by a couple of routes. I took well-built cutts to 20 inches at Deadman a decade ago. I'd like to fish here again, and also to check on a smaller lake 2 miles to the southwest that I've heard an interesting report on.

In "West Slope—Central Region," I described Middle Fork Lake (see page 152), which is in the central portion of the Bridger Wilderness and is generally reached from the Boulder Lake Trailhead. Just a mile north of Middle Fork Lake, a trail crosses the divide at Kagevah Pass (11,400 feet) and descends in 3 miles to Sonnicant Lake on the reservation. **Sonnicant** (136 acres, 10,100 feet) is on the North Fork of the Little Wind River. This drainage harbors half the trout lakes on the reservation. There are many good lakes within a 4-mile radius of Sonnicant. I've taken brook trout and cutthroats to 15 inches from Sonnicant but have not fished the lake thoroughly.

At **Lake Heebeecheeche** (102 acres, 10,356 feet), just 2 miles north of Sonnicant by trail, I've seen small brook trout and a few cutthroats. Several smaller, off-trail lakes above Heebeecheeche are worth exploring. At one I caught a half dozen cutthroats to 24 inches in just a few hours. Another trail climbs south from Sonnicant into a cirque that has three big lakes—**Solitude, Moraine,** and **Polaris**—which I haven't fished. They contain mainly brook trout and some cutthroats, and sound worth exploring.

Heading downstream along the North Fork of the Little Wind River from Sonnicant, you'll quickly reach **Wykee Lake** (55 acres, 9,843 feet), which has brook trout and cutthroats, as do two more lakes just down the trail. **Raft Lake** (330 acres, 9,154 feet) reportedly has four species of trout—rainbow, mackinaw, cutthroat, and brook. I've been within a mile of this huge mountain lake but haven't fished it. Six miles due south of Raft, I've taken some cutts to 20 inches at **Roberts Lake** (107 acres, 10,745 feet). The **Twenty Lakes,** a string of smaller lakes between Raft and Roberts, offer fast action for decent cutts.

I have leads on several more trophy-cutthroat lakes, plus a brook trout lake that has produced some 4-pound fish. I've caught larger goldens and have found many more good golden lakes off the reservation than on it, yet I look forward to exploring the reservation further. At the very least, I expect to find some more outstanding cutthroat fishing.

Nonresident one-day fishing permits are currently $20. Nonresident season fishing permits are only $80, so if you'll be fishing more than a few days, the season permit is a better buy and lets you move on and off the reservation at will (it's nice to have such flexibility on a trip when you're fishing the reservation and adjoining national forest). All permit holders must also have a $5 recreation stamp. Permits and fishing regulations are available at Tribal Headquarters in Fort Washakie, 15 miles north of Lander. Permits are also sold in sporting goods stores in Lander, Dubois, and Pinedale. If you plan to build campfires, also obtain a free fire permit.

I usually hike into the reservation from adjacent wilderness areas, but there are a number of dirt access roads and trailheads on the reservation. Some of these roads are too rough for two-wheel-drive vehicles, and some are closed to all but tribal members, so inquire about any road you plan to use.

For information contact:

Wind River Indian Reservation
Fish and Game Office
P.O. Box 217
Fort Washakie, WY 82514
Phone: (307) 332-7207

THE EAST SLOPE—POPO AGIE WILDERNESS

The Popo Agie Wilderness of the Shoshone National Forest covers 101,000 acres and contains the bulk of the backcountry waters on the southeastern slope of the Winds. There are also a couple dozen backcountry lakes in roadless country just to the east of the wilderness.

Worthen Meadow Reservoir, at about 9,000 feet, is the most heavily used trailhead in the area. Worthen Meadow can be reached by driving up the Middle Fork of the Popo Agie River from Lander or by taking Louis Lake Road, which connects with Wyoming 28 near Atlantic City and South Pass. Either route takes you over an all-weather road that's washboarded and dusty but is suitable for two-wheel drive. Worthen Meadow has a forest service campground, and there are several more campgrounds along the road. You can also camp for free in various meadows.

Leg Lake, just 5 miles from the trailhead, has nice golden trout, but there's no established trail to take you there. You'll need the USGS 7.5-minute quadrangle of Cony Mountain, Wyoming. This topo map was produced in 1953, before Worthen Meadow Reservoir and the present trailhead existed, so refer to a Shoshone National Forest Map for these features. To get to Leg, hike out of Worthen Meadow on the trail that heads to the Stough Creek Basin. Less than ½ mile after leaving the gravel road, you'll reach **Roaring Fork Lake** (10 acres, 9,023 feet), which holds small brook trout. This is where you leave the trail and start navigating on your own. Skirt the lakeshore and find the inlet stream at the southern end. This is Roaring Fork Creek, and you basically follow it southwest all the way to Leg Lake. If you can find it and stay with it, a faint trail will take you to timberline in about 3 miles. You'll also catch occasional glimpses of a sheer rock wall that crests at 11,600 feet. Leg sits in a cirque right at the base of this imposing wall.

Scattered along the various branches of Roaring Fork Creek are more than a half dozen lakes and ponds with brook trout. For the most part, these lakes are not overpopulated with fish, and because they see few anglers, the fish have a chance to grow. I've never taken anything big here, but if you put in some time, a 2-pound brookie is doable.

Just south of Leg is **Gap Lake** (10 acres, 10,300 feet). Gap and a couple of ponds just below it have grayling. Most are under a foot long, but I've taken a couple to 14 inches—the biggest I've seen in the Rockies. You have to cradle a grayling in your hands to really appreciate its iridescence.

Leg Lake (41 acres, 10,500 feet) has furnished a lot of enjoyable fishing over the years when I wanted to catch some nice goldens and had only a couple of days to do it. I've never cracked the 20-inch mark here, but it was a hot lake for beefy goldens to 17 inches when I first started fishing it in the mid-1980s. The last time I was here, in 1995, there were a lot more small fish, and the top-end fish weren't quite as stout, so maybe spawning in the outlet stream has been a little too successful. I wouldn't be adverse to eating small fish here, but let the nice ones go.

From Gap Lake I've hiked cross-country straight west over Roaring Fork Mountain, topping out at 11,100 feet, before dropping into **Stough Creek Basin** just a mile away. This basin is a big cirque with a cluster of two dozen lakes. Most of the trout lakes are near or above timberline and range from 10 to 30 acres. It's all brook trout and cutthroats, with some decent fish to a couple of pounds. From a base camp anywhere in the basin, you can easily fish several lakes a day. You won't be alone, because the basin is just 8 miles by trail from Worthen Meadow.

A few miles west of Stough Creek, at the head of Tayo Creek, is **Mountain Sheep Lake** (23 acres, 10,200 feet). In the mid-1980s I heard a rumor of big brook trout from this lake. I did catch a fat brookie over a foot long, but that was all I could muster. This lake reportedly has goldens and cutthroats, too, but they didn't materialize for me either, so maybe the trout were deep. **Coon Lake** (50 acres, 10,534 feet) is just a mile west of Mountain Sheep and has golden-cutthroat hybrids that top 15 inches.

Four miles straight north of Mountain Sheep are the **Ice Lakes,** which are mostly fishless or contain small brook trout. A mile north of those are **Deep Creek Lakes**—three lakes that range from 33 to 68 acres and sit at 10,500 to 10,800 feet. The upper two have goldens that occasionally top a couple of pounds; the lower lake has golden-rainbow hybrids.

Just north of Deep Creek Lakes are **Echo Lakes** and **Baer Lakes,** a group of four brook trout waters all about 7 acres in size and tucked in the timber at 10,000 feet or so. All four lakes can produce brook trout over a foot long. A mile west of Baer Lakes on Volcano Creek is **Hidden Lake** (68 acres, 10,100 feet). Hidden has golden-rainbow hybrids that occasionally push 20 inches. Echo, Baer, and Hidden Lakes all drain into the North Fork Popo Agie River and are just a mile south of it. If you take the North Fork Trail west from this area, it's only about 7 miles to the Cirque of the Towers, which can also be reached by a 10-mile hike from the Big Sandy Openings.

Lakes in the northern portion of the Popo Agie Wilderness are easiest to reach from the Dickinson Park Trailhead, at about 9,500 feet. Dickinson Park has a forest service campground; it lies at the end of an improved dirt road that starts near Fort Washakie and climbs for 20 miles. The Bears Ear Trail runs straight west out of Dickinson, crossing high, open country at nearly 12,000 feet before dropping to Valentine Lake in about 10 miles. **Valentine** (45 acres, 10,399 feet) was one of the best golden lakes in the range before my time; it now holds a mix of small goldens and cutthroats. **Upper Valentine Lake** (23 acres, 10,544 feet) is a better bet for slightly larger goldens.

Washakie Lake (115 acres, 10,363 feet), 2 miles west of Valentine, used to kick out some golden-rainbow hybrids to 7 pounds, but this action has slowed. Washakie also has some goldens, brook trout, and decent rainbows. The lake is used quite heavily by outfitters, so I don't fish it much.

From Valentine Lake the Bears Ear Trail runs west and north along the South Fork of the Little Wind River. **Spearpoint Lake** (20 acres, 10,599 feet) is about 600 feet above and a mile west of the trail. A decade ago I caught goldbows here to 18 inches, but I haven't been back.

Five miles from Valentine is **Grave Lake** (200 acres, 9,964 feet). Grave has average cutthroats and supposedly has some lake trout, although I haven't fished for them. From Grave Lake it's just a 3-mile hike over the divide at Hailey Pass to reach Pyramid Lake and the East Fork Lakes—some good golden waters described in "West Slope—Southern Region" (see page 154).

A couple of miles west of Grave is **Baptiste Lake** (178 acres, 10,828 feet). Most of Baptiste is on the reservation, where you need a permit to fish, but an arm does extend into the wilderness. Baptiste is a fine lake for cutthroats that can top 3 pounds.

The Fiddlers Lake Trailhead (9,417 feet) is less than 10 miles south of Worthen Meadow. From Fiddlers Lake it's just an 8-mile hike west to **Thumb Lake** (33 acres, almost 11,000 feet), at the head of Silas Canyon. A maintained trail takes you 5 miles to Upper Silas Lake. A bit west of Upper Silas you break out of the timber and follow **Silas Creek** past **Island Lake** (average cutthroats) and right to Thumb. Thumb is on the same USGS quadrangle (Cony Mountain, Wyoming) as Leg Lake. It's a pretty cirque lake above timber, and considering how easy it is to reach, Thumb is a pretty good golden lake. I've taken as many as a half dozen nice goldens in an afternoon. The largest was a hefty 19-incher that ran all over the lake. This is a lake where everything should be released.

Two miles south of Thumb, at the head of Atlantic Creek Canyon, there are decent goldens in **Windy Lake** (30 acres, 10,700 feet), although I've never had the kind of action here that I've enjoyed at Leg and Thumb. From Island Lake below Thumb, you can hike cross-country to **Atlantic Creek** and then follow this creek up to Windy Lake; you'll want the adjoining USGS quadrangle of Christina Lake, Wyoming. There are small brook trout in Atlantic Creek, Silas Creek, and several lakes scattered along both.

MAPS AND SERVICES—EAST SLOPE

The map of the Shoshone National Forest (south half) shows the east slope of the Winds except for portions of the reservation; the scale is ½ inch to the mile. The two Earthwalk Press maps (see page 155) also cover the east slope, except for parts of the reservation, and a few lakes east of the Popo Agie Wilderness, including Thumb and Leg. I've never seen a useful map of the entire reservation. I carry USGS topo maps of all areas not covered on the Earthwalk maps.

Lander lies at the southern end of the east slope, Dubois at the northern. Both towns offer all services. Lander has better grocery stores. Dubois is a smaller, more traditional western town with a trout stream running right under Main Street. The Good Place, on the main drag in Lander, and Whiskey Mountain Tackle, in the center of Dubois, are full-line sport shops that can fill you in on conditions on local and back-country waters.

CHAPTER 24

Teton Wilderness
(Wyoming)

The northwestern corner of Wyoming is blessed with an abundance of fine cutthroat waters, including Yellowstone Park, the powerful Snake River in Jackson Hole, and a wealth of alpine lakes. But few anglers visit the finest cutthroat fishing in the area—the Thorofare country of the Teton Wilderness.

The Teton Wilderness covers more than a half million acres and is buffered by large tracts of wildlands. The remote southeastern corner of Yellowstone Park is just to the north, and the Washakie Wilderness of the Shoshone National Forest is directly east. Together these areas constitute one of the largest roadless tracts in the Rockies.

The wilderness is physically similar to Yellowstone Park—much of it is plateau country covered with lodgepole pine and large meadows. The western two-thirds of the wilderness is relatively gentle, with elevations ranging from 7,500 to 10,000 feet. The eastern third is more rugged, with sharply defined canyons and peaks, including 12,165-foot Younts Peak at the very headwaters of the Yellowstone River. Big game is abundant. Much of the Jackson Hole elk herd summers on the grassy plateaus. This is core grizzly country. I've seen more grizzlies here than in the back-country of Yellowstone Park.

A unique feature of the wilderness is Two Ocean Creek, which forks atop the Continental Divide. Atlantic Creek flows into the Yellowstone and eventually to the Atlantic; Pacific Creek flows into the Snake and eventually to the Pacific. Two Ocean Pass is the only place on the continent where this phenomenon is known to occur.

Deep in the Thorofare region, some 20 miles south of Yellowstone Lake, is cutthroat trout paradise. In early summer a major migration of cutthroats from Yellowstone Lake surges up the Yellowstone River to spawn in the wilderness. During the peak of the run, trout infiltrate many miles of wilderness waters. The upper **Yellowstone River** and **Thorofare Creek** receive the bulk of the migration, but several tributary streams to those rivers are also good.

Most lake-run cutts are 16 inches right on the button, but there are some larger fish. At the peak of the run, fly fishers can hook several dozen fish a day. Peak migration can shift by a couple of weeks, depending on spring weather and the severity of the previous winter, but most years fish complete spawning by late June. After spawning, many trout linger and feed as they drop back to Yellowstone Lake, but by late July fish density in the Thorofare drops sharply. Even though fish numbers are dropping, I like to visit the area in early July. There are still plenty of fish around, and they're intent on feeding rather than spawning, so the angling is more interesting.

Straddling the park boundary is the 7-mile-long **Yellowstone Meadow.** My favorite stretch of water is the Yellowstone River upstream of the park boundary. Here the Yellowstone is a classic meadow stream with an inviting mix of large pools, long slicks, gravel riffles, and swift, deep runs with undercut banks. Most of the meadow is grass or low willows. The stream can be fished effectively in hiking boots, but lightweight waders, or even hippers, are an advantage. In wet years be warned that the meadow has pockets of standing water, which produce plenty of mosquitoes; biting flies join the fracas as well.

The stream holds a superb strain of resident cutts. I've caught and released many of these resident fish in the 2 miles of water just downstream from the Hawks Rest pack bridge. The resident cutts are stockier and much stronger than the lake fish—in fact, they have the best body type of any cutts I've taken in the Yellowstone drainage. The lake fish tend to feed and hold in the slower pools, slicks, and eddies, where they can be seen throughout the day. The resident fish prefer swift runs with undercut banks, and they vanish between significant hatches. On my latest trip I lucked into daily hatches of green drakes in the meadow. The duns started showing around noon and came off for about two hours.

There were never more than a few duns in sight at once, but they were juicy enough to pull the resident fish out from beneath the cut banks. Often I'd spot a big dun at a distance and watch it drift until a fish inhaled it. Then I'd stalk the fish and put my imitation right on its platter. A #12 Industrial-Strength Dun Green Drake was seldom refused. After the fish shredded my last Green Drake, I switched to a big Wood-Duck Adams, and the trout gobbled that, too.

There's too much water in the Thorofare to fish it all. I've fished the Yellowstone upstream from the park boundary for about 7 miles (the river winds so much it's tough to estimate river distances accurately). Above this are more than 5 miles of sizable meadow water and many miles of smaller, timbered water that I haven't seen. A trail follows the river all the way to the headwaters.

Heavy rains can turn the upper Yellowstone chalky and slow the fishing, but it normally clears in a day or two. If the river is roiled, check out the lower reaches of Atlantic Creek, which meets the Yellowstone about 3 miles south of the park. I found a big pool stuffed with enough lake-run cutts to entertain me for an afternoon. A glance at a topo map will reveal all kinds of seldom-fished tributary streams that widen as they wind through the meadow.

Thorofare Creek is actually a freestone river that's as big as the Yellowstone where the two meet a couple of miles inside the park. From its headwaters on Thorofare Mountain (12,058 feet), the creek runs through the Teton Wilderness for more than 20 miles. It blossoms into a sizable river about 10 miles above the park, where it's mostly timbered and has an abundance of gravel riffles that are ideal spawning habitat. Thorofare Creek probably attracts as many lake-run fish as the Yellowstone and has some resident cutts to boot. Waders or hippers are a big advantage, because the banks are mostly tree lined. A trail follows the river all the way to the headwaters.

I've seen hatches of pale morning duns on both the Yellowstone and Thorofare Creek. Small yellow stoneflies and a variety of caddis are also abundant. Attractor drys, like Humpies and Wulffs, take fish, but I have more fun matching hatches. Since rising fish are usually available, I don't spend much time nymphing.

I like to set up a base camp near Hawks Rest—an imposing formation that looms 2,000 feet above the Yellowstone Meadow. This puts me right on a productive stretch of the Yellowstone, and I can easily day hike to other waters. Atlantic Creek and Thorofare Creek lie within 2 miles. A pack bridge over the Yellowstone at Hawks Rest provides quick access to either bank. There's also springwater spilling from a wooden sluice just below the Hawks Rest patrol cabin, so you don't have to purify river water. A wilderness ranger who lives in the cabin most of the summer told me that horse parties pass through almost daily, but he sees only about a dozen hiking parties a summer.

In the heart of the Thorofare, Hawks Rest is a long way from any-where, but you can get there several ways. From the north you can skirt the eastern shore of Yellowstone Lake and hike up the Yellowstone River (this 35-mile route is described in chapter 43). Outfitters from the Cody area, to the east, ride in from the South Fork of the Shoshone River, cross the divide at Ishawhooa Pass (9,870 feet), and descend to upper Thorofare Creek. This route is around 40 miles long and climbs more than 3,000 feet from the Shoshone River to the divide. I was set to come in this way once, but the trail was temporarily closed because grizzlies were eating a dead horse on it. The problem was dissipated (lit-erally) with explosives.

The shortest and easiest route for hikers and horse parties alike is from Turpin Meadow south of the wilderness. Turpin Meadow (7,000 feet) is 15 miles east of Moran Junction, Wyoming, and accessible by good roads from U.S. 287. The trailhead has a forest service campground and corrals. I've met folks at the trailhead who hauled in their own horses from as far away as Michigan and Texas.

To reach Hawks Rest from Turpin Meadow, you hike up the North Buffalo Fork Trail and catch a trail that pops over Two Ocean Pass. The "Parting of the Waters" is just north of the trail. From the pass you descend Atlantic Creek to the Yellowstone River. It's 26 miles from Turpin Meadow to Hawks Rest, and the entire route, including Two Ocean Pass (which sits at only 8,200 feet), is pretty gentle. On my last trip, I hiked in to Hawks Rest in a day, despite the fact that I was on muddy trails with a 60-pound pack and wasn't in top condition. Backcountry river fishing in the Rockies doesn't get much better or wilder than this. If you go to the Thorofare, pack some grub and stay a while.

During the half-hour hike from Hawks Rest to Thorofare Creek, you go right by **Bridger Lake** (104 acres, 7,858 feet). This is a fertile lake where I've taken a couple of cutts over 20 inches, but given the abundance of moving water in the region, I haven't fished Bridger a lot. The shores were torched pretty thoroughly in the 1988 fires. The last time I was here, in the early 1990s, there were still a lot of standing snags, and it was not a safe or attractive place to camp. Waders will buy you some backcasting room.

Since Yellowstone Park is so close, you should be aware that area rivers and streams in the park do not open to fishing until July 15. To fish in the park, you need a valid park fishing permit; to camp, you need a permit for an assigned backcountry campsite. With so much fine water in the Teton Wilderness, however, there's no pressing need to enter the park. In the wilderness you can keep two fish a day (only one over 20 inches). I usually eat a trout or two.

The other large streams and scattered lakes of the Teton Wilderness are mostly west of the divide. Turpin Meadow is a handy trailhead for reaching many of them. The **North** and **South Forks of the Buffalo River** converge just inside the Teton Wilderness boundary, 2 miles east of Turpin Meadow. Trails run up both forks. The Buffalo runs dirty during runoff or heavy rain; before hiking, check the color of the river where it crosses the road to Turpin Meadow. The lower 10 miles of the South Fork, below Lower Pendergraft Meadow, hold mostly cutts that average 12 inches. Higher up, the South Fork holds mostly smaller brook trout. At Upper Pendergraft Meadow, 15 miles above the confluence, the South Fork loses much of its size.

The **Angle Lakes** are just south of Upper Pendergraft Meadow. All are small, but the largest, including Rainbow, Golden, Mackinaw, and Bertha, are tightly bunched in the timber at 8,500 feet and hold mostly cutthroats to 15 inches. Many small, unnamed ponds in the vicinity have small brook trout.

From Upper Pendergraft Meadow, a trail runs north for 5 miles to **Ferry Lake** (45 acres, about 8,300 feet). I haven't been to Ferry, but it reportedly has fair action for small golden trout. Just west of Ferry, along the **Soda Fork,** is **Crater Lake** (80 acres, 9,950 feet), with small cutts. You can complete a 40-mile loop trip back to Turpin Meadow by continuing west down the Soda Fork, which has some good pockets and a few nice trout.

The first time I hiked into the Thorofare, I used the Pacific Creek Trailhead, which is north of Moran Junction and just east of Grand Teton Park. The lower 10 miles of **Pacific Creek** have some sizable meadow sections and enjoyable fishing for pan-size cutts, although the runs are seldom deep. There are some beautiful campsites on open terraces above the creek that offer great views of the Tetons. **Gravel Lake** (about 15 acres, 7,990 feet) is 5 miles north of Pacific Creek in dense timber. It's stuffed with small cutts.

The trail up Pacific Creek heads right to Two Ocean Pass in about 20 miles. On the way you can swing by **Enos Lake** (178 acres, 7,750 feet), which is by far the biggest lake in the vicinity and has good action for cutts that average over a foot.

There are small lakes of 5 acres or less scattered throughout the wilderness. Many of them are up creek drainages that have no trails. Most of these small, isolated lakes hold small trout, but there are exceptions. I know of a fertile pond (that shall remain a mystery) in the southeastern corner of the wilderness that produces a few fat rainbows of over 20 inches, plus some nice brook trout. Locals who hunt, fish, and travel the southeastern part of the wilderness extensively take a few big brook trout from the many ponds in this region, but going in there and sorting the better ponds out on your own could take weeks of bushwhacking.

In addition to the major streams and rivers I've discussed, the Teton Wilderness is laced with small streams that have moderate gradients by mountain standards and rarely see an angler. If you're looking for moving water and a place to bend a light rod in real solitude, this wilderness has an abundance of fun streams.

MAPS AND SERVICES
The map of the Bridger-Teton National Forest (Buffalo and Jackson Ranger Districts) shows the entire Teton Wilderness, including access roads to the trailheads at Turpin Meadow and Pacific Creek. The map has a scale of ½ inch to the mile and a contour interval of 50 meters.

If you plan on approaching the Thorofare from Cody, you should also have the map of the Shoshone National Forest (north half), which shows the Washakie Wilderness, trailheads along the South Fork of the Shoshone River, and several passes on the divide from which you can descend to the Thorofare.

If you're planning to fish this region, you'll also want the USGS 15-minute topo map of Two Ocean Pass, Wyoming, which shows much of the Thorofare in detail, including Two Ocean Pass, the entire Yellowstone Meadow, Hawks Rest, Bridger Lake, and the lower 8 miles of Thorofare Creek.

Dubois, about 40 miles east of Turpin Meadow, is a nice, quiet town with all services. Jackson, an hour to the southwest, is the most bustling tourist town in Wyoming. Jack Dennis runs a top-notch fly shop and outdoor store on the square in Jackson.

CHAPTER 25

Absaroka–Beartooth Wilderness (Montana–Wyoming)

The Absaroka–Beartooth Wilderness encompasses a million acres of rugged high country just north and east of Yellowstone Park. The bulk of this wilderness lies in Montana, although its southern tip extends into Wyoming. It has over four hundred trout lakes with a variety of species. There are some fine trophy fisheries. In all of the Rockies, only the Wind River Range surpasses the Beartooth Mountains for sheer numbers of good, high lakes.

The Absaroka Mountains, in the western half of the wilderness, feature sharply eroded volcanic peaks and forested valleys. Lakes are few and scattered. Small to large streams abound, and most have small to pan-size trout. Slough Creek, an outstanding cutthroat stream that lies partially in the Absarokas, is discussed with Yellowstone Park waters in chapter 43. **Buffalo Creek,** 5 miles west of Slough, also begins in the Absarokas and flows south into the park. I haven't fished Buffalo Creek, but I've heard that north of the park, it holds rainbow trout, including a few nice fish. I plan to fish the wilderness portions of the Buffalo when I revisit Slough. Grizzlies roam the forested western and southern regions of the wilderness adjacent to the park but are uncommon in the open plateau country to the east.

The majority of lakes are clustered on the Beartooth Plateau and several smaller plateaus in the eastern half of the wilderness. The plateau country is primarily uplifted granite and boasts the highest mountains in Montana; Granite Peak at 12,799 feet is the tallest. Many lakes are above timber in relatively gentle country, and opportunities for cross-country travel are frequent. On exploratory trips it's possible to visit several lakes a day. I've made fifteen trips to these plateau lakes, which might sound like a lot, but half of my trips were made primarily to fish just two lakes. There are entire drainages I haven't set foot in. A word of warning: The plateau country has hundreds of potholes that produce mosquitoes. In early summer the air can fairly hum.

I've broken my discussion of the plateau region into its northern and southern trailheads. Virtually every lake on the plateau is within 15 miles of a trailhead, but there are so many out-of-the-way waters that many are lightly fished.

SOUTHERN TRAILHEADS OF THE PLATEAU REGION

If you've driven the spectacular Beartooth Highway (U.S. 212) from Red Lodge, Montana, to Cooke City and Silver Gate at the Northeast Entrance of Yellowstone Park, you've driven right over the Beartooth Plateau. Several high-elevation trailheads spaced along the Beartooth Highway provide quick access to dozens of lakes just to the north. I often recommend this area to fly fishers who want to give high-lake fishing and backpacking a whirl, because it's so easy to pack in to good lakes.

The Clarks Fork Trailhead (about 8,000 feet) is 4 miles east of Cooke City and provides access to dozens of lakes in the Clarks Fork drainage. Day hikers parade to the lakes within a few miles of the trailhead, so I bypass these. Of the local lakes, **Rock Island** (137 acres, 8,666 feet), about 3 miles east of the trailhead, is reputed to hold a few big brook trout and cutthroats. An angler I once talked to on the trail was packing a float tube for fishing island areas of Rock Island Lake that can't be reached from shore.

From the Clarks Fork Trailhead, I usually head up Russell Creek to **Russell Lake** (small brook trout) at the 6-mile mark. From Russell Lake the trail climbs quickly above timber and in the next 3 miles is flanked by creeks and several small lakes that have more brookies. **Fossil Lake** (165 acres, 9,900 feet) is 10 miles from the trailhead. It has the most convoluted shape of any high lake I've seen, with arms and legs sprawling all over. Fossil actually sits at the very head of the East Rosebud drainage and is the hub of activity in the area (the USGS 15-minute quadrangle of Cooke City, Montana-Wyoming, shows Fossil and the surrounding lakes). Fossil used to be known for big fish, but I've camped here several nights en route to other waters, and the best fish I've taken or seen were 15-inch cutts.

Three miles northwest of Fossil, in the Clarks Fork drainage, is a pair of very big, productive lakes. At **Upper Aero** (292 acres, 10,140 feet) look for big cutthroats cruising the shore. I've taken well-built fish to 20 inches, but not many. **Lower Aero** (190 acres, 9,995 feet) has cutts, plus some solid brook trout to 15 inches. Also look for nice cutts stacked up in the deeper pools in the ½ mile of stream between the two lakes. Upper Aero is a windy locale; stake your tent down well. Also, don't urinate near your tent anywhere in this plateau country. Mountain goats crave the salt that's deposited in this fashion. They'll paw and eat the ground, soil and all, and keep you awake all night.

Scattered between Fossil and Aero Lakes is a bunch of brook trout lakes. **Rough Lake** (102 acres, 10,150 feet) is by far the biggest and is full of small brook trout. I took a photo of Rough on a calm evening when so many trout were rising it looked like it was raining. Rough also has some grayling. Brook trout and grayling can reach respectable size in **Lone Elk Lake** (80 acres) just downstream.

During a trip in July 1991 I checked out several small, off-trail lakes south of Lone Elk that reportedly yield a few big brook trout. At most of these lakes, I came up empty or encountered small fish—but I did find an off-trail lake in the vicinity of Fossil Lake that was and still is an exceptional brook trout lake for both numbers and size. Starting in 1991 I fished this lake for five straight years, and after a couple of years off, I'm now getting the itch to go back.

I made my first trip to the Beartooths in 1980. On that trip I also hiked out of the Clarks Fork Trailhead, but instead of swinging north toward Fossil Lake, I worked my way east past Widewater Lake and spent nine days exploring a bunch of lakes in high, open country in the center of the Beartooth Plateau. **Jordan Lake** (36 acres, 9,625 feet) has nice cutthroats and is a good place to set up your base while fishing the surrounding lakes (which are shown on the USGS 15-minute quadrangle of Alpine, Montana-Wyoming). North of Jordan, on Farley Creek, is a chain of three lakes a bit above 10,000 feet. As you move up the drainage, you'll encounter **Anchor Lake** (12 acres), **Big Butte Lake** (22 acres), and **Desolation Lake** (31 acres). When I was here in 1980, I took a few nice cutthroats in these lakes. Apparently the cutts were not reproducing well, however, because since then golden trout have been introduced to all three lakes. I haven't heard anything about the fate of these goldens, but the lakes are capable of growing nice trout and could be worth checking if you're in the area.

Canyon Lake (67 acres, 8,780 feet) is 2 miles west of Jordan and downstream in the timber along Farley Creek. Canyon has nice rainbow-cutthroat hybrids. The remaining lakes near Jordan, including **Farley, Mariane,** and **Otter,** have mostly small brook trout.

Access to the eastern end of the Beartooth Plateau is easiest from the Island Lake Trailhead (9,516 feet), just off the Beartooth Highway. From this high-elevation trailhead, it's a mostly level stroll to many lakes above timber. The only catch to hiking out of Island Lake is that it's in Wyoming, and the Montana line is just 4 miles north; depending on your destinations, you may need valid fishing licenses for both states. I use the trailhead primarily to fish lakes in Montana. Most of the Wyoming lakes are so close to the trailhead that they see a lot of day and weekend hikers.

From Island Lake I head for **Becker Lake** (80 acres, 9,639 feet), 5 miles to the north. Becker is nearly 2 miles long and has pan-size brook trout, but it's mainly a guidepost on the route to other waters. As you skirt its eastern side, you'll emerge from the trees and find clear sailing to **Albino Lake** (39 acres, 10,000 feet), which is about 7 miles from the trailhead and a mile into Montana. Albino has steady fishing for cut-throats to 15 inches.

To reach the best lake in the area, climb through a little swale northwest of Albino and drop down to **Jasper Lake** (55 acres, 10,150 feet) at about the 9-mile mark. I've had two fun trips to Jasper (the latest in 1991) for cutthroats to 20 inches. The fish are well fed and can be uncooperative, but if you hit the lake right, you'll find good numbers of them cruising the flats and shelves. Put a scud imitation or a Soft-Hackle Woolly Worm in front of these fish. Jasper has limited natural reproduc-tion—it occurs in an inlet stream on the northern side of the lake—so a variety of fish sizes are always present, but the fishery is largely main-tained by stocking at eight-year intervals. In fact, quite a few cutthroat lakes in the wilderness require stocking, and the Montana Department of Fish, Wildlife and Parks does an excellent job of adjusting stocking intervals and densities to produce nice fish. As a result, there are some outstanding and readily accessible cutthroat lakes, like Albino, on the plateau.

On my first trip to Jasper, I scouted the **Clover Leaf Lakes,** a trio of small (20- to 30-acre) lakes above timber at 10,150 feet that are a

2-mile cross-country hike west of Jasper. All of these lakes have a few cutts, but they don't rival Jasper's fish for size.

A few hundred yards below Jasper is **Golden Lake** (49 acres, 10,130 feet). Some cutthroats drop down to Golden from Jasper. The stream between the two lakes also has some nice pockets that can hold mature fish, especially in early summer.

If you hike southwest down the outlet stream from Golden, in 2 miles you'll reach **Hidden Lake** (18 acres, 9,500 feet), right at the edge of the timber and just north of the Montana line. Hidden contains cutthroats that have dropped down from Jasper and Golden.

Just south of Hidden and back in Wyoming is a slew of small brook trout lakes: Wonder, Net, T, Rocky, Gus, Halfmoon, Ewe, Surprise, and Native are only some of the names. Most of these lakes are from 5 to 15 acres in size and near 10,000 feet, which puts them just above or below timber. Some are loaded with small trout, but a few produce good numbers of respectable brookies in the 10- to 13-inch class and occasionally bigger. Some of these small lakes are susceptible to winterkill. Fish that filter in from creeks and survive a few years can beef up. I've taken several fat brook trout to 2 pounds, and this is an interesting area to explore. All of the lakes are an easy 4- to 6-mile hike from the Island Lake Trailhead, making this an ideal destination for a family or group outing—especially after mid-August, when the skeeters slack off. The USGS 7.5-minute quadrangle for Beartooth Butte, Wyoming, shows all these lakes. Some are too small to be named.

One year I made a short four-day trip to the Hellroaring Plateau in the far southeastern corner of the wilderness. About 15 miles west of Red Lodge, and before the Beartooth Highway begins to climb through a big series of switchbacks, take a side road that leads to a group of campgrounds (Greenough, Parkside, and Limberpine). This side road turns to dirt and runs southwest for about 8 miles to dead-end at a trailhead at 8,600 feet. From here it's just a 2-mile climb to **Glacier Lake** (177 acres, 9,818 feet). Glacier is actually a reservoir with a dam at its southern end. (The dam is in Wyoming; the bulk of the lake is in Montana.) It's reputed to have slow fishing for nice cutthroats and the biggest brook trout in the range. I must have caught one of these slow periods; during my two days at the lake, all I managed was a single 15-inch cutt, and I didn't see another fish. I caught more and larger cutthroats at **Triangle Lake** (8 acres, 9,730 feet), just north of Glacier (in Montana), and at **Emerald Lake** (40 acres, 9,750 feet), just south of Glacier (in Wyoming).

NORTHERN TRAILHEADS OF THE PLATEAU REGION

Between Livingston and Columbus, Montana, several roads run south from Interstate 90 to trailheads on the northern side of the plateau region. I regularly use the Box Canyon Trailhead on the headwaters of the Boulder River to access the Lake Plateau, which holds a concentration of lakes in the northwestern part of the wilderness. Boulder River Road (Montana 298) heads south from the interstate at the town of Big Timber, 30 miles east of Livingston. It's a 50-mile, three-hour drive to the Box Canyon Trailhead. The last 25 miles of road are improved dirt but are passable by car (there are several forest service campgrounds, but no services, along this section). The improved road ends at Box Canyon (6,700 feet), although a four-wheel-drive road continues south for several miles.

From the trailhead a trail runs east up the **East Fork of the Boulder River,** which is a big stream with good fishing in spots for pan-size brook trout and rainbows. In about 7 miles you'll hit the first trail junction, near a fishless pothole named Lake Kathleen. The East Fork Boulder Trail bears south and runs to the headwaters of Slough Creek, reaching the fourth meadow on Slough (described in chapter 43) in about 15 miles. If you head this way, you'll want the USGS 15-minute quadrangle of Cutoff Mountain, Montana-Wyoming.

If you take the trail that forks to the left up Rainbow Creek, on the other hand, you'll continue east and then north and climb to the first lakes on the Lake Plateau at about the 10-mile mark. All of the plateau lakes I'll discuss are shown on the USGS 15-minute quadrangle of Mount Douglas, Montana. At **Fish Lake** (18 acres, 9,472 feet) I've caught only small cutts. **Rainbow Lakes,** a half dozen small lakes of 2 to 18 acres at about 9,500 feet, are on the headwaters of Rainbow Creek. They have plenty of open shoreline and decent fishing for mostly pan-size rainbows. I see a lot of large groups and outfitters operating in this vicinity, and most of them routinely kill the better trout they catch. **Mirror Lake** (16 acres, 9,740 feet) is about a mile west of Rainbow Lakes, but it's off trail so it sees less traffic. Mirror has good action for foot-long rainbows.

From Rainbow Lakes ,hiking cross-country to the northwest for a mile puts you on **Squeeze Lake** (7 acres, 9,535 feet). This long, skinny lake is periodically stocked with cutthroats. I took a nice, 2-pound fish of 17 inches in a brief evening visit, but that was all I saw. **Narrow Escape Lake** (12 acres, 9,340 feet), just north of Squeeze, is said to have wild cutthroats to 3 pounds, but I ran out of daylight and never got there.

A trail running west from Rainbow Lakes goes to **Horseshoe Lake** (16 acres, 9,490 feet) in 2 miles. Horseshoe has mostly small cutts and sits right on the western edge of the Lake Plateau. If you continue west down Upsidedown Creek, in about 6 miles you'll drop 3,000 feet to Hicks Park on the Boulder River. Hicks Park is just a couple of miles north of the Box Canyon Trailhead; it has a forest service campground and a small trailhead. I hiked Upsidedown Creek on my first trip to the Lake Plateau, but I like the longer, gentler, more scenic route out of Box Canyon better.

Back at Rainbow Lakes on the Lake Plateau, if you continue east by trail for 2 miles, you'll reach **Wounded Man Lake** (50 acres, 9,248 feet). This lake has average cutthroats and rainbows but is heavily used as a base camp by outfitters, so I bypass it. **Martes Lake** (17 acres, 9,150 feet) is 2 miles due south of Wounded Man. To get there, take the trail south through Jordan Pass, then hike cross-country. Martes was first stocked with cutthroats in 1969, and many of these fish reportedly grew to 5 pounds. I fished Martes only once, in 1993, and never saw a fish. This is one of those lakes about which you might want to check with the state—find out when it was last stocked, then shoot for the third to sixth year after that.

The main reason I go to the Lake Plateau is to fish **Lightning Lake,** which is the premier golden trout lake in the Beartooths. From Wounded Man Lake, it's a spectacular cross-country hike of about 5 miles to Lightning. To make this trip, head north from Wounded Man for a mile on the trail that drops to the West Fork of the Stillwater River. The first lake north of Wounded Man is **Diaphonous** (9 acres, 9,631 feet), which was stocked with rainbows in 1980, but I've never seen fish here. At Diaphonous, leave the trail and begin a 2-mile ascent right over the top of Chalice Peak (11,153 feet), which is almost a vertical mile above the trailhead. Just head north as you climb the grassy south face of Chalice. The Mount Douglas topo map shows a narrow corridor only a few hundred yards wide over Chalice Peak—shoot for the top, and this corridor will become evident as you climb. It's a sheer drop to the east or west, so you've nowhere to go but north. As you top out and begin to descend, the route runs over boulder fields and begins to widen, and you'll see Lightning Lake (63 acres, 9,340 feet) far below you. There are several ways down to the lake, but all are steep drops, so take your pick. The total distance to Lightning from Box Canyon is about 20 miles. I've made the trip out in a day. Going in, I take two days, because it's late afternoon by the time I reach the base of Chalice Peak. By then I've already climbed almost 3,000 feet in 15 miles, and tackling the peak fresh in the morning is a more inviting option.

Lightning is out of the bag, because it has been producing state-record goldens in the 4-pound class in recent years. I've taken goldens considerably larger in several lakes in Wyoming, but in Montana this is big enough to draw golden aficionados from near and far for a crack at the record. On my first trip to Lightning, in August 1991, the lake did not disappoint: My very first Lightning Lake golden, taken on a #12 Fast-Sinking Scud, was a fat 21-inch fish that probably weighed more than the official state record. My next fish, taken a few minutes later on the same fly, cast from the same rock, was only slightly smaller. These turned out to be the two biggest fish I've taken in four trips to Lightning.

On my second trip, in August 1993, I landed better than two dozen goldens from 15 to 18 inches long. They were all solid, hot-running fish, but I couldn't crack the 20-inch mark. Most were taken in the evening on a single reef. When fish have been on this small, rocky reef, I've had fun at Lightning; otherwise, I've had to work hard for scattered fish. It's possible to fish completely around the lake, but it takes most of the day, and you'll have some cliffs and dense timber to deal with.

On my last two trips to Lightning, in 1994 and 1995, I arrived at the lake to find several other anglers already pounding the water. This is never conducive to good golden fishing, and predictably, I saw slower action than during my first two trips. Most anglers are killing their better fish at Lightning, in pursuit of records or fish to mount; some are fishing live bait, which inevitably results in high mortality to released fish. Unfortunately, Lightning can be reached in a day from a trailhead on the West Fork of the Stillwater, and some locals are using this route to pop in to the lake for a couple of days on a regular basis and to pack out trophy fish. It's about an 8-mile hike up the Stillwater. The last 2 miles to the lake from the river are a steep climb through timber, and there's not an official trail, but it's still a shorter, easier route than going over Chalice Peak. If you have a week, though, I still recommend the route over Chalice, which is much more scenic and provides the option to fish many other lakes on the Lake Plateau.

As the best golden lake in the state, Lightning clearly merits special protection in the form of catch-and-release regulations and, perhaps, a delayed opening date to protect spawning fish. Lacking these, everyone who values this extraordinary fishery should voluntarily practice catch-

and-release so that the lake can reach its potential. Tasty, pan-size goldens are plentiful in **Little Lightning Lake** just a couple hundred yards downstream, so there's no justification for eating fish from the big lake.

If you exit Lightning Lake via Chalice Peak, you can fish the lakes on the plateau that I've already discussed—and you have more options, too. Head north by trail from Wounded Man and Diaphonous Lakes and you can follow the **West Fork of the Stillwater River** downstream for many miles. The river offers good action for rainbows that occasionally top a pound in its wooded, hard-to-reach sections. Small meadows scattered along the river provide enjoyable camping, although the meadows tend to be heavily fished compared with the wooded sections.

A mile northeast of Wounded Man and Diaphonous is **Lake Pinchot** (54 acres, 9,260 feet), at the head of Flood Creek. Pinchot is popular with outfitters and has rainbow-cutthroat hybrids. There's no maintained trail down Flood Creek, but a path takes you to three more lakes in the next 2 miles. **Dreary Lake** (15 acres, 9,040 feet), **Lake Surrender** (9 acres, 8,625 feet), and **Cimmerian Lake** (19 acres, 8,580 feet) are all in the timber and all offer good action for colorful cutthroat-rainbow-golden hybrids that can grow fairly large.

A half mile downstream from Cimmerian, a tributary enters Flood Creek from the south. Bushwhacking up this tributary for 2 miles takes you to the **Sisters Lakes**—four lakes all under 10 acres and mostly above timber at about 9,500 feet. I haven't been to these lakes, but goldens were introduced in the 1980s, so I suggested them to two other anglers who were heading for the Lake Plateau. Both reported some goldens to 14 inches, so apparently the introduction has resulted in a wild population.

From Lake Surrender you can travel cross-country northwest up Rabbit Gulch to **Jay Lake** (24 acres, 9,600 feet), which is above timber and tucked up against the sheer eastern walls of Chalice Peak. Going over Chalice, you can look down on Jay from a height of 1,500 feet. Jay reportedly produced big cutthroats in the 1980s, but when I fished it in 1995, it appeared to be overpopulated with rather skinny fish that topped out at 16 inches.

Several northern trailheads also provide access to the main concentration of lakes on the Beartooth Plateau. The most popular of these trailheads is at East Rosebud Lake (6,208 feet). I haven't used this entrance, but a hike of 10 to 15 miles takes you to various lakes north of Fossil (which I reach from the Clarks Fork Trailhead).

MAPS, BOOKS, AND SERVICES

The Absaroka–Beartooth Wilderness spills into three national forests—the Custer and Gallatin in Montana and the Shoshone in Wyoming. A forest service map titled "Absaroka–Beartooth Wilderness" covers the entire wilderness. Its scale is slightly larger than ½ inch to the mile; the contour interval is 50 meters. Because there are scores of off-trail lakes, you'll want USGS topo maps of all areas you plan to visit.

The Beartooth Fishing Guide, by Pat Marcuson, describes species and general fish sizes for more than four hundred lakes; there's no other book as detailed about any other major range in the Rockies. Marcuson personally devoted more than a decade to sampling fish and aquatic life and surveying over a thousand lakes for the Montana Department of Fish, Wildlife and Parks. He was instrumental in formulating management plans that introduced trout to barren waters and created new golden trout fisheries. He also structured stocking policies to produce larger cutthroats in many lakes that lack significant natural reproduction. The Beartooths remain the most effectively managed high-lake country in the West. Marcuson's book was published in 1985, and much of the data predates its publication by several years. The fishing in some lakes has changed, and management goals were not achieved at some lakes, but as a general guide to the productivity of Beartooth Lakes, this book is still mandatory reading. It also has line drawings of all the drainages and will help you locate many lakes that aren't named on forest service or USGS maps.

Along the Beartooth Highway, Cooke City, Montana (near the Northeast Entrance to Yellowstone Park), and Red Lodge, Montana (at the eastern foot of the Beartooths), offer all services. Ronnie Wright, who operates Beartooth Plateau Outfitters in Cooke City, is the premier guide in the region, offering horseback trips into the Absaroka–Beartooth Wilderness and Yellowstone Park. His shop in Cooke City also has fly-fishing tackle and current information on local conditions.

North of the range, Livingston, Montana, offers all services, plus a pair of great fly shops just off the interstate. George Anderson's Yellowstone Angler, conveniently located at the southern end of town on the highway to Gardiner and Yellowstone Park, maintains one of the most knowledgeable staffs and classiest shops in the West. Dan Bailey's in downtown Livingston is one of the oldest and most famous fly shops in the West.

The South Fork of the Flathead River deep in Montana's Bob Marshall Wilderness is the best westslope cutthroat stream left in Montana.

The very best high-altitude lakes are usually off trail or very remote. The author pauses on a 40-mile trek to a favorite golden trout lake in the Wind River Range of Wyoming.

A cozy, one-man camp in rock and ice country above timberline in the Wind River Range. Small tents, like this solo bivy, can be pitched in the lee of boulders. When big wind roars through a cirque, a big tent can be trashed in a flash.

Most of the author's favorite backcountry flies are his own designs or significant variations on established patterns. Top row (left to right): *Industrial-Strength Dun (Adams), Industrial-Strength Dun (Green Drake), Wood-Duck Adams, Hare's Ear Wulff.* Second row: *Duck Shoulder Dun (Flav), Duck Shoulder Dun (Callibaetis), Upland Caddis (Tan), Upland Caddis (Gray), Grizzly Caddis.* Third row: *Rusty Spinner, Topwater Midge, Rusty Floating Nymph, Chocolate Hare's Ear, Pheasant-Tail Midge.* Fourth row: *Soft-Hackle Woolly Worm (Black and Grizzly), Soft-Hackle Woolly Worm (Black and Hot Orange), Fast-Sinking Scud (Olive/Gray), Mega Scud (Orange Flashback).* Fifth row: *Soft-Hackle Wet Fly (Partridge and Green), Muddler Minnow.* Bottom row: *Soft-Hackle Bi-Bugger, Bobbing Baitfish (Gold).* (*All flies tied by Rich Osthoff.*)

The Beartooth Plateau, just northeast of Yellowstone Park, has scores of good lakes that can be reached by relatively short hikes. Eric Osthoff leads a nice Beartooth brook trout to shore.

The Beartooth Plateau on an August afternoon. When the weather is nice, the high country is beautiful. When the weather's bad, it's sublime.

Big Creek, a superb catch-and-release cutthroat river, flows through Idaho's Frank Church Wilderness. As Big Creek nears the Middle Fork of the Salmon, the country becomes arid.

The St. Joe River in northern Idaho. Thanks to catch-and release regulations, fine west-slope cutts once again thrive in sparkling emerald runs.

Storm clouds hover above Hawks Rest, which stands sentinel over the upper Yellowstone River, deep in the Teton Wilderness. The cutthroat fishing in the Thorofare country is as good as it gets on moving water.

Brook trout have been widely introduced throughout the high Rockies. As common as they are, they're still uncommonly beautiful, even after you've caught thousands.

This high Montana lake has a trophy-trout profile, including extensive food-producing shallows, a deep center bowl to sustain trout through winter, and limited spawning habitat, as there's no sizable inlet stream. Best of all, it's not on a trail. Big cutts reside here.

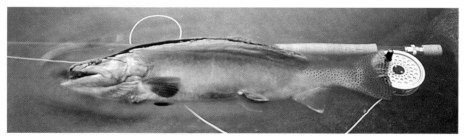

This 22-inch golden trout is a striking dark ebony across the back. The author caught the fish over a dark, algae-covered reef. Trout are chameleonlike in their ability to hide from overhead predators. Note how the dorsal surfaces of other trout pictured in this section blend with the aquatic habitat.

This gorgeous golden trout is bigger than it looks. The 7-weight rod with fighting butt is sitting high on a rock and is out of proportion. At just under 25 inches and an estimated 6 pounds, the trout fell for a Fast-Sinking Scud.

Slab-sided rainbows dwell deep in the bowels of the Black Canyon of the Gunnison in Colorado.

Scores of alpine waters are overpopulated with stunted brook trout, but where brookies find plenty of forage, they can quickly balloon. The trout the author is holding has a girth that rivals its length of 18 inches.

CHAPTER 26

Bob Marshall Wilderness (Montana)

The Bob Marshall Wilderness Complex in northwestern Montana extends into four national forests—the Flathead, Lewis and Clark, Lolo, and Helena. The Bob Marshall Wilderness itself covers over a million acres; the Great Bear Wilderness, which abuts the Bob to the north, and the Scapegoat Wilderness, which flanks the Bob to the south, add almost a half million more.

My trips to the Bob have primarily been to fish the South Fork of the Flathead River, which lies just west of the Continental Divide and is the best backcountry river in Montana—perhaps in the West—for west-slope cutthroats. The South Fork has many miles of prime water and is discussed separately in chapter 54.

My first two trips to the South Fork originated at the Holland Lake Trailhead 25 miles north of the town of Seeley Lake on Montana 83. Using this trailhead provides opportunities to fish other waters on the way to or from the South Fork. From Holland Lake the trail climbs a couple thousand feet to **Upper Holland Lake** (about 30 acres, 7,000 feet). I've taken foot-long cutts from this lake, which sees a lot of passing traffic. From Upper Holland trails fork every which way, and you can follow any of several major creeks that make long descents to the South Fork. All of the routes to the South Fork from Holland Lake are about 25 miles.

Gordon Creek is the southernmost route and runs to the head-waters of the South Fork near Big Prairie. Gordon is a pretty stream that tumbles through timber and a few small parks, and offers fun fishing for pan-size cutts and a few small bull trout. From the headwaters of Gordon Creek, a side trail runs south for a couple of miles to **Doctor Lake** (about 40 acres, 5,645 feet), which has small cutts. **Koessler Lake** (about 45 acres, 6,070 feet), a mile west of Doctor, is harder to reach because there's no trail, but it has some nice cutts. There are no other lakes on this route to the South Fork.

Holbrook Creek descends from the Upper Holland Lake area to hit the South Fork near Murphy Flat—one of my favorite stretches of river. Holbrook is similar in action to Gordon Creek but is smaller and more difficult to fish. From the headwaters of Holbrook, a trail runs south for a mile to **Lena Lake** (about 60 acres, 6,732 feet), which I haven't visited but is stocked with cutts. Opposite the mouth of Holbrook Creek, the **White River** enters the South Fork from the east. Fording the South Fork to reach the White River has always looked a little too risky to me in July, so I've never tried it. As a major tributary to the South Fork, though, the White undoubtedly has cutthroats and bull trout; it should be well worth fishing, especially in its large lower reaches.

From Upper Holland Lake the northernmost route to the South Fork follows **Big Salmon Creek.** One trail from Upper Holland to the headwaters of Big Salmon Creek swings by the **Necklace Lakes,** a series of small lakes with some decent cutts. As you descend Big Salmon Creek, you'll pass Barrier Falls (about 15 miles from the trailhead and 4 miles above Big Salmon Lake). Above the falls the fishing is similar to that in Gordon and Holbrook Creeks; below the falls the cutts run a little nicer. **Big Salmon Lake** (4,300 feet) is 4 miles long and has cutts that average 12 inches, plus some good bull trout, which start running up the creek in late summer as the fall spawning season approaches. The trail follows the entire northern shore of the lake, so you have plenty of opportunities to wet a line, even if you're just passing by on your way to the South Fork. As with most of the lakes in the Bob, the shores of Big Salmon Lake are heavily wooded, so waders or a float tube would be a major asset. The outlet of Big Salmon Lake is a sizable stream that hits the South Fork in about a mile (there's a pack bridge over Big Salmon Creek just above the South Fork). The fishing in Big Salmon Creek below the lake is comparable with the South Fork's: You'll find good stonefly and mayfly populations, nice cutthroats, and some good bull trout.

Other than the few lakes I've just described, however, there is very little lake fishing within 15 miles of the South Fork in any direction. The only other sizable lake on the western side of the Bob is **Sunburst Lake** (about 100 acres, 5,322 feet). Sunburst lies about 17 miles northwest of Big Salmon Lake and 10 air miles west of the South Fork; it's easy to spot on a map, because it's big and isolated. To hike to the lake from the river would be a round-trip of better than 30 miles. An acquaintance once showed me pictures of some fat, 4-pound cutts from Sunburst, but I've never made the trip. I was also told that it's tough to fish the lake without a tube or raft and that outfitters use the lake regularly.

There's a wealth of large and small creeks spilling into the South Fork from all directions. A small-rod addict could spend a summer exploring just the larger ones. Most of the sizable tributaries, such as Gordon, Holbrook, and Big Salmon Creeks and the White River, are followed by trail for many miles. **Little Salmon Creek,** which spills into the South Fork a few miles north of Big Salmon Creek, is another major tributary that's followed by trail for many miles. Spawning cutthroats from the South Fork ascend many tributaries to spawn in June and to seek out cool water in their lower reaches during hot summers. Bull trout, some of them big, begin ascending tributaries by late summer. Depending on the time of year and conditions, poking your nose up any of the tributaries can pay off.

The **Middle Fork of the Flathead River** begins in the Bob Marshall Wilderness and flows north through the Great Bear Wilderness for over 40 miles before crossing U.S. 2 just south of Glacier Park. From a trailhead just east of the highway bridge over the river, a trail follows the eastern bank of the Middle Fork all the way to its headwaters. The first 30 miles of river above the trailhead are mostly in shallow canyon. I've fished for only 10 miles above the trailhead. It's a scramble to reach the river from the trail in many places. You'll want to tackle the inclines in hiking boots and hang your pack in camp while you fish.

The Middle Fork does not compare with the South Fork for fish numbers, but the action is respectable for nice cutthroats that average 12 to 14 inches, plus some better fish. Big dry flies and big stoneflies or Woolly Worms dead-drifted deep take most of the cutts. Baitfish imitations are a good bet for enticing bull trout, which ascend the wilderness portion of the Middle Fork from midsummer on.

Schafer Meadows, about 30 miles above U.S. 2, has a dirt landing strip where wilderness raft trips begin. Above Schafer the Middle Fork has about 12 miles of sizable water that are not in canyon and reportedly hold good numbers of nice bull trout by late summer. If you want to fish the headwaters of the Middle Fork above Schafer, the shortest hike is from a road that runs up the **Spotted Bear River.** To get there, drive to the southern end of Hungry Horse Reservoir (this drive is described in chapter 54). From the Spotted Bear Ranger Station, a road runs another 30 miles up the Spotted Bear River; numerous trails depart this road for the Middle Fork. The Spotted Bear hosts a spawning run of cutthroats from Hungry Horse Reservoir and seems to always hold some nice resident cutts and bull trout. The bigger water and fish are primarily below the wilderness boundary. If you're looking for some semi-wild road fishing, this river and the 10 miles of the South Fork immediately above the reservoir can provide it.

There's only a handful of wilderness lakes in the upper Middle Fork drainage. The best I've fished are the **Tranquil Lakes,** which are east of the Middle Fork and a 4-mile hike from the trailhead on U.S. 2. The trail in to the lakes peters out on a knife ridge above the lakes. Rather than plunge 700 feet down the extremely steep slope to the bigger lake, as I did on my approach, bypass the big lake and descend more gradually to the small one. Once you're there, you can cut back west to the big lake (about 20 acres, 6,256 feet). The bigger of the two Tranquil Lakes has a classic high-lake profile that you can clearly see from above. It's completely rimmed by shelves and extensive flats that drop to a deep center bowl. The lake is right at the head of a cirque with no substantial inlet stream, so cutthroat reproduction is marginal. The lake is not hopping with fish. I caught only three westslope cutthroats in two days, but all were well built and pushing 3 pounds. This lake has all the indications of a trophy fishery, and I wouldn't be surprised if it holds some cutts in the 5-pound class—although much of it is flanked by steep or wooded shores and is tough to fish. Be warned that I also spent a restless night here after finding a half-digested candy bar wrapper in a sizable pile of fresh bear crap. The Tranquil Lakes are just 2 miles south of Glacier Park, and the entire Bob Marshall Complex has some of the best grizzly habitat in the lower forty-eight. The forest service has implemented strict food-storage regulations similar to those used in Yellowstone and Glacier. At night or when away from camp, backpackers must hang all food at least 10 feet high and 4 feet from tree trunks or sizable branches.

MAPS AND SERVICES
The forest service offers a topographic wilderness map that covers the entire Bob Marshall Complex, including the Great Bear and Scapegoat

Wilderness Areas. There are very few off-trail waters in the complex, so I don't pack USGS topos.

The town of Seeley Lake, some 20 miles south of the Holland Lake Trailhead, offers most services, though I'm not aware of any fly shops. Holland Lake has a forest service campground, and you'll find large forest service campgrounds at Lake Inez and Lake Alva just a few miles north of Seeley Lake. There are very limited services at the southern end of Hungry Horse Reservoir. Stock up on gas and groceries before tackling the dirt roads that run to the Spotted Bear area above the reservoir.

CHAPTER 27

Selway–Bitterroot Wilderness (Idaho–Montana)

The Bitterroot Mountains stretch along the Idaho–Montana border for roughly 200 miles. Much of my fishing in the Bitterroots has been on Kelly Creek and the St. Joe River—two of Idaho's best westslope cutthroat rivers, which headwater on the northern end of the range and are described separately in part 9, "Premier Westslope Cutthroat Rivers."

The biggest block of wild country associated with the Bitterroot Mountains is the Selway–Bitterroot Wilderness, which, at nearly 1½ million acres, was once the largest classified wilderness in the lower forty-eight (it has since been surpassed by the Frank Church Wilderness). The Selway–Bitterroot Wilderness sprawls into four national forests—the Nez Perce, Bitterroot, Clearwater, and Lolo. Most is in Idaho, but the eastern portion is in Montana adjacent to the Bitterroot River Valley.

The **Selway River** flows through the Idaho portion of the wilderness for more than 40 miles and is followed by trail for this entire length. With so much mileage to explore, the river is really a destination in itself. Elevations along it average only around 2,000 feet. The river corridor is mostly forested—although there are some open slopes—and the summer climate is dry and warm, with temperatures frequently nudging into the 90s Fahrenheit. By August the river can be warm enough that midday fishing is slow. In hot weather look for trout off the mouths of cold tributary streams. When the evening shade hits the river corridor and starts creeping up the adjoining slopes, the fishing usually picks up.

The Selway is over 100 feet wide in places. Wading puts you in better position to cover rising fish on the far side of big pools and runs. I pack shorts and a pair of old running shoes for wet wading on the many sand and gravel bars. I don't hike along the river for any distance in shorts or soft shoes, because the entire corridor is prime rattlesnake habitat.

Fishing for trout on the wilderness portion of the Selway River is catch-and-release with artificial lures and a single, barbless hook. The angling is good, but for action and size, I wouldn't rank the Selway on a par with Idaho's top westslope cutthroat rivers—Kelly Creek, Big Creek, the St. Joe River, and the Middle Fork of the Salmon. Most days I take a dozen or more trout around a foot in length, with an occasional fish of 15 inches or slightly better. Still, the fishing and the water are interesting, and I love the atmosphere along the river. The Selway isn't a spot I normally fish hard all day. To beat the midday heat, I usually kick back for a few hours on one of the big white sandbars beneath the shade of a towering red cedar and watch the river glide by. After weeks in cold, wet alpine country, I always enjoy getting into a warm, dry river bottom and letting the heat seep into my bones for a few days. The Selway is ideal for this. The sandbars also make gorgeous campsites.

There are trailheads on both ends of the wilderness section of the Selway, so it's possible to complete a through-hike up or down the river. To reach the Race Trailhead on the downstream (northern) end of the wilderness, follow U.S. 12 along the Lochsa River to the mouth of the Selway, then drive about 20 miles up the Selway on an improved gravel road to the trailhead. To reach the Paradise Trailhead on the upstream (southern) end of the wilderness, drive to Conner, Montana, which sits on U.S. 93 at the head of the Bitterroot River Valley about 70 miles due south of Missoula. From Conner a series of paved and gravel roads runs west, crossing into Idaho at Nez Perce Pass and dropping to the Selway. Once you're on the river, drive downstream as far as you can go and you'll hit the Paradise Trailhead. From Conner it's roughly 60 miles to the trailhead. The road is single lane in spots but passable by a two-wheel-drive vehicle.

From the Race to the Paradise Trailhead is about a 45-mile hike. Selway Lodge, a guest lodge with an airstrip, is about 15 miles downstream from Paradise. There are also a couple of private ranches in the vicinity.

In early to midsummer, a limited number of parties float through the wilderness. Floaters are primarily recreational rafters, rather than anglers. By August, as water levels drop, traffic along the river is reduced to a trickle of hikers and an occasional horse party. In two late-summer trips along the Selway in the early 1990s, I met only a couple of other hikers more than 5 miles into the wilderness, and I never saw a float party.

Dozens of tributary streams spill into the Selway within the wilderness, and most of the larger ones provide fair to good action for small to average cutthroats. Trails climb out of the river corridor and ascend many creek drainages, but most of these are used primarily by hunters. If you fish your way up any of the smaller tributaries, your chances of seeing another angler are just about nil. **Bear Creek,** which flows from the east to enter the Selway near Selway Lodge, is a good-size stream in its lower 5 miles; a maintained trail runs right up its northern side. **Moose Creek** is the biggest tributary to the Selway. It flows south to enter the Selway about 20 miles upstream of the Race Trailhead. In hot weather Moose Creek can fish better than the Selway. I've fished only a few miles up from the mouth, but you can follow Moose and then its East Fork upstream for many miles through a valley with a fairly gentle gradient. Fifteen miles northeast of the Selway, where the East Fork of Moose Creek first becomes a sizable stream, the elevation is only 3,200 feet—just 1,000 feet higher than the Selway.

A few small, widely scattered lakes can be reached from the river corridor, but in most cases it takes a long, grueling climb and a two- to three-day commitment to check out a single lake. Although most of the peaks on the Idaho side are in the 6,000- to 8,000-foot range, don't let the modest elevations deceive you: This wilderness has more than its share of rocks, brush, and rough terrain, and when you start from a base elevation of 2,000 feet, it's a significant climb to 7,000 feet. Not many people are willing to invest this kind of effort, so there are lakes in the heart of the wilderness that rarely see an angler.

Before hiking in to a remote and isolated lake, you should obtain fisheries data to learn what you can about stocking rotations, fish sizes, and fish abundance. A number of the remote lakes in the Idaho part of this wilderness that lack significant natural reproduction are stocked from the air with westslope cutthroat fingerlings about every three years.

In 1992 I trekked in from the Paradise Trailhead to fish a trio of lakes east of the Selway. From the trailhead I hiked up White Cap Creek for 3 miles and caught a trail north to **Emerald, Bills,** and **Brushy Fork Lakes;** all are about 20 acres and sit at about 6,500 feet high on Brushy Fork Creek. It's about 12 miles in to Emerald. The lakes are strung out in a line: Bills is a mile east of Emerald, and Brushy Fork a mile east of

Bills. Action was steady for cutthroats and rainbows that averaged about a foot, with a few fish each day between 16 and 18 inches.

A glance at a map shows a smattering of lakes in the northern part of the wilderness that can be reached from trailheads along the Lochsa River. There are also a couple dozen lakes along the Montana side of the wilderness, which can generally be reached by hikes of less than 10 miles from trailheads along the Bitterroot River Valley. Some peaks on the rugged Montana side of the Bitterroots top out at nearly 10,000 feet.

MAPS, GUIDEBOOKS, AND SERVICES

A topographic map of the entire Selway-Bitterroot Wilderness is sold by the Forest Service Northern Region; the scale is ⅝ inch to the mile, and the contour interval is 50 meters. The visitor map of the Nez Perce National Forest shows the entire Selway River between the Paradise and Race Trailheads. If you stick to the river, detailed topo maps aren't needed; if you plan to bushwhack up any tributaries or climb to any off-trail lakes, you'll definitely want detailed USGS topos.

Montana Fly-Fishing Guide (western volume), by John Holt, briefly describes the fishing action in many lakes on the Montana side of the wilderness.

Gas and limited groceries are available along the lower Lochsa River on the northern side of the wilderness. The Lochsa River, which is followed by U.S. 12 for many miles, is a good westslope cutthroat river by roadside standards, with a long catch-and-release section.

The Paradise Trailhead is the main access from the south. As far as I know, gas and groceries aren't available after you leave Conner, Montana.

In the Bitterroot Valley to the east of the wilderness, the towns of Victor, Hamilton, and Darby offer all services.

CHAPTER 28

Frank Church
River of No Return Wilderness
(Idaho)

The Frank Church River of No Return Wilderness in central Idaho is, at 2.3 million acres, the largest classified wilderness in the lower forty-eight. If you're panning for solitude, you should be able to hit pay dirt here. Most of my fishing in this area has been on the Middle Fork of the Salmon River (described in chapter 47) and on Big Creek (described in chapter 53). Together these two outstanding cutthroat rivers have nearly 140 miles of water. Either is a destination in itself, and both are worth going back to repeatedly. It's tough to break away from such excellent river fishing to explore the rest of the wilderness, but there's a lot more country out there.

On my first trip to the Middle Fork, I entered the wilderness on its eastern side from the Bighorn Crags. The Crags Campground and Trail-head are a 50-mile drive from the town of North Fork, Idaho, on the main Salmon River (the drive to the trailhead is described in chapter 47). The Crags top out at a bit over 10,000 feet and are the highest peaks in the wilderness. There are about three dozen lakes scattered throughout the Crags. Most are at about 8,000 feet, smaller than 20 acres, and within an easy 5- to 10-mile hike of the trailhead, so they see some angling pressure. My friend Clark Heindl and I had good action at several lakes one year, mostly for pan-size cutthroats, rainbows, and hybrids. (Big Clear Lake was supposed to have golden trout, but the bloodlines looked pretty diluted.) That trip took place in early July. Because of the heavy snow pack, we had to park more than a mile short of the trailhead. Daily snow squalls and freezing temperatures prevented us from fishing as many lakes as we'd planned to.

From the Crags the Waterfall Creek Trail plummets more than 6,000 feet in 13 miles to the Middle Fork of the Salmon. **Waterfall Creek** is the most rugged and scenic route to the Middle Fork. Just looking west from the Crags toward the heart of the Frank Church Wilderness should get your blood pumping—wave on wave of timbered mountains roll to the horizon.

To descend Waterfall Creek from the Crags, you pop over a pass above Heart Lake at about 9,000 feet. **Terrace Lakes,** a set of four small lakes at the head of Waterfall Creek, hold average cutthroats. Waterfall has cutts all the way to the Middle Fork, although the trail runs high above the stream for the last few miles.

On a long through-hike in this wilderness, I left the Middle Fork near the mouth of Waterfall Creek and headed through the mountains to the main Salmon. Trails climb more than 4,000 feet to the old Stoddard Creek Lookout Tower (7,536 feet), which overlooks miles and miles of the Middle Fork gorge. Three miles northwest of the tower are **Stoddard Lakes** (8,200 feet); I caught nice cutthroats to 2 pounds at the larger of these two small lakes. My route through the mountains to the main Salmon, which lies in the second deepest gorge in the continental United States, was an adventure. Trail #169, which runs high above the Middle Fork and about a mile to the west, plunges some 3,000 feet to cross Stoddard Creek, then climbs again abruptly. There are a couple more creek drainages to cross, and then the final steep descent to the Salmon. I came off that little roller-coaster ride with fluid build-up in both my knees. This also happened to me on the Appalachian Trail in northern Maine, which blasts straight up and straight down mountains rather than following contours, but it's never happened elsewhere in the Rockies.

To fish **Big Creek,** the largest tributary to the Middle Fork, you generally enter the wilderness on the western side. The Big Creek Trailhead (described in chapter 53) is about 25 miles northeast of the small town of Yellow Pine. From the trailhead you can fish your way down Big Creek for 35 miles, all the way to the Middle Fork. Just 10 miles below the trailhead, **Monumental Creek** flows into Big Creek from the south. I invested several days in visiting a small, isolated lake high in the Monumental drainage. I didn't see any huge fish, but I did catch a couple of fat, hard-fighting westslope cutthroats of about 4 pounds. This off-trail lake is just an inconspicuous blue blip on a very big map, but it has trophy potential, including very limited natural reproduction. Undoubtedly there are other isolated lakes scattered throughout this massive wilderness that are well worth fishing, but scouting any number of them on foot would burn up many weeks. The best approach is to gather whatever fisheries data you can, then go after an interesting lake or two. Most lakes in the wilderness have wooded shores, so waders are an advantage.

Monumental Creek is a large freestone stream (20 to 30 feet wide) that offers many miles of cutthroat fishing in solitude. Some of the slopes in this drainage support the finest stands of ponderosa pines I've seen in the Rockies. Mature ponderosas have horizontal limbs and tend to distribute sparsely, like prairie oaks. Beneath the yellow-barked trees, the ground is as open as a city park. On a warm summer day the aroma wafting from the carpet of downed needles and duff is intoxicating. I can sit for an afternoon in a glade like this and never glance at my watch.

Every now and then you bump into an abandoned cabin in this wilderness, like the one up Monumental Creek. Most were built by gold miners and are now protected as historic sites, so removing artifacts is prohibited. But if the door is open, it's fun to look around and wonder about the people who worked and lived here, deep in the woods.

I've hiked up the West Fork of Monumental Creek to **Cougar Basin,** which holds a half dozen small lakes at about 8,500 feet. I caught average cutthroats in a couple of lakes, but I fished only briefly in passing. From Cougar Basin the trail swings north and descends Lick Creek to hit the access road within a couple of miles of the Big Creek Trailhead. The Big Creek–Monumental Creek loop is about 50 miles, counting side trips to fish a few lakes.

The bulk of the Frank Church Wilderness, including the Middle Fork and Big Creek drainages, is south of the main Salmon, which flows through the wilderness for more than 50 miles and, like the Middle Fork, is popular with rafters. The Salmon is no longer a great trout river, but cutthroats and some rainbows are present, especially near the mouths of cold tributaries. Dozens of neglected trout streams tumble from the mountains to feed the Salmon. Most of these high-gradient streams are

5 to 10 miles long and offer fast fishing for small cutthroats or rainbows in their upper reaches, plus a shot at a few fish of over a pound in the lower sections. Even the few streams that are followed by trails are rarely fished. My brother Eric took his first teaching job in Elk City, Idaho, not too far north of the Salmon. When he got hungry for trout, he'd drive south to **Crooked Creek,** a tumbling tributary to the Salmon that flows just inside the eastern boundary of the Gospel Hump Wilderness. We spent a day together here once, stair-stepping our way down several miles of stream and taking eager little trout from every thigh-deep pocket. Both banks of the Salmon are veined with creeks like this.

North of the Salmon and east of Elk City, there are another three dozen lakes in the Frank Church Wilderness. Right after school ended in early summer, Eric usually backpacked into **Lake Creek Lakes.** This trio of lakes is in the timber at about 7,500 feet, a 6-mile hike south of Dry Saddle on the Nez Perce Trail, a four-wheel-drive road that runs from just south of Elk City all the way east to hit the Selway River not far from the Paradise Trailhead. In early summer Eric always took a few nice cutts to 20 inches in these lakes. We came here for a couple of days one August and managed only small fish. It was, by the way, the only backpacking trip I ever made with a dog. Our German shorthair, Browning, was a wonderful bird dog spending his retirement years in Elk City with Eric, and he went with us to Lake Creek Lakes. One evening, as we were hiking around a lake to fish the far shore, Browning locked up on point. I approached from behind, looking for a spruce grouse or something with wings. Instead I saw hair—and a lot of it. Glaring back at us from the lake edge, with weeds and water dripping from his mouth, was a bull moose.

MAPS AND SERVICES

The Frank Church Wilderness extends into six national forests—the Nez Perce, Bitterroot, Boise, Challis, Payette, and Salmon. The north-half and south-half maps of the Frank Church River of No Return Wilderness show the entire area. Both have a scale of 1½ miles to the inch and a contour interval of 50 meters; they're available in waterproof versions.

The major trailheads for fishing the Middle Fork and Big Creek are described with those waters, in chapters 47 and 53. There are many more trailheads. Challis and Salmon (to the east) and McCall (to the west) are the largest towns near the wilderness and offer all services.

CHAPTER 29

High Uintas Wilderness (Utah)

The Uintas, in northeastern Utah, are the only major mountains in the lower forty-eight that run east to west. This distinctive-looking range is built of uplifted sedimentary rock. Weathered peaks of layered stone overlook sprawling glacial basins dotted with numerous lakes. Elevations range to 13,528 feet atop Kings Peak, the highest point in Utah.

The High Uintas Wilderness of the Wasatch and Ashley National Forests covers 470,000 acres in the heart of the range. The Uintas harbor an estimated six hundred trout lakes, the bulk of which are in the wilderness area or in roadless country adjoining it. In two trips to the Uintas in the mid-1980s, I saw steady to excellent action at many lakes but very few fish over 15 inches. Based on my research and experience, when it comes to producing sizable trout, the Uintas definitely don't rank with the Winds and the Beartooths, or even with many smaller ranges that have far fewer lakes. Still, given the size of the area, the sheer abundance of lakes, and the steady action, I rate this wilderness as a major back-country destination. And with so much water, there are bound to be some large trout somewhere. Hit enough lakes and maybe you'll find them.

Most lakes in the wilderness are stocked by air on a three- to five-year rotation. Cutthroat trout and, to a surprising extent, brook trout are the primary species being stocked. Lakes tend to be tightly bunched in glacial basins above 10,000 feet, and most shorelines provide unobstructed casting. Maintained trails run to most of the larger lakes, but many small lakes can be reached only by hiking cross-country. The major lake basins are drained by sizable creeks that offer many miles of fun fishing for small to pan-size brook trout and cutthroats.

My first trek through the Uintas covered about 60 miles and began at the Hayden Pass Trailhead (10,200 feet), which is at the western end of the wilderness on Utah 150 about 50 miles south of Evanston, Wyoming. The Highline Trail runs east from the pass across the northern portion of the wilderness.

About 8 miles east of Hayden Pass, the Highline Trail crosses Rocky Sea Pass (11,500 feet). A couple of miles east of the pass, side trails run north to a cluster of small lakes at the head of Rock Creek. The western lakes in this bunch are mostly at 10,400 to 10,800 feet, which puts them near or above timberline. **Helen Lake** (8 acres) and **Lightning Lake** (14 acres) are the biggest in the bunch. **Jack, Jill,** and **Ouray** are 3 to 4 acres each. All have good action for small to average brook trout or cutthroats; some lakes have both. Just to the east, in a wide-open alpine basin, are some higher trout lakes. **Reconnaissance Lake** (9 acres, 11,150 feet) has average brook trout. **Boot Lake** (9 acres, 11,100 feet) has plenty of pan-size cutts.

The Highline Trail continues east across Dead Horse Pass (11,400 feet), about 16 miles from the trailhead. **Ledge Lake** (3 acres, 10,850 feet) is a brook trout pond right on the trail just a mile south of the pass. At **Continent Lake** (27 acres, 11,280 feet), a high, open lake just southwest of the pass, I saw good action for average cutthroats and brook trout.

In the next 15 miles there are few lakes on or close to the Highline Trail. I buzzed west through Porcupine Pass (12,200 feet). Just east of it, though, I caught some nice cutthroats to 16 inches—my best fish of the trip—in **North Star Lake** (about 10 acres, 11,600 feet) and **Tungsten Lake** (about 15 acres, 11,400 feet).

At Tungsten Lake I left the Highline Trail and dropped south a few miles to sample several lakes at about 11,000 feet in **Garfield Basin,** where I saw the standard array of small to average brook trout and cutthroats. **Five Point Lake** (about 90 acres) is the biggest lake in the basin, thanks to a dam; here I managed a few more cutts to 16 inches, but the average trout was quite a bit smaller. From Garfield Basin I hiked another 15 miles down Garfield Creek, then Yellowstone Creek, to the Swift Creek Trailhead, one of several trailheads stretched along the southern side of this wilderness.

My second trip to the Uintas was to fish Krebs and Atwood Basins, which are about 10 air miles east of Garfield. This trip began at 8,000 feet at the trailhead on the **Uinta River,** which is about a 25-mile drive north from Roosevelt, Utah. The Uinta is one of the larger streams draining the range and has many miles of fishable water above the trailhead.

A few miles upstream from the trailhead, a trail veers west to the four **Chain Lakes** in Krebs Basin. The Chain Lakes, a couple of which are dammed, range in elevation from 10,600 to 10,800 feet; the two largest, Lower and Upper Chain, are about 75 acres. All are loaded with small brook trout.

From the Chain Lakes, I climbed north over Roberts Pass (11,200 feet) and dropped into **Atwood Basin,** which has a half dozen lakes at about 11,000 feet. **Lake Atwood** (about 200 acres) is by far the largest. Atwood still had some small, pretty goldens when I was here in 1988, but they were vastly outnumbered by small brook trout and probably doomed.

There are two more lake basins about 15 miles straight north of the trailhead at the headwaters of the Uinta River. Two of the larger lakes in these basins, **Rainbow** and **Fox,** reportedly have some nice fish.

MAPS, BOOKS, SERVICES, AND A BONUS FISHERY

The forest service offers a map titled "High Uintas Wilderness," with a scale of about 1 inch to the mile. The map of the Ashley National Forest also shows the wilderness; its scale is ½ inch to the mile. There are forest service campgrounds near all trailheads.

Several booklets in a series titled *Lakes of the High Uintas* cover various drainages and briefly describe trout species and general sizes for most lakes in each drainage. These booklets are available from the following:

Utah Division of Wildlife Resources
1596 West North Temple
Salt Lake City, UT 84114
Phone: (801) 538-4700

Several towns south of the range, including Vernal, Roosevelt, and Duchesne, offer all services.

From Vernal it's just a one-hour drive north to the fabulous tailwater fishery on the Green River below Flaming Gorge Reservoir. The Green draws throngs of anglers from around the country, but there are ways to beat the pressure and fish in relative solitude. From the access just below the dam to the next access point at Little Hole is 7 miles. A foot trail runs right along the river throughout the canyon, and you can easily spot undisturbed fish from the trail. Midday pressure from floaters and walk-in anglers is heavy, but most floaters clear off the upper 4 miles of river by dinnertime, and most walk-in anglers are within a mile of an access by evening. I like to hike and fish my way downstream over the course of the day so that I'm at least 3 miles below the dam by early evening. Then I can turn around and fish my way upstream for a couple of miles in virtual solitude. Full dark usually finds me a mile or two below the dam; midging is usually great in the evening, and fishing with big drys can be dynamite at twilight. I pack an extra flashlight for hiking out of the canyon—it's pitch black down there on moonless nights.

PART SIX

Smaller Mountain Ranges and Wilderness Areas

CHAPTER 30

Small Is Relative

Scattered across the Rockies are dozens of smaller mountain ranges and wilderness areas that offer good backcountry fishing. In fact, there are so many areas that fall into this category that it's tough for anyone to visit even a fraction of them. I've visited many, but I don't key on small areas to the extent that I do large ones—for several reasons.

In small areas streams normally flow beyond wilderness boundaries before they have the opportunity to grow or flatten much and become the type of moving water that holds a lot of nice trout. Small areas invariably do have small, tumbling creeks with plenty of small to average trout, but the largest, most productive backcountry streams and rivers are generally in large wilderness areas.

Small areas also tend to have a limited number of lakes, and most of these have trails running right to them. In a range with only two dozen lakes, local anglers and outfitters can keep tabs on them all. It's just very tough for a lake with exceptional fishing to remain a secret for long. Once a good lake is discovered, locals will pound it repeatedly. In small ranges meat anglers can pop into most lakes on weekends and crop off the larger trout. Smaller backcountry blocks are consequently the areas that would benefit the most from catch-and-release regulations. Local anglers and fly-fishing clubs should let area fish managers know that they want to see special regulations extended to a few backcountry lakes in their area that have the right conditions to grow trout to several pounds.

As it is, exceptional angling in small ranges tends to be temporary and is usually dependent on opportune conditions rather than inaccessibility. New beaver ponds, barren lakes being stocked for the first time, lakes being stocked after a fallow period, or lakes that are prone to winterkill but happen to catch a series of mild winters—any of these habitats can produce a season or two of great fishing before conditions change or the word travels too far.

Fishing, like almost everything else, is relative. If you've been deep in big wilderness areas whaling on nice trout for six weeks, a trip for average trout in a small area may not float your boat. But if you're on your first trip of the summer or have never fished the backcountry, catching foot-long brook trout from a sparkling lake or stream just a few miles into the mountains may be great recreation. I tend to visit small ranges on shakedown cruises in preparation for longer trips. At the onset of summer, just being back in the mountains, catching some colorful trout, and finding my stride are exhilarating. If I'm driving through a region anyway and I can squeeze in a few days, I'll often visit a small range just to take it in. Even if the fishing isn't good enough to bring me rushing back, I always enjoy seeing new country.

Don't mistakenly assume that small wilderness areas are a cinch to travel. Routes tend to be shorter than in big wilderness areas, but the terrain can be just as demanding. And the term *smaller* as I've applied it to the areas in this part of the book is relative. Many of the wilderness areas I include here cover several hundred thousand acres and would be considered huge wild tracts anywhere east of the Rockies. For size and sheer abundance of water, however, they don't rank with the top wilderness areas in the West.

CHAPTER 31

Rawah Wilderness (Colorado)

The Rawah Wilderness of the Roosevelt National Forest is in north-central Colorado northwest of Rocky Mountain National Park. The wilderness is small—27,000 acres—but rugged and scenic. It stretches along the eastern side of the Continental Divide for about 15 miles and is about 4 miles wide. Peaks along the divide top out at well over 12,000 feet.

The best concentration of lakes is in the center of the wilderness. A few lakes range from 20 to 30 acres, but many ponds scattered along the creek drainages are much smaller. Most of the lakes and ponds are near or above timberline at 10,000 to 11,000 feet and can be reached by trail.

Because the wilderness is easily reached from the heavily populated Denver–Fort Collins area, I'm sure it sees significant traffic on weekends and holidays. I used the area for a four-day tune-up hike one year in early July. On a midweek trip I saw only one group of hikers and enjoyed the fishing. I also had bighorn sheep near my camp most evenings.

Brook trout are the predominant species in most of the streams and ponds. Action is good and the brookies reach respectable size. In a couple of ponds I caught solid fish that averaged 9 to 11 inches, with a few topping a foot. The streams linking the ponds are also fun to explore and full of brookies.

At **Rawah Lakes,** within a mile of the divide, I took a few cut-throats to 15 inches. **Kelly Lake,** just west of the divide in the Colorado State Forest, yielded the state-record golden trout (3 pounds, 12 ounces) in 1979.

The main trailhead is near the Tunnel Creek Campground, which is east of the wilderness and 5 miles due north of Chambers Lake. A 20-mile round-trip from this trailhead will show you the majority of lakes in the wilderness. Chambers Lake is about 60 miles west of Fort Collins via Colorado 14.

MAPS AND SERVICES
The entire Rawah Wilderness is shown on the visitor map of the Arapaho/Roosevelt National Forests; the scale is ½ inch to the mile. Topo maps are handy for reaching a few off-trail lakes or for crossing the divide to access the Colorado State Forest.

Fort Collins (an hour's drive to the east) and Walden (an hour's drive to the west) offer all services.

CHAPTER 32

Mount Zirkel Wilderness (Colorado)

Colorado has the only major metropolitan area in the Rockies, plus a thriving resort community in nearly every mountain valley, so it's tougher to find real solitude here than in the more desolate reaches of Montana, Wyoming, and Idaho. Still, the western half of Colorado boasts range upon range of spectacular mountains, including many peaks over 14,000 feet. Most of the high country is publicly owned, and nearly every range has a small wilderness area with interesting fishing. The Mount Zirkel Wilderness of the Routt National Forest in north-central Colorado is a case in point. This 140,000-acre wilderness lies just east of the bustling resort town of Steamboat Springs. The area straddles the Continental Divide for about 25 miles and averages about 5 miles in width. The Park Range within the wilderness has more than a dozen peaks that approach or top 12,000 feet.

I made my only trip in this wilderness in 1988 and found good cutthroat fishing in several lakes. I hiked out of the Buffalo Pass Trailhead, which is a 12-mile drive east of Steamboat Springs on an improved dirt road. The trailhead sits at the southern end of the wilderness at 10,600 feet, making for a fairly level hike to a group of sizable lakes about 10 miles to the north. Forest Trail #1101 runs along the divide and gradually climbs above 11,000 feet. About 7 miles north of the trailhead, you can catch a trail that descends to several off-trail lakes that are actually west of the wilderness boundary but have no road access. **Luna Lake,** the biggest in the group, is ½ mile long and sits at about 10,500 feet a mile west of the divide. It has good fishing for pan-size cutts.

Hiking west from Luna for 2 miles, you'll continue to drop to **Mirror Lake,** a pothole where I took plump, foot-long cutts. Just west of Mirror is a group of four lakes, all at about 10,000 feet. **Margaret Lake** (about 30 acres) is the largest and highest in the group. Clear and with extensive shallows, Margaret is a place where you can put your fish-spotting skills to good use. I spent a sunny afternoon circling the lake and looking for scattered cruisers and landed better than a dozen cutthroats to 16 inches. The shoreline is mostly lodgepole pine, but I found enough backcasting alleys to work pretty effectively from land. Within a mile to the west of Margaret are the three smaller lakes, which average about 10 acres. **Fish Hawk Lake** is the smallest and lowest, offering good fishing for cutts.

About 10 miles north of the trailhead, you can catch a trail that descends to Roxy Ann Lake a couple of miles east of the divide. **Roxy Ann** (about 10,200 feet) is a good-size lake of about 50 acres. I saw good action here for cutts that averaged about 13 inches; a couple ran to 17 inches. Action was good off the mouth of an inlet stream and along some sharp drop-offs.

There are a couple dozen more lakes scattered throughout the wilderness. The Seed House Campground (about 30 miles north of Steamboat Springs) provides access to lakes in the northern half of the wilderness. Cutthroat and brook trout are the most common species, but rainbows and goldens are found in a few lakes. There are many small ponds scattered along creek drainages in and near the wilderness.

MAPS AND SERVICES
The map of the Routt National Forest shows the entire Mount Zirkel Wilderness; its scale is ½ inch to the mile. There's a forest service campground at Summit Lake near Buffalo Pass.

Steamboat Springs, to the west, offers all services, including fly tackle. Walden, to the east, also has all services. Roads running west from Walden provide access to the eastern side of the wilderness, but many are four-wheel-drive roads in their final miles.

CHAPTER 33

West Elk Wilderness
(Colorado)

The West Elk Wilderness is in the Gunnison National Forest in west-central Colorado not too far west of Crested Butte. This 176,000-acre area is about 15 miles in diameter, with elevations that top out at almost 13,000 feet. Its many notable features include the largest blue spruce trees I've seen and fine stands of mature aspens that were turning a brilliant gold when I visited in September 1992. At the same time, however, cattle damage to trails, meadows, and stream banks was the most severe I've seen in a classified wilderness area.

I went to the West Elk for my final trip that summer primarily to catch my first golden trout in Colorado. A wildlife biologist had tipped me off to a pair of lakes with naturally reproducing fish, describing one as the best self-sustaining golden trout fishery in the state. When I inquired about the size of the fish, the biologist became evasive, saying that it was a wonderful fishing experience and worth the trip. So I went.

I hiked out of the Lost Lake Campground and Trailhead (9,600 feet), which is 10 miles west of Kebler Pass and about 20 miles west of Crested Butte. From here I hiked south through Beckwith Pass (10,000 feet) to reach **Costo Lake** (7 acres, 9,900 feet) in about 10 miles. At this small, stagnant-looking lake in the timber, I saw slow action for brook trout, although the pair of fish I did catch were about 15 inches and looked to be eating pretty well. Just north of Costo Lake is **North Castle Creek,** which has lots of willows and many beaver ponds. There are plenty of small to average brook trout in both creek and ponds.

After leaving the creek, I continued west for a couple of miles to Castle Pass (11,057 feet); from here you can travel cross-country north for about a mile to the top of Storm Ridge (11,800 feet). Once on top you'll see the golden lakes just to the east. Make a little buttonhook around the highest part of the ridge and drop back south to reach them.

North Golden Lake (8 acres, 11,040 feet) is only about 10 feet deep. On a sunny afternoon I was able to survey virtually the entire lake bottom and I couldn't spot a fish. Given the elevation and the lack of a permanent inlet stream, I'm sure this shallow lake is subject to winterkill some years. Interestingly, the shore is covered with spruce and fir, which illustrates how high timberline is here in the southern Rockies.

South Golden Lake (4 acres, 11,080 feet) is a small, scruffy lake sitting in a talus bowl just a few hundred yards to the south. Like North Golden it's primarily a seep lake that receives most of its water directly from snowmelt and rain. South Golden is apparently deep enough to sustain trout, because goldens are here and in pretty good numbers. The bulk of the fish are under 10 inches long, however, and even the top-end fish are just over a foot. If a few could find their way downstream to the northern lake and manage to survive for a couple of winters, they might pack on some weight while feeding in seclusion. Otherwise, this is small-golden water that wouldn't rate anything close to "wonderful" if it were in Wyoming.

From Castle Pass I descended a couple of miles to the west and caught a trail south to **Sheep Lake** (about 7 acres, 10,505 feet), where I caught rainbows to 14 inches. Cutting back to the north, I completed a 30-mile loop to the trailhead.

There are no lake concentrations in this wilderness, but you will find some other small lakes scattered about.

MAPS AND SERVICES
A forest service map titled "Gunnison Basin Area" shows the entire West Elk Wilderness; its scale is ½ inch to the mile. Trails Illustrated offers a topo map titled "Kebler Pass West, Colorado," which shows the northern portion of the West Elk, including the Castle Pass area. The scale is 1½ inches to the mile, and the contour interval is 40 feet.

Crested Butte to the east offers all services.

CHAPTER 34

Flat Tops Wilderness (Colorado)

The Flat Tops Wilderness lies primarily in the White River National Forest in northwestern Colorado. At 235,000 acres and roughly 20 miles in diameter, it's the third largest wilderness in Colorado and one of the most distinctive in the Rockies. As its name implies, much of the wilderness is high, gently undulating plateau. Once you're atop this plateau, a short, steep climb of about 1,500 feet from most trailheads, you can cruise for miles through sparsely timbered meadows with very little change in elevation. Most of the plateau lakes lie between 10,600 and 11,200 feet in elevation and have wide-open shorelines, where you can double-haul to your heart's content. Trails run to or near most lakes, but cross–country travel options are unlimited.

There are trailheads on all sides of the wilderness. One of the most popular entry points is Trappers Lake, which lies 50 miles east of Meeker, Colorado, at the head of the North Fork of the White River; access is by improved dirt road for the last 20 miles. **Trappers Lake** (200 acres, 9,627 feet) is a good cutthroat lake right on the wilderness boundary, but it's heavily fished by boat anglers from several nearby forest service campgrounds. A 3–mile hike south from Trappers Lake puts you on top of the plateau and within a day's hike of most lakes in the core of the wilderness.

Just 4 miles south of the trailhead is **Wall Lake** (about 50 acres, 10,986 feet), where I've taken a few nice cutts to 16 inches, but Wall is positioned to see plenty of traffic from people entering or leaving the plateau. Two miles east of Wall, there are many small, off-trail ponds near the headwaters of Frazier Creek. Most of these nameless ponds are fishless, but at one I've taken cutts to 2 pounds. **Surprise Lake** (about 15 acres, 11,128 feet), just east of Frazier Creek, has brook trout, including a few nice ones. There are also brook trout in most of the plateau streams in this region.

Hiking about 8 miles south from Wall Lake takes you to **Shepherd Lake** (about 40 acres, 10,762 feet). Shepherd is a seep lake. There's no permanent inlet stream, and the outlet stream runs almost dry in summer. Like many lakes on the plateau, Shepherd has a shallow, dished profile. Because of its lack of depth, lack of permanently flowing inlets, and considerable elevation, the lake can experience at least partial winterkill during years of heavy snow, but brook trout were thriving when I fished here following some easy winters in the late 1980s. Shepherd has extensive shallows and is one of the most fertile lakes I've fished at this elevation. The shallows support reeds, weeds, and mats of moss that are loaded with scuds. The Fast-Sinking Scud was the only fly I needed on this lake, and most of the time I fished it blind on a sinking-tip line just over or along the edge of weeds. Over the course of two trips, I fished Shepherd for more than a week; most days I caught three dozen hefty brookies that averaged around 14 inches, with an occasional fish to 18 inches. I don't know how Shepherd is fishing now, but for numbers and average size, it was one of the top handful of high-country brook trout lakes I've seen. In fact, I had trouble prying myself away to visit other lakes on the plateau.

Much of the timber around Shepherd Lake and elsewhere on the plateau has been killed by insects. You're better off camping in the open than close to standing snags; just make sure you camp in depressions, where you're somewhat protected from lightning. The plateau, with its extensive meadows, is also ideal summer range for elk. As you fish in the evening, you may enjoy fifty or more elk nearby, grazing, cavorting, and making all kinds of strange vocalizations.

Just a mile west of Shepherd is **Rim Lake** (about 25 acres, 10,804 feet), which has some nice cutthroats and supposedly has lake trout. **Sweetwater Creek,** the outlet stream from Rim Lake, spills off the plateau just south of the lake. There's good action for brook trout in the stream and in beaver ponds several hundred feet below the plateau. A couple of miles north of Rim is Shingle Peak. At **Shingle Lake** (about 5 acres, 11,214 feet), a small, off-trail lake on the northern side of this peak, I saw good action for nice cutthroats.

After climbing to the plateau from Trappers Lake, you can swing west to **Twin Lakes** (10,998 feet) at about the 6-mile mark. The bigger of these two lakes is about 60 acres and looks pretty shallow all the way across. The lakes are supposed to have cutts, but I didn't find any. Another 5 miles to the west are **Marvine Lakes** (about 80 acres each, 9,300 feet). To reach these lakes, where I experienced good action for small brook trout and pan-size cutts, you have to drop off the plateau into the Marvine Creek drainage. I saw the twisted wreckage of a single-engine plane lying in this deep ravine—one of several wrecks I've seen in the backcountry.

From Yampa, Colorado (30 miles south of Steamboat Springs), you can drive up the Bear River on an improved road to several trailheads on the eastern side of the wilderness. From Upper Stillwater Reservoir (9,700 feet), a trail runs north to the four **Mandall Lakes** (10,600 to 10,800 feet) in the northeastern corner of the wilderness (in the Routt National Forest). I haven't fished the Mandalls, but I've been told they offer challenging fishing for a mix of cutthroats, brook trout, and rainbows, including an occasional trophy.

From Stillwater Reservoir (10,225 feet) at the end of the road, trails run south to **Hooper Lake** and **Keener Lake.** A few miles south of these are **Solitary Lake** and **Deer Lake.** I've heard interesting reports on all of these lakes, which are less than 10 miles east of Trappers Lake and could easily be fished on the way to the Shepherd-Rim area if you climb to the plateau from the Bear River.

MAPS AND SERVICES

The map of the White River National Forest shows the entire Flat Tops Wilderness, access roads, and numerous public campgrounds; its scale is ½ inch to the mile. Trails Illustrated offers a series of topo maps that cover the wilderness. Most of the lakes I've discussed appear on the map titled "Flat Tops NE, Colorado."

Meeker (to the west), Glenwood Springs (to the south), and Steamboat Springs (to the east) offer all services.

CHAPTER 35

Weminuche Wilderness (Colorado)

The Weminuche Wilderness is in the Rio Grande and San Juan National Forests in southwestern Colorado. At 459,000 acres this irregularly shaped wilderness is the largest in the state. Elevations are equally impressive: The Needle Mountains in the western portion of the area have several peaks over 14,000 feet. Sweeping alpine ridges and basins allow expansive views of distant mountains.

Several sizable streams drain the wilderness and offer good action for pan-size trout, including brookies, rainbows, and cutthroats. The Los Pinos River and Vallecito Creek are large mountain streams that drain into Vallecito Reservoir just south of the wilderness (and just northeast of Durango). Trails follow both streams for more than 10 miles to their wilderness headwaters.

Ute Creek drains into Rio Grande Reservoir just north of the wilderness (and southwest of Lake City). The best concentration of lakes is in the northwestern part of the wilderness in and near the headwaters of Ute Creek. From Rio Grande Reservoir (9,500 feet), it's a 12-mile climb to the **Ute Lakes** and **Twin Lakes,** which are all in high basins at, or just over, 12,000 feet. I spent most of a week attempting to fish these lakes but was pinned in my tent by intense thunderstorms much of the time. One evening, during a short break in the weather, I made a dash up to Ice Lake, about a mile south of my camp at Ute Lake. At **Ice**

Lake (about 5 acres, 12,300 feet) I ran into extremely spooky rainbows but managed to midge a couple of fine fish in the 18-inch class, plus a dozen small ones, before the weather closed in again.

The only other good lake fishing I had on that trip was at Twin Lakes, which sit in a big meadow at 12,300 feet. The southern lake (about 20 acres) is separated from the northern lake (about 5 acres) by a strip of land about the width of a two-lane highway. This may be the only spot where I've taken trout in two different lakes while casting from the same position. The fish are cutthroats and brook trout that mostly range from 10 to 14 inches.

There are several more very high lakes within 3 miles of Twin Lakes that could easily be fished on the same tour. **Emerald Lake** (200 acres, about 10,500 feet) is the biggest lake in the wilderness; it's about 6 miles south of Twin Lakes, as the crow flies, but quite a bit farther by trail. It's actually easier to reach by hiking up the Los Pinos River from a trail-head just east of the Vallecito Reservoir. Emerald reportedly has good fishing for rainbow-cutthroat hybrids.

There are a couple dozen small lakes scattered in the very high peaks of the Needles Mountains. Most are off trail and probably too high to support fish, but a few of the larger ones could be worth researching. There are also a few additional lakes scattered along the many creek drainages throughout this wilderness.

MAPS, SERVICES, AND A BONUS FISHERY

To cover the entire wilderness, you need the maps of the San Juan and Rio Grande National Forests; the scale of each is ½ inch to the mile.

Lake City (to the north) and Durango (to the south) offer all services, including fly shops.

From Durango it's just a one-hour drive to the catch-and-release water on the San Juan River below Navajo Dam. On the average the rainbows here in the San Juan are the largest I've caught in any western river. You can easily wade-fish most of the river and camp on the cheap in Navajo State Park. Most days there are dozens of cars in the more popular parking lots by 9:00 A.M. If you want to see how well this river can really nymph, make it a point to be on the water at first light, when the fish are undisturbed. You'll catch more fish in that first hour than most anglers will catch all day.

CHAPTER 36

Bighorn Mountains (Wyoming)

For travelers heading west on Interstate 90, the Bighorns are an invigo-rating sight. After the long drive through flat farm country and rolling ranch lands, the Rockies suddenly waft on the horizon. The highway runs right at the Bighorns, which become more distinct with each pass-ing mile. Granite peaks dotted with snowfields and blue-timbered slopes flanked by sweeping meadows snap into focus. Even on a nice day in the outlying basins, there's often a cluster of thunderheads clashing over Cloud and Bomber Peaks. Sheets of rain drape from the distant storm while shafts of sunlight play on the surrounding mountains.

As you leave the four-lane at the foothill town of Buffalo, Wyoming, and begin to climb into the Bighorns on U.S. 16, the high-plains heat dissipates and the cool mountains embrace you. The air is saturated with the scent of freshly washed pines, and you taste each gulp in the basement of your lungs, as if you haven't breathed down there in a long time. Sleek mule deer graze on the road shoulder. Cobblestone creeks of startling clarity bound down the mountainsides. For me the prospect of shoul-dering the pack and immersing myself in all this splendor always makes me quiver with anticipation, like a hard-charging bird dog about to be unleashed on a snappy fall morning.

I made my very first solo backpack trip in the West in the Bighorns in 1976. It doesn't seem possible that nearly twenty-five summers have passed since that sunny June morning when I buckled on the pack and hiked up the South Fork of Clear Creek. The Bighorns were often the first mountains I played in on my way West other years, too, so they figured prominently in several of those early, carefree summers when getting back into the mountains was what I lived for. Often I would hit the range without a plan. I was just happy to be back in the high country and wandering wherever I pleased.

The Bighorns are not a big range by Rocky Mountain standards, but they're still big country to a backpacker. The core of the range is encompassed within the 137,000-acre Cloud Peak Wilderness, which runs north to south for nearly 40 miles and is close to 15 miles across at its widest point. From the east the mountains present an imposing facade, with their vertical walls of granite that plunge 5,000 feet. Cloud Peak, at 13,176 feet, stands sentinel over the range. There are more than fifty sizable lakes here, plus many small creeks and ponds.

U.S. 16 runs over the southern shoulder of the range from Buffalo to Ten Sleep and provides access to several trailheads and many lakes. Just 15 miles west of Buffalo, a side road leads to the North Fork Picnic Ground and Hunter Corrals—a popular jumping-off point for trips into the wilderness. If you have a four-wheel-drive vehicle and want to camp in solitude, there are numerous road spurs in this area that dead-end in high meadows just east of the wilderness. Most of the creeks in the meadows, including the **North** and **Middle Forks of Clear Creek,** have enough small brook trout to entertain you for an evening as you stretch your legs after the long drive west.

From Hunter Corrals (about 8,000 feet) a trail runs west for 5 miles to the **Seven Brothers**—a tight cluster of seven lakes ranging from 5 to 30 acres in size and nestled in a cirque just below timber at about 10,000 feet. In the late 1970s I was taking nice rainbows to 17 inches from a couple of these lakes, although the action was never fast. The lakes are still stocked regularly with 'bows; several also hold lake trout.

From Hunter Corrals (or the Seven Brothers) you can catch a trail north for about 7 miles to **Cloud Peak Reservoir** (106 acres, about 9,500 feet), where I've also seen fair action for nice rainbows to a couple of pounds, plus a few cutthroats. **Mead Lake** (27 acres), just above and to the west of the reservoir, has pan-size cutthroats.

U.S. 16 crosses the South Fork of Clear Creek about 18 miles east of Buffalo. From the South Fork Campground (7,800 feet) you can pick your way west up the creek for a couple of miles to the **South Fork**

Ponds, a rash of small ponds in the timber at about 8,500 feet. These ponds are all under 2 acres and hold a mix of brook, brown, rainbow, and cutthroat trout that are mostly small to average in size. Just north of the South Fork Ponds at **Sherd Lake** (4 acres, about 9,000 feet), I was catching heavy cutthroats to 19 inches in the late 1970s. Sherd is dependent on stocking, and I don't know whether the fish are growing as well these days. A couple of miles southwest of the South Fork Ponds are the three **Firehole Lakes.** These range from 7 to 19 acres and hold a smattering of trout, including a few goldens that are primarily stocked.

U.S. 16 continues west to cross Powder River Pass (9,677 feet), before descending toward Ten Sleep. A dozen miles west of the pass, an improved road runs north for 8 miles to West Tensleep Lake (9,100 feet), which has a forest service campground and a well-used trailhead that provides access to many lakes on the western side of the Cloud Peak Wilderness. A 4-mile hike straight north from the trailhead takes you to **Lake Helen** (45 acres); just north of Helen are **Lake Marion** (12 acres) and **Mistymoon Lake** (28 acres). All three are at about 10,000 feet and offer good action for small brook trout.

From Mistymoon a trail climbs to Florence Pass (about 11,000 feet) a couple of miles to the east. Just west of the pass are **Gunboat Lake** (16 acres) and a couple of smaller waters that offer decent action for small goldens. At **Florence Lake** (10 acres) just east of the pass, I've taken average cutts. The trail through the pass continues east down the North Fork of Clear Creek for almost 10 miles to the Seven Brothers area. Three miles east of the pass, watch for a tributary stream from the north. This is the outlet from **Powell Lakes,** which are above 10,000 feet and about a mile north of the trail. The two biggest lakes in this group are about 15 acres and have good fishing for cutts. The lakes are stocked about every four years, so fish size depends on when you're here, but I've taken a few trout to 2 pounds. If you continue down the North Fork of Clear Creek for 2 more miles, you'll pass **Deer Lake** (2 acres), just north of the trail. It has fun fishing for pan-size brook trout.

From Mistymoon Lake (back on the west side of Florence Pass) a trail runs west down **Paint Rock Creek,** which has good action for brook, rainbow, and brown trout that are mostly pan size but sometimes run larger. Some of the best fishing is below the wilderness boundary, where the creek gathers some size.

U.S. 14 crosses the northern end of the Bighorns. Forest roads running south from this highway provide access to scattered lakes and trails in the northern half of the Cloud Peak Wilderness, where I've spent little time.

MAPS AND SERVICES

The map of the Bighorn National Forest shows the entire Bighorn Range, including the Cloud Peak Wilderness and all access roads. Its scale is ½ inch to the mile.

The Most Complete Guide to Wyoming Fishing, by John Baughman, lists fish species and approximate size for most lakes and streams in Wyoming, including those in the Bighorns.

Buffalo, on the eastern side of the range, offers all services, including fly shops.

CHAPTER 37

Spanish Peaks
(Montana)

The Spanish Peaks are just west of the Gallatin River in the Gallatin National Forest about 20 miles northwest of Yellowstone Park. At one time these peaks were managed as a separate primitive area, but this 78,000-acre unit is now part of the larger Lee Metcalf Wilderness (which also encompasses the Madison Range). I've spent more time looking up at these mountains—while fishing the Madison and Gallatin Rivers— than hiking in them. But because they're close to some of my favorite roadside rivers, I've poked around in them a bit.

My best fishing in the Spanish Peaks came on a short, 15-mile round-trip up Deer Creek. The Deer Creek Trail starts at about 6,000 feet, where Deer Creek spills into the Gallatin a few miles north of the road to Big Sky Village. A bridge over the Gallatin provides access to the trail on the western side of the river. The trail climbs 3,000 feet in 6 miles to **Moon Lake,** which is less than 10 acres and still in the timber at just under 9,000 feet (the peaks top out at a bit over 11,000 feet). I didn't find a lot of trout at Moon, but the rainbows ran nice (13 to 18 inches), and I stuck almost every cruiser I laid eyes on. At **Deer Lake,** a slightly larger water just north of Moon, I caught small grayling. The evening I exited along Deer Creek, I reached the Gallatin just before dark and camped on the western side of the river opposite the highway. In the last half hour of light, I had a couple of big pools all to myself and banged several good rainbows on caddisflies, including a heavy 19-inch fish. Too bad Robert Redford wasn't there with his camera crew! (Most of the fishing scenes in *A River Runs Through It* were filmed on the Gallatin.)

I haven't researched the Lee Metcalf Wilderness thoroughly, but I've heard it holds some pretty good cutthroat and rainbow lakes, plus a few with golden trout. Most lakes can be fished in round-trips of less than 20 miles. Given the proximity of the wilderness to Yellowstone Park and many fine rivers, it's a handy area for anglers looking for a short getaway on some backcountry lakes.

MAPS AND SERVICES
The forest service offers a topographic map of the entire Lee Metcalf Wilderness, including the Spanish Peaks. The map of the Gallatin National Forest (west half) also shows the Spanish Peaks.

Bozeman, to the north, and West Yellowstone, to the south, offer all services, including excellent fly shops.

CHAPTER 38

Mission Mountains
(Montana)

The Mission Mountains lie in western Montana north of Missoula and southeast of Flathead Lake. The 80,000-acre Mission Mountains Wilderness stretches along the eastern slope of the range and contains better than three dozen trout lakes, ranging from 300-acre affairs to small ponds. The Tribal Wilderness Area of the Flathead Indian Reservation covers much of the western slope and contains a couple dozen more lakes that are open to persons who are not tribal members by permit.

This north-south range is long but narrow, with numerous trailheads on both slopes. A hike of under 10 miles will take you to most of the lakes in a given basin. A few sizable lakes are not accessible by maintained trails. Most lakes are in timbered cirques at elevations of 5,000 to 7,000 feet and have steep, brushy shores, so waders or a float tube would be an advantage.

The Mission Mountains Wilderness is accessible from several trailheads west of Montana 83 between the towns of Seeley Lake and Condon. Most trailheads are reached by drives of under 10 miles on improved dirt roads. As on all winding dirt roads in the West, turn on your headlights and watch for oncoming logging trucks.

The best lake I've fished in the Missions is **Gray Wolf Lake** (6,646 feet), at the far southern end. The trailhead is on Forest Road 906, which heads west from Montana 83 about 15 miles north of Seeley Lake. The hike to the lake is a bit under 10 miles. At 334 acres Gray Wolf is an exceptionally big backcountry lake with a wild population of healthy westslope cutthroats. The biggest fish I took was 18 inches, but the lake holds some better trout. When I was here one August, I found trout cruising the shores mainly in the evening. Although much of Gray Wolf's shore is difficult to navigate, the eastern side has the best camping and easiest access.

High Park Lake is another very big water just 1½ miles north of Gray Wolf, but there's no trail between the two. Hiking cross-country is doable but difficult. Instead, from the same trailhead you used to reach Gray Wolf, you can make a trail connection to **Crystal Lake** (186 acres, 4,755 feet), which has cutthroats. The inlet stream to Crystal forks ½ mile west of the lake. The fork that descends from the southwest is the outlet stream from **High Park** (220 acres, 6,377 feet); I had good action here skating caddisflies for pan-size westslope cutts. The fork from the northwest descends from **Lost Lake** (109 acres, 6,227 feet), which reportedly has slow fishing for nice Yellowstone cutts. Either lake is about 6 miles from the trailhead, including a steep 2-mile climb from the head of Crystal Lake.

On the reservation (the western slope) I've fished only a couple of small cutthroat lakes that I reached from the eastern slope. The Flathead Reservation has an active fish management program that now emphasizes westslope cutthroats, although there are brook and rainbow trout in some high lakes, as there are on the eastern slope. More than a half dozen trailheads east of Pablo and St. Ignatius provide access to the Tribal Wilderness Area. Season and short-term permits are priced very reasonably. Certain areas on the reservation are closed to nonmembers. The reservation also features a grizzly bear management area in the center of the Missions that's closed to travel for much of the summer. The range has a small resident grizzly population, and additional bears wander through from the Bob Marshall Wilderness to the east.

MAPS, GUIDEBOOKS, AND SERVICES

The map of the Flathead National Forest (south half) shows all lakes, all access roads, and most maintained trails in the Missions, including the Flathead Reservation. Its scale is ½ inch to the mile. The forest service also offers a Mission Mountains Wilderness map with a scale of 1¼ miles to the inch and a contour interval of 40 feet. You'll want USGS topos for most cross-country travel.

For additional maps and information on the Tribal Wilderness, contact the Flathead Reservation's permit agent:

Tribal Permit Agent
P.O. Box 278
Pablo, MT 59855
Phone: (406) 675-2700

A book titled *Montana Fly-Fishing Guide* (western volume), by John Holt, has brief descriptions of many lakes on both slopes of the range.

Seeley Lake, on the eastern side of the range, offers all services. Polson, at the southern end of huge Flathead Lake, is a big town on the western slope with all services.

CHAPTER 39

Jewel Basin Hiking Area
(Montana)

The Jewel Basin Hiking Area is in western Montana just west of Hungry Horse Reservoir. Like the Mission Mountains, it's close to Glacier Park and provides an alternative high-lake destination if you have trouble getting a park permit or just want to see more country. At about 15,000 acres and 10 miles long by 4 miles wide, this small area has about two dozen lakes and 35 miles of trail. It really is a hiking area; motorized equipment and pack stock are prohibited. Cutthroat trout are the predominant species, although rainbows inhabit or share several lakes.

The main trailhead is located 17 miles east of Kalispell at the end of Forest Service Road 5392, an improved dirt road. A trail heading east winds and climbs to **Black Lake** (50 acres, about 5,800 feet), where I caught a few nice cutthroats to 2 pounds. Because Black Lake is so accessible from the main trailhead, it sees more traffic than any other lake in the area. Just north of Black are the four **Jewel Lakes,** small lakes of 2 to 5 acres each, scattered in the timber at about 6,000 feet. They have mostly average cutts.

From Black Lake trails head north or south to most of the other waters in the area. I've heard two reports that **Lower** and **Upper Three Eagles Lakes** (9 and 11 acres, 5,705 and 6,340 feet) and **Lower Pilgrim Lake** (29 acres, 6,365 feet), in the southeastern corner of the wilderness, have good fishing for westslope cutthroats to 3 pounds. The two sets of lakes are tucked into neighboring basins that lack maintained trails, so they see lighter use than other lakes. The easiest approach is from the east. Graves Bay is a prominent finger about halfway down the western shore of Hungry Horse Reservoir. Three Eagles and Pilgrim Lakes drain into this bay. An unimproved road runs west from Graves and ends within a couple of miles of the lakes. Your net elevation gain as you hike will be about 1,500 feet. You'll want a topo map to help you pick your way up the drainage and to plot a cross-country route between the two lake basins, which are just a mile apart.

MAPS AND SERVICES

The Jewel Basin is shown on the map of the Flathead National Forest (south half). Its scale is ½ inch to the mile. Contact the Flathead Forest for additional information and maps of the area.

Kalispell, Montana, a half hour west of the area, offers all services and fly shops. If you enter the area from the east, stock up on gas and supplies before you start the drive around Hungry Horse Reservoir.

CHAPTER 40

Sawtooth Wilderness
(Idaho)

The 217,000-acre Sawtooth Wilderness is part of the Sawtooth National Recreation Area in central Idaho. The wilderness is about 25 miles long by 15 miles wide; it lies just west of the headwaters of the Salmon River and north of Sun Valley. The Sawtooths are rough-cut mountains with many exposed granite and sedimentary spires over 10,000 feet.

The Sawtooth Wilderness has several dozen glacial lakes, which are mostly under 10 acres and tucked into rocky basins. The primary angling destinations here are the dozen largest lakes, which range in size from 20 to 100 acres. All of these larger lakes are directly on maintained trails and are mostly dependent on stocking, so there's not a lot of good, undiscovered fishing. Cutthroats and brook trout are the primary species, with a smattering of rainbows, goldens, bull trout, and grayling.

My first trip in the Sawtooths was in early July 1978, which was an unusually cold summer all over the high Rockies. I entered the wilderness on the northeastern side at Redfish Lake (6,547 feet) and climbed about 1,000 feet to **Hellroaring Lake** (about 15 acres, 7,407 feet) in 6 miles. At Hellroaring, which is really a fringe lake that sees a lot of traffic, I had spotty action for small rainbows, but at least I found open water. The next lake up the trail, **Imogene** (8,436 feet), was still frozen. That put a damper on the trip and dissuaded me from exploring any higher.

In 1983 I made a trip across the wilderness, starting at **Yellow Belly Lake** (6,900 feet) on the eastern side and climbing to a group of sizable lakes—**Edna, Vernon,** and **Ardeth**—in about 8 miles. These three lakes range from about 15 to 40 acres and are all around 8,500 feet. At Edna I caught a half dozen cutthroats in the 2-pound class (my best fish of the trip). I took small brook trout and rainbows at some smaller lakes to the south.

I exited by hiking down the **South Fork of the Payette River** for 15 miles to the Grandjean Trailhead (about 7,000 feet) on the western side of the wilderness. The Payette is the longest and largest stream draining the wilderness, and I took small rainbows and cutts from pockets and pools. Hot springs are common in central Idaho, and there are a couple of small ones on the Payette at Grandjean. Here tired hikers can soak their carcasses—although hot springs support some funky bacteria, so you're better off not submerging your head.

If you're looking for additional high lakes, check out the White Cloud Peaks on the eastern side of the Sawtooth NRA. These peaks are not managed as wilderness, but they harbor a couple dozen small lakes in off-road basins above 9,000 feet. These lakes are reputed to be more fertile than those in the Sawtooths and to produce larger trout.

MAPS AND SERVICES

The map of the Sawtooth National Forest shows the Sawtooth Wilderness, the White Cloud Peaks, and all access roads. The scale is ½ inch to the mile. The forest service also offers a topographic map of the Sawtooth Wilderness; its scale is about 1 inch to the mile. There are numerous public campgrounds in the NRA, although some regularly fill to capacity. You'll find additional campgrounds on adjoining national forest lands.

Stanley, on the northern side of the NRA, offers all services, including groceries. Ketchum/Sun Valley, just south of the NRA, is a major resort area with all services, including fly shops.

Silver Creek, a famed spring creek with big rainbows, prolific insect hatches, and some public access, is less than an hour south of Sun Valley.

CHAPTER 41

Eagle Cap Wilderness
(Oregon)

At the mention of Oregon, most anglers envision coastal rivers shrouded in mist spilling from the lush Cascades—but this is a big state with a varied climate. The mountains in arid eastern Oregon more closely resemble the northern Rockies than the Cascades. In fact, the Wallowa Mountains of northeastern Oregon run right to the Idaho border and are physical extensions of the Idaho mountains.

In the footloose summer of 1980, after a couple of months of fishing and hiking in the Rockies, I hitched to the Pacific Coast on an impulse. In western Oregon I hiked in the Cascades near Sisters, and on Mount Jefferson, and in the Oregon Dunes right on the ocean. On my way west I'd swung through the Wallowas for the first time and hiked in the Eagle Cap Wilderness in the Wallowa-Whitman National Forest. At 358,000 acres this is now the largest classified wilderness in Oregon; it's also an exceptionally beautiful and rugged area. Granite peaks approaching 10,000 feet overlook broad, U-shaped, glaciated valleys similar to those in Glacier Park. The streams spilling from the Wallowas carry some of the most transparent water I've seen.

I hiked out of the Wallowa Lake Trailhead (4,645 feet), which is at the end of a paved road just south of the peaceful Wallowa Valley towns of Enterprise and Joseph. After hiking about 7 miles upstream (south) along the West Fork of the Wallowa River, I swung west a few miles into **Lakes Basin,** where I spent a few days fishing more than a half dozen brook trout lakes that range to 40 acres in size and are at about 7,500 feet (Douglas, Horseshoe, Mirror, and Moccasin are the biggest in the group). The fishing was on the slow side for small to average brook trout, but the fish and the lakes were worth seeing.

From the basin I hiked south over Glacier Pass (8,500 feet) and dropped to a pair of rainbow lakes. At **Prospect Lake** (14 acres, 8,328 feet) I saw excellent action skating Elk Hair Caddis for rainbows to 2 pounds. **Glacier Lake** (41 acres, 8,166 feet) also has rainbows. From here I exited via several creek drainages to the Cornucopia Trailhead above the town of Halfway on the southern side of the Wallowas.

There are several dozen more lakes scattered about the central and southern portions of the wilderness. Brook trout are the dominant species, but there are rainbows in more than a dozen lakes and golden trout in a couple. Almost all lakes can be reached by trail, but many are tucked in out-of-the-way basins; you'd have to walk a long way to see them all.

The northern and western parts of the wilderness are a series of long, parallel ridges and valleys. There are few lakes in this region, but if you're looking for solitude and moving water, you might want to research one of the major streams, such as the Minam River, which flows through the western part of the wilderness for many miles.

MAPS AND SERVICES
The forest service offers a special contour map of the Eagle Cap Wilderness. Its scale is ½ inch to the mile; the contour interval is 160 feet.

Joseph and Enterprise, to the north, and Halfway, to the south, offer all services.

CHAPTER 42

Putting Up with Park Policies

Several national parks in the Rockies provide fine backcountry trout fishing amid splendid scenery. This should be enough to satisfy any angler, but in recent years I've found myself steering clear of the parks more and more. Restrictive backcountry regulations can take much of the adventure and flexibility out of a trip. Throw in throngs of jostling tourists in area towns and campgrounds, plus the customary traffic jams, and I'm prone to head for classified wilderness areas, where I can hike and fish with less hassle.

Backcountry camping in the national parks is at assigned campsites and by permit only. Demand often exceeds the available permits on popular routes. Most parks are now issuing backcountry camping permits by advance reservation (for a fee). If you know your trip dates and route in advance, it's best to reserve a permit. As such reservations catch on, there will obviously be fewer permits available to hikers who arrive at a park without a reservation. Already I'm finding that when I try to secure a backcountry permit on short notice, I'm often out of luck on my preferred route. Even with a reservation, you must stop at a ranger station or park office during open hours to pick up your permit and be briefed on backcountry regulations, etiquette, and safety.

I find that having to camp in specific spots on specific nights hurts my flexibility and success as an angler. Indeed, on a trip in unfamiliar country, assigned campsites rarely put you in position to fish the best water at the prime times. At times you'll have to leave productive water or walk away from a hatch prematurely just to make your campsite by nightfall. Other times you'll hustle to reach your next camp with several hours to fish, only to discover that the surrounding water is marginal trout habitat compared with what you bypassed. If bad weather hits at the wrong time, or if you underestimate hiking time, you can wind up with only a brief fling at the lake or section of river that was your primary destination.

Still, I don't want to leave the impression that park backcountry isn't worth fishing, because it is. And over time, permit systems, user fees, and more restrictive backcountry camping regulations will likely be implemented for popular classified wilderness areas in the Rockies. When I'm old and completely bald, I'll probably prattle wistfully to the grandkids about the good ol' days when I could hike wherever I wanted whenever I wanted without a permit. And they probably won't believe me.

Be sure you have the required state or park fishing license and read regulations carefully. Most parks have special fishing regulations, and some waters are closed to angling to provide undisturbed fishing grounds for bears, pelicans, and other wildlife.

CHAPTER 43

Yellowstone Park
(Wyoming-Montana-Idaho)

Yellowstone Park is mostly plateau country and quite gentle in relief compared with much of the Rockies. Though the high mountains surrounding the park are peppered with small glacial lakes and tumbling creeks, Yellowstone itself has only scattered lakes and a wealth of moving water. Nearly all of my backcountry trips in Yellowstone have been to fish large streams and rivers that glide through vast lodgepole forests, snake through spacious meadows, or thunder through steep-walled canyons.

The variety of wildlife found in the park today is nearly identical to what John Colter encountered in 1807 when he passed through, or very near, present-day Yellowstone—and into legend as the first white man to see the natural wonders of the region. The park supports black and grizzly bears, bison, moose, elk, mule deer, antelope, bighorn sheep, mountain goats, cougars, coyotes, and wolves, plus an abundance of predatory birds, waterfowl, and small animals. The abundance of wildlife alone makes Yellowstone a special place to hike and fish.

Incidentally, bison injure far more people in the park than bears do. Because bison frequent river meadows, keep an eye peeled for them while you fish, and avoid close contact. In parks large game animals often lack much fear of humans. Moose and even elk can turn aggressive when disturbed.

The geothermal wonders that made Yellowstone our first national park boost the alkalinity of park streams and help sustain fine trout fishing. Most streams and rivers here support native cutthroat trout or wild populations of introduced trout (the last stockings were in the 1950s). Current management is aimed at sustaining wild trout, especially cutthroats. Since the mid-1970s nearly all of the park's streams and rivers have been managed as catch-and-release. Only artificial lures are allowed on most waters, and some streams allow flies only. Special regulations have restored cutthroat numbers in roadside waters such as the Yellowstone River below Fishing Bridge and have also benefited heavily fished backcountry streams like Slough Creek. Anglers who are sixteen or older must purchase a park fishing permit (no state license is required). The park prohibits the use of lead split shot; as of this writing, however, lead wire wrapped on the hook shank during fly tying is still allowed. Read the regulations carefully; some park waters don't open until July 15, and some are closed permanently.

Backcountry camping permits can be obtained in person no more than forty-eight hours in advance of a trip. Advance reservations can be made (for a fee) beginning in April of each year. All backcountry camping in Yellowstone is at assigned campsites, so you have to plan your trip carefully and stick to your schedule. In my experience backcountry use in Yellowstone is moderate compared with that in Glacier and Rocky Mountain Parks, perhaps because Yellowstone covers much more area. Still, when applying for permits, it's wise to have an alternative route in mind in case the campsites on your preferred route are filled. The maximum stay at any campsite varies from one to three nights. Some sites don't allow wood fires. You must suspend all food at night or when leaving it unattended; most campsites are furnished with a wooden bear pole that looks like a goalpost. I hang my entire pack from the crossbar. Technically you must also obtain permission for off-trail travel in the park. If you plan to fish along rivers and lakeshores away from trails, mention this to the ranger who issues your permit so you'll be advised of any closures or dangers you're not aware of.

Only groups of four or more people are issued backcountry permits for some of the regions in the park that grizzlies frequent. When it comes to avoiding bear attacks, there is some safety in traveling with a group. Still, this policy reminds me of the two good backpacking buddies, Moe and Joe. Every night before crawling into his sleeping bag,

Moe laces on his running shoes. One evening Joe finally remarks that no man can outrun a grizzly, even in track shoes.

"I don't have to outrun a grizzly," Moe replies. "I just have to outrun you."

BLACK CANYON OF THE YELLOWSTONE

In the first meandering miles below Yellowstone Lake, the Yellowstone River flows clear and smooth with long, undulating weeds, like a giant spring creek. On a typical summer day throngs of fly fishers from around the country ply their lines in the braided channels around Buffalo Ford, where large cutthroat trout rise almost continuously to a smorgasbord of insect hatches. This is the placid image that most anglers have of the Yellowstone River in the park.

But there are places where the Yellowstone adopts a different character and relatively few anglers venture. The Black Canyon of the Yellowstone is such a place. Before exiting the park at Gardiner, Montana, the Yellowstone tumbles for 20 miles through a remote canyon flanked by soot-colored volcanic outcroppings and steep, timbered slopes. Here the Yellowstone is a brawling freestone river with deep green pools, boulder-strewn riffles, whitewater chutes, and tumbling falls.

The canyon holds cutthroats, rainbows, and cutthroat-rainbow hybrids, plus scattered brook and brown trout; most are smaller than the fish in the insect-rich meadow sections of the river just below Yellowstone Lake. In two trips into the canyon, my largest trout have been scrappy rainbows to 18 inches, but one look at some of the huge pools will convince you that larger fish must exist.

Water clarity is the key to good fishing here. A few miles before entering the canyon, the Yellowstone receives the waters of the Lamar River. Thunderstorms wash silt into the Lamar, turning it chocolate, and it in turn discolors the Yellowstone in the canyon. When the water is clear or clearing, fishing in the canyon turns on, but for a day or more after the Yellowstone receives a fresh surge of muddy water, fishing shuts down. Before hiking into the Black Canyon, check the clarity of the Yellowstone where it runs through Gardiner, or check the Lamar where it crosses Northeast Entrance Road just east of Tower Junction. If the water is muddy in either location, you're better off fishing elsewhere until it clears. When you're in the canyon, take advantage of clear water by fishing as much as possible while conditions are favorable. Thunderstorm activity on the upper Lamar some 30 miles distant will eventually discolor the Yellowstone, and the mud can arrive suddenly, even during bluebird weather in the canyon. If the river becomes dirty, check out **Hellroaring Creek,** which empties into the Yellowstone near the head of the Black Canyon. This fast, tumbling stream usually runs clear and provides fast action for pan-size cutthroats and some rainbows.

Even during dry weather, the Yellowstone in the Black Canyon is not crystal clear, and you must generally fish the water rather than sight-cast to specific fish. I've had good action on a Muddler Minnow. Bottom bouncing with large stonefly nymphs or Woolly Worms is also productive. I've encountered adult stones into mid-July; also look for good caddis hatches.

To fish the entire Black Canyon, you begin in Gardiner and travel upriver 20 miles before exiting near Tower Junction. There's no clear trailhead in Gardiner—just park in town and find the trail, which runs along the northern side of the river throughout the canyon. From Gardiner to Knowles Falls, where the river plunges 15 feet, is 6 miles. The banks in this stretch are high and steep, making fishing a scramble, but you'll find several immense pools and abundant pocket water. There are high walls and practically unfishable water scattered throughout the canyon, but above the falls the river becomes more fishable with somewhat gentler banks and some swift meadow runs. Lightweight waders, good wading shoes, and caution let you fish some runs more effectively than you can from shore.

Through the lower two-thirds of the canyon, the trail stays within a few hundred yards of the river. For several miles at the head of the canyon, though—around Hellroaring Creek—the trail swings nearly a mile away from the river. I've had some of my best fishing in the upper canyon by following Hellroaring Creek to the river and working downstream from the mouth. A couple of miles upstream from Hellroaring Creek, the trail crosses the Yellowstone on a suspension bridge. From here it's a 1-mile hike to Mammoth-Tower Road a few miles west of Tower Junction.

The trail climbs only 1,000 feet over the length of the canyon, so the hiking is fairly easy. Elevations are only around 6,000 feet, making the canyon the hottest, most arid region in the park, especially in its lower reaches near Gardiner. The lower canyon is the only place you might see a rattlesnake in the park. You will see dozens of bleached skeletons— remnants of elk that starved while attempting to winter in the canyon.

Park regulations prohibit the collecting of teeth, bones, antlers, or other natural objects. Grizzlies frequent the area.

If you'd rather fish just a few miles of river in the middle of the canyon, you can enter and exit by the **Blacktail Deer Creek** Trail, which heads north from Mammoth-Tower Road to strike the Yellowstone near Crevice Lake (no fish), some 8 miles upstream of Gardiner. The trail drops 1,000 feet in slightly more than 4 miles to the river. There's good fishing for pan-size brook trout in the creek. A suspension bridge lets you cross the Yellowstone to reach the main trail along the northern side of the river.

You can also fish just the head of the Black Canyon, around Hellroaring Creek, by entering and exiting near Tower Junction. This area can even be fished on a day hike.

I've seen a few hikers but no other serious fly fishers in the heart of the Black Canyon. If you'd like to fish the Yellowstone in solitude, this is the place to go.

THE LAMAR RIVER

The Lamar is a popular and productive cutthroat river in its lower reaches, where it winds through the open Lamar Valley. Northeast Entrance Road follows the river through the valley for more than 10 miles, offering easy angling access and excellent opportunities to view scattered herds of buffalo. From the junction with Soda Butte Creek, the Lamar River Trail heads south for 25 miles, tracing the river to its wilderness headwaters high in the rugged Absaroka Mountains.

In the summer of 1984 Duffy Brungardt and I hiked and fished to the headwaters of the Lamar. I'd like to tell you that we slayed dozens of huge cutthroats in the wild headwaters. We did catch dozens of trout, but the farther upstream we traveled, the smaller the fish ran. The average trout above the mouth of Miller Creek was under 10 inches, and we didn't catch any cutts over a foot long. Still, the action was steady, and the fish rose eagerly to Elk Hair Caddis and other hairwing dry flies. Above Miller Creek the Lamar dwindles to a large creek with gravel riffles and thigh-deep runs. Given the easy wading and willing fish, this is a river that young or less experienced anglers should enjoy. Quite a few guided horse parties head for this region.

Just after leaving the trailhead, the trail crosses Soda Butte Creek and runs through open meadows for 3 miles. It then crosses Cache Creek and enters the timber. The scenery doesn't change much after this; you're in timber most of the way, except for small meadows spaced along the river. In July we encountered scattered buffalo bulls in these clearings, and one rainy morning a huge bull blundered into camp and eyeballed us maliciously from about 30 feet before lumbering off. On a trip up the Lamar, you'll discover why it runs dirty after downpours. Where the river cuts into hillsides, exposed dirt banks tower more than 50 feet above the water.

The trail up the Lamar runs along its eastern side all the way to Cold Creek Junction, which sits 18 miles from the trailhead at about 7,300 feet. This is only 500 feet above the trailhead, so the hiking is pretty mellow. Just above Cold Creek Junction, the trail leaves the river for good. You could bushwhack east for another 10 miles into the very remote and rugged headwaters of the Lamar, but I doubt the fish get any bigger.

During our trip up the Lamar, we intended to cross Mist Creek Pass and fish **Pelican Creek** before exiting near Fishing Bridge. In fact, Pelican Creek was our primary angling destination. But a lone backpacker had recently been killed and partially eaten by a grizzly, so we were prevented from completing this route and wound up exiting to the North Fork of the Shoshone in the Shoshone National Forest. The Pelican Valley is indeed a grizzly haven and is rumored to have good cutthroat fishing in a meadow setting, but that was as close as I've come to seeing it. It's possible to fish Pelican Creek by day hiking from a trailhead located near Squaw Lake a few miles east of Fishing Bridge. The 2 miles of Pelican upstream from its mouth are permanently closed to fishing, however, to protect the spawning habitat of cutthroats that run into the creek from Yellowstone Lake.

SLOUGH CREEK

This superlative cutthroat stream winds through a series of broad, scenic meadows in the northeastern corner of Yellowstone Park. Far from being slack and stagnant in character, as its name would imply, Slough Creek is a pretty meadow stream with a firm sand-and-gravel bottom. The hike-in water above Slough Creek Campground is loaded with large cutthroats. Below the campground there are also rainbows and rainbow-cutthroat hybrids.

In the last decade Slough Creek has become the most heavily fished hike-in stream in the park. A lot of day hikers now fish the upper meadows; on a recent August day I counted over sixty vehicles at the trailhead. Several backcountry campsites in the upper meadows also fill up most nights. Camping in the meadows lets you enjoy uncrowded fishing in the evening after the day hikers clear out.

From the trailhead near the Slough Creek Campground, it's an easy 2-mile hike through aspen and lodgepole pine to the first meadow. The trail is actually a horse-drawn wagon road that's used to ferry guests and supplies to the private Silver Tip Ranch just north of the park boundary. The first meadow has better than a mile of stream and offers good fishing, but it's easily reached by day hikers, so these fish see more pressure and are tougher to fool than the ones upstream.

To reach the second meadow, continue along the wagon road through sparse timber. At the 5-mile mark, you'll cross Plateau Creek, which is in the second meadow. This meadow has more than 3 miles of excellent water. The backcountry campsites along Slough begin near Plateau Creek, but the second meadow is still within striking range of day hikers. My wife, Dawn, took a couple of nice cutts here on a day hike. Follow all camping and food-storage regulations, because grizzlies roam the area. My brother Eric and his wife, Neysa, heard a bear—easily imagined to be a monster silvertip—woofing and snapping brush near camp one night.

If you stay on the wagon road, you'll pass through ½ mile of timber and cross Elk Tongue Creek at the 8-mile mark. When you break out of the timber, you're in the third meadow, which extends almost to the park boundary 11 miles from the trailhead. The stream is very serpentine, so the meadow actually has about 5 miles of very good water. Given the minimum 16-mile round-trip from the trailhead, the third meadow sees limited day use. If you want to camp on Slough with little competition from day anglers, shoot for a campsite here.

If you want to camp on Slough but can't get a park permit, there's a fourth meadow in the Gallatin National Forest about 3 miles north of the park boundary and 14 miles from the trailhead. This meadow has 4 miles of good water and is lightly fished compared with park waters. The USGS 7.5-minute quadrangle of Cutoff Mountain, Montana-Wyoming, shows the meadow in detail. As long as you don't camp in the park without a permit, it's legal to hike through the park and camp up here. You can also reach the fourth meadow via national forest trails from Cooke City and the Lake Plateau in the Beartooths.

All of the upper meadows on Slough have gravel riffles and long, smooth runs with undercut banks. When it's sunny you can clearly see good fish in every run. Slough is an excellent terrestrial stream—take ant, flying ant, beetle, and hopper imitations. Also pack the kind of convincing mayfly and caddis patterns that you rely on for fishing spring creeks. These cutts see plenty of imitations and by late summer respond best to convincing flies and careful presentations. In four trips into the upper meadows, I've consistently had my fastest fishing on drizzly or overcast days. Even on slow days, you're usually working to visible or rising fish, and it's not unusual to take a dozen or more nice trout in an afternoon.

Once spring runoff is over, the stream generally remains clear, even in rainy weather. The meadows are dry grass and short sagebrush. Hiking is easy, visibility is good, and casting is unobstructed. Hip boots are all you really need to cross the stream at the riffles and to fish effectively.

I've had several anglers tell me, without batting an eye, that the average Slough Creek trout pushes 20 inches, and larger fish are common. Actually, the average cutthroat on Slough is a tad over 16 inches, and a 20-incher is a good fish. One afternoon Duffy Brungardt and I spent some time observing a big corner pool in the third meadow that was stacked with a couple dozen fine trout. I rigged a Fast-Sinking Scud and caught what was clearly the longest, heaviest fish in the pool—it measured 20 inches right on the button and was the largest of many fish we caught that day. As a general rule, you can take what most anglers tell you about fish size in Slough Creek—or other backcountry water in the Rockies—and whack 3 to 4 inches right off the top.

BECHLER RIVER

The Bechler is a marvelous little meadow river tucked away in the lightly visited southwestern corner of Yellowstone. Much of the river is swift and tumbling and holds pan-size trout, but 4 miles of glassy and difficult water in the Bechler Meadows hold some big rainbows and a few nice Snake River cutthroats.

The first time I saw the Bechler was on a weeklong 70-mile exploratory hike that began near Lewis Lake, ran across the Pitchstone Plateau to the Falls River, turned up the Bechler to the west arm of Shoshone Lake, and ended near Old Faithful Lodge. The Bechler Meadows were definitely the find of the trip. Although I didn't catch anything noteworthy in the few hours I fished here, I saw a couple of trout that definitely grabbed my attention. In three more trips to the meadows, I've caught some nice fish and tangled with one of the largest rainbows I've ever hooked in the Rockies.

Since that first trip, I've always hiked into the Bechler Meadows the easy way—from the Bechler Ranger Station. This station and scenic Cave Falls on the Falls River lie up a dead-end road 26 miles east of Ashton, Idaho. Much of the road is gravel, but it's very passable. Backcountry permits can be secured right at the ranger station. I've had good luck getting permits for this corner of the park on short notice. From the ranger station it's a flat 5-mile hike to the upstream end of the meadows, where the river breaks out of the Bechler Canyon. The meadows can be fished by day hiking, but camping on the river lets you fish right through the evening hours—which often bring the best surface activity of the day. If you can get the campsite near the suspension bridge that crosses the river in the upper end of the meadows, you'll be right on productive water. If this site is filled, there are a couple more sites upstream, near the mouth of the Bechler Canyon.

Within the meadows the Bechler runs gin clear, but the bottom is dark and fish are difficult to spot. The river has gravel riffles, long glassy runs with undercut banks, and some deceptively deep pools on its outside bends. Hip boots will let you cross at some of the riffles. Waders can be packed in to the meadow easily enough, but attempting to wade into casting position will scare most fish. The trout here are among the spookiest I've encountered in or out of the backcountry—false casting anywhere near a fish, even in low light, will put it down. Because of irregular bank and bottom contours, the river's surface wells and boils with conflicting currents that make dry-fly presentation tricky. Don't expect to see or hook the numbers of fish you'll encounter on many other park rivers. At midday you'll often have to walk and observe water for an hour to locate a good fish rising sporadically along a cut bank or holding in an open run. To catch a few good fish a day in these meadows, you have to convert a high percentage of limited and difficult opportunities. This means staying completely out of sight in the grass as you crawl into position and doing everything right on your first presentation. In bright sun expect to be humbled. On rainy or overcast days the playing field is a bit more level.

When trout are inactive, the Bechler can appear almost devoid of fish, but nearly every deep run and pool holds a good trout or two. Most adult trout in the meadows are fat, hard-fighting rainbows to 18 inches, but there are a few truly big 'bows. While midging I once hooked a rainbow in the 7-pound class that busted my 6X tippet, although I had several good looks at the fish before and after I hooked it. The Bechler was originally a cutthroat river, and there are still some native Snake River cutthroats in it. If you think all cutthroats are listless fighters, you haven't hooked a hot one in the Bechler Meadows. I had an 18-inch Bechler cutt take me into my backing faster than a foul-hooked freight train, and I had to hustle after the fish to land it.

The scenery on the Bechler reminds me of the Railroad Ranch section of the Henrys Fork of the Snake. Flat, expansive meadows are flanked by lodgepole forests and mountains. The backside of the Tetons is visible to the southeast. Unfortunately, hatches are not as prolific throughout the summer as on the Henrys Fork. In August, when I've always fished the Bechler, I've yet to see a major mayfly or caddis hatch, although fish usually rise to midges in the evening. During nonhatch periods Bechler fish are not super-selective—a small Adams or beetle will produce if your presentation is up to snuff. The meadows reportedly host a green drake hatch in early summer that brings the good fish up— I'd like to see it. I've nymphed a few visible fish from open runs, but good fish in the meadows are so scattered that blind nymphing doesn't yield much.

The best density of big fish seems to be in the upper half of the meadows. Traveling downstream through the meadows toward the junction with Boundary Creek, you'll pass through extensive willow stands. Watch for bedded moose—I once jumped a group of four bulls that rose and held their ground while I backed off. Below the mouth of Boundary Creek, the Bechler increases in size and gradient as it reenters the timber. From the creek downstream to its confluence with the Falls River—about 3 miles—the Bechler is mostly shallow riffles with small fish and a few big ones.

Two miles upstream from the Bechler Meadows, the river plunges 100 feet over spectacular Colonnade Falls. Between the falls and the meadows, the river winds through timber for 2 miles. On my most recent trip, I caught quite a few small rainbows and saw several big schools of rainbow fry in logjams in this area. Bechler rainbows received catch-and-release protection only in 1990, so perhaps populations are on the upswing.

There are small cutthroats in the Bechler Canyon above Colonnade Falls, but the scenery and a fabulous thermal pool on the **Ferris Fork**

of the Bechler are the big draws. It's an 8-mile hike from the Bechler Meadows to Three River Junction, where three streams merge to form the Bechler; keep an eye open for huckleberries. About ½ mile up the Ferris Fork is the most glorious hot spring I've ever soaked my tired bones in. It's one of the park's few backcountry hot springs in which swimming is allowed—but make sure it's still legal if you plan to visit. A powerful jet of hot water gushes upward through a fissure in the streambed. The fissure is in the middle of a big pool that's about 5 feet deep—stand right next to it and you'll feel the rocks vibrate. You can just drift around in this pool and find any temperature you like. The Ferris Fork has good action for small cutthroats.

By August the Bechler Meadows are usually dry, but in wet years they're a mosquito factory. When the sun is high and the mosquitoes retreat, the biting gnats and deerflies pick up the slack. Take a head net—you may need it.

FIVE-MILE AND SEVEN-MILE HOLES

The Grand Canyon of the Yellowstone is the most spectacular sight in the park. On any summer day thousands of tourists view and photograph the Upper and Lower Falls from Artist and Inspiration Points. And on any summer day a few ambitious anglers trek to the canyon floor to camp and wet a line in a truly grand setting.

From the Boulder Trailhead near Canyon Village, a trail runs along the north rim of the canyon, providing superb views for the first mile. After 3 miles the trail descends 1,500 feet to the canyon floor. The total distance into Seven-Mile Hole from the Boulder Trailhead is actually about 5 miles; Five-Mile Hole is a newer backcountry camping site and a slightly shorter hike.

Fishing for cutthroats in the canyon is good. Most of these cutts run from 14 to 18 inches and fall for streamers, big nymphs, and attractor dry flies. You might also catch an occasional rainbow, brown, or brook trout anywhere in the Yellowstone below the falls. Even after you reach the canyon floor, however, access along the river is restricted by steep walls. To fish even a couple hundred yards of river in Five-Mile Hole, I had to scramble along steep banks. Twice I've failed to get a backcountry permit for Seven-Mile Hole, but according to friends who've fished there, it has more fishable water than in Five-Mile Hole. In either location you should fish in hiking boots for reliable footing along the banks; the current in the canyon is powerful, and I saw little advantage in wading.

To an experienced mountain hiker, the 1,500-foot climb out of the canyon is a routine elevation gain, but for the legions of inexperienced backpackers who tend to flock to national parks, a climb like this can be gut wrenching. An angling acquaintance of mine vomited on this ascent. Watch your step.

THE FALLS RIVER

The Falls River winds across the southwestern corner of the park for about 30 miles before exiting. The bulk of the river in the park is lightly fished, because it's approached by trails in only a few places.

I've fished the river a few miles below its headwaters near Grassy Lake Reservoir, which can be reached by a dirt road that begins near Flagg Ranch at the South Entrance. The upper Falls River is a forested freestone stream with good action for cutthroats and rainbows that reach respectable size. My largest fish in an evening in this area was a 15-inch rainbow.

I've also fished briefly where the river meets the South Boundary Trail a few miles east of Cave Falls. There are some meadows in this area that I'd like to explore more on a short one- or two-night trip. Several miles of the Falls River in the park can be fished by day hiking from the Cave Falls area. The Falls and the Bechler can be fished on the same backcountry trip.

HEADWATERS OF THE YELLOWSTONE RIVER

The Yellowstone River is born south of the park in the Teton Wilderness of Wyoming. It gathers feeders as it flows north for some 30 miles through the remote Thorofare region before entering Yellowstone Lake. In June throngs of cutthroats, averaging 16 inches, migrate out of Yellowstone Lake and surge into the upper Yellowstone and its tributaries to spawn.

To protect these spawning trout and to prevent conflicts with grizzlies that converge to feast on them, all Yellowstone Lake tributaries within the park, including the upper Yellowstone and its feeder streams, are closed to fishing until mid-July. By then many trout have completed spawning and reentered the lake.

There are no roads into the Thorofare from any direction. To reach the upper river where it enters Yellowstone Lake requires a 20-mile hike that traces the lake's entire eastern shore. Above the lake there are 14 miles of river within the park. Most of this mileage flows through boggy, bug-infested meadows with dense willows. Since the Thorofare is Grizzly

Central, the park service issues backcountry permits only to groups of four or more people. To get in on the cutthroat migration as a solo act, I hike into the Thorofare region of the Teton Wilderness from its Jackson Hole side and fish the Yellowstone and many miles of productive tributaries above the park boundary. This route and its excellent fishing are described in detail in chapter 24.

THE LAKES OF YELLOWSTONE

Here's the bottom line on fishing the small backcountry lakes scattered throughout Yellowstone: If you do your homework and target a select few lakes, you can enjoy good action on cutthroats that average 16 inches or a bit bigger. This is decent fishing, of course, but you can catch cutthroats as large or larger in hundreds of hike-in lakes throughout the Rockies, and you don't have to contend with the park's crowds, regulations, and grizzlies to do it. I go to Yellowstone primarily for the rare opportunity to fish large, fertile streams and rivers in backcountry settings, and I do most of my lake fishing elsewhere.

If you do elect to fish backcountry lakes in the park, you're probably better off concentrating on a few truly big ones that offer some unusual opportunities.

Yellowstone Lake

At nearly 90,000 acres, Yellowstone Lake is the largest natural lake and the largest wild cutthroat lake in the high Rockies. It sits at 7,733 feet in a gigantic, 50-mile-diameter volcanic crater in the center of the park. About 30 miles of its northern and western shores are rimmed by road, but the remaining 80 miles of shore are in backcountry. Even the shores along the road are lightly fished. Day hiking or backpacking just a few miles from the road will usually put you in solitude.

The Thorofare Trail runs for 20 miles along the eastern shore of the lake, mostly through timber. From the trail the lake is visible only periodically, and you have to walk through trees for a few hundred yards to reach the water in most spots. I've hiked along this shore and enjoyed good wade fishing when the onshore wind wasn't too stiff. Backcountry campsites along the Thorofare Trail begin around Park Point, 6 miles south of the Lake Butte Trailhead.

Yellowstone Lake is infamous for sudden storms. The water stays cold all summer, too, so tubing, canoeing, or even boating in a motorized craft can turn lethal in a hurry—respect wind and lightning at all times. To use any watercraft in the park, including a float tube, you must purchase a permit. (Virtually all flowing water in the park is closed to craft of any kind.)

Most of Yellowstone Lake is open to motorboats, but its remote south and southeast arms, beyond the tip of the Promontory (a 7-mile-long peninsula), are closed to motors. The southeast arm, where the upper Yellowstone River enters, is known for excellent fishing and attracts some canoe traffic. Canoeing to the southeast arm is a trip that intrigues me. Along with my brother Stu, I've been making annual canoe trips to the Quetico-Superior country to fly-fish for smallmouth bass, walleye, northern pike, and lake trout. I recently bought a solo canoe, and I'm planning some trips in the Quetico and farther north in Canada. Some summer I'd like to make a western swing with the canoe to paddle Yellowstone and Shoshone Lakes (described below).

Since the mid-1970s regulations on Yellowstone Lake have allowed the harvest of two cutthroats under 13 inches. Trout of 14 to 17 inches are once again abundant. In fact, don't count on catching any trout small enough to keep. The lake opens to fishing June 15. All moving water in the Yellowstone River drainage above the Upper Falls at Canyon opens July 15, including tributaries to Yellowstone Lake.

The lake reaches depths of 300 feet, but the cutts feed and cruise primarily in the shallows, where water temperatures are moderate and forage is abundant. Plenty of fish can be taken by wading and tubing. The trout rise to damselfly, midge, and midday *Callibaetis* hatches. During nonhatch periods try stripping a scud, damselfly nymph, or swimming mayfly nymph imitation along the bottom.

Shoshone Lake

At over 8,000 acres, Shoshone is the largest park lake that's completely in backcountry. Shoshone Lake sits at the headwaters of the Lewis River and drains into Lewis Lake through the 4-mile-long Lewis Channel. You can canoe to Shoshone Lake by paddling across Lewis Lake, then paddling and portaging up this channel. Motors are allowed in Lewis Lake but not in Shoshone or the channel.

The southeastern shore of Shoshone, where the channel exits, can be reached by hikes of 4 to 7 miles on trails that originate just north of Lewis Lake. Shoshone's northern shore can be reached by a 3-mile hike down De Lacy Creek from a trailhead 9 miles west of West Thumb. The only time I've been to Shoshone was on the last day of a 70-mile swing through the southwestern corner of the park. Plans to wet a line in the lake were thwarted by an all-day downpour. Our party of three wet, tired hikers voted unanimously to keep right on trudging; we reached Old Faithful Lodge and showered just in time to be the last party served in the dining room that night. Thus the following information on the lake is secondhand but solid.

Shoshone contains mostly brown and lake trout, which reach trophy size. Lakers retreat to the cold depths for much of summer, so plan on fishing deep with a large streamer if you want to hook one. While canoe fishing in Canada, I've been taking all kinds of deep-water game fish, including lake trout, on a #2 Bobbing Baitfish and a 9-weight extra-fast-sinking line. This rig can be cast from shore and retrieved, but often I troll and slowly pump the fly while drifting with the wind or paddling slowly.

Shoshone Lake isn't known for fast action in midsummer, but in October the Lewis Channel attracts anglers from around the country. That's when big brown and lake trout move into the channel to spawn. By then I'm usually hunting grouse and woodcock in northern Wisconsin, but maybe some year.

Heart Lake
At more than 2,000 acres, Heart Lake, near the South Entrance, is the other large backcountry lake in the park. It's reached by hiking 8 miles east from a trailhead just north of Lewis Lake. The lake can also be reached by a 12-mile hike that starts at the South Entrance and follows the upper Snake River for the first several miles. The **headwaters of the Snake** offer decent action for cutthroats that are generally under 12 inches long.

I haven't been to Heart, but it's reputed to hold cutthroats that can run a bit bigger on the average than those in Yellowstone Lake. Heart also holds some huge lake trout. A 43-pounder was taken in the 1960s. In late October lake trout spawn in the shallows, but to have a legitimate shot at taking a laker most of the summer, you'll need a float tube, a fast-sinking line, and big streamers. Cutthroats can be caught from shore.

MAPS AND SERVICES
The USGS publishes a topo map titled "Yellowstone National Park, Wyoming-Montana-Idaho," which covers the entire park at a scale of ½ inch to the mile; the contour interval is 80 feet. Earthwalk Press publishes an easy-to-read, updated, waterproof topo map that covers the entire park. Trails are clearly highlighted, and backcountry campsites are shown.

The Yellowstone Fly-Fishing Guide, by Craig Mathews and Clayton Molinero, is a valuable reference that contains angling descriptions ranging from brief to detailed of virtually all trout waters in the park, including backcountry waters.

Most of the park's drive-in campgrounds fill early in the day, so you may have difficulty finding a campsite in the park between backcountry trips. Following are some convenient places to drive-in camp near the park.

The town of West Yellowstone, at the West Entrance, has more fly-fishing shops per capita than anywhere else in the world. I always stop at Blue-Ribbon Flies to hand-select natural fly-tying materials from its extensive stock. West Yellowstone also has the best array of grocery stores, restaurants, and motels of any town on the park boundary. Between back-country trips in the park, I often camp and fish along the Madison River below Quake Lake; other famous waters, including Henrys Fork of the Snake, are also within a short drive of West Yellowstone.

Gardiner, at the North Entrance, offers all services. You can camp for free at state fishing accesses on the Yellowstone River north of Gardiner.

Cooke City, at the Northeast Entrance, offers all services, though groceries are limited. National forest campgrounds along the Beartooth Highway just a few miles east of Cooke City are conveniently located for forays into the eastern half of the park or the Beartooth Plateau.

The East Entrance has limited services. You can usually find a site in one of several campgrounds along the Shoshone River just outside the park. Cody, Wyoming, an hour east of the park, offers all services. The North Fork Angler in Cody is a full-service fly shop close to good waters that aren't as famous or crowded as many park waters.

The South Entrance offers limited services. Flagg Ranch is a large, privately owned campground just south of the park. Call ahead if you're planning on camping at Flagg Ranch, though: If it's full, you may have to drive south through Grand Teton Park or beyond to find a campground.

A dead-end gravel road runs to the lightly used southwestern corner of the park from Ashton, Idaho. A little-used Targhee National Forest campground located between Cave Falls and the Bechler Ranger Station is an excellent base for overnight trips into the Bechler region. From here you can also day hike to the lower Bechler or to roadless stretches of the Falls River both in and out of the park. There are no services after you leave Ashton.

CHAPTER 44

Glacier Park
(Montana)

Glacier Park is still being shaped by small glaciers, but it took big ones to sculpt the broad, U-shaped valleys and jagged sedimentary peaks and walls that give the park its distinctive scenery. For sweeping grandeur Glacier may well be the crown jewel of the U.S. Rockies. On clear summer days, lush, emerald slopes laced with glittering cascades seem to hang from an impossibly blue sky, and there is not a more gorgeous setting for fly fishing anywhere in the West.

As the last great glaciers retreated, roughly ten thousand years ago, the valleys and cirques they left behind filled with water. Native westslope cutthroats and bull trout navigated to the long, narrow lakes in the lower valleys. Much later the park service introduced trout to the small, barren cirque lakes in the high country. Stocking in Glacier ended in the late 1960s. Today self-sustaining populations of trout inhabit about sixty lakes. With the exception of the large valley lakes, which offer spotty fly fishing, most park lakes are in the backcountry and can be reached only by hiking or on horseback.

Like other mountain regions, Glacier enjoyed some boom years following the introduction of trout, including exotic rainbow, brook, and lake trout to virgin waters. I have a book on the history of sport hunting and fishing in America that includes a 1938 photo of a Glacier Park angler unhooking what must be a 15-pound lake trout. I doubt that this fish was released, because the foreground of the photo shows an even bigger laker and a whopper cutthroat that have already been dispatched. Today the average size of park fish is considerably under 15 pounds, but Glacier still offers some good high-lake angling. The uplifted sedimentary rock that's clearly visible in peaks and walls throughout the park boosts the fertility of many lakes. Because of their high gradients, however, most of the park's beautiful, cascading backcountry streams are barren or support only small fish.

Glacier is not a popular fly-fishing destination, although it attracts about two million tourists a year. Plenty of backpackers, who may or may not pack fishing tackle, compete for a limited number of backcountry permits. Permits can now be reserved in advance beginning May 1 of the current year. As reserving permits becomes the norm, obtaining them on a drop-in basis will likely become more difficult than it already is.

Backcountry trips in Glacier are limited to a maximum of six nights. All camping is at designated sites—designated campgrounds, really. Backcountry sites on any given lake are so closely grouped that several parties hang food from the same bear pole and prepare meals in a central area (wood fires are prohibited at many sites). The number of sites in a campground ranges from two to seven; a maximum of four people are allowed per site. Even aside from the obvious aesthetic drawbacks of this arrangement, I don't like camping near strangers in bear country, because I have no control over what they do. On Lake Ellen Wilson, for instance, an angler from a neighboring site walked within feet of my tent while dripping a trail of fish slime from a freshly soaked canvas creel.

In bear country I like to hang my entire pack, but the bear poles provided in Glacier are inadequate for this: They're rather flimsy metal poles with several hooks for hanging food sacks. Not everyone complies with food-storage regulations, either. Although Glacier may be the most beautiful backcountry I've camped in, the camping experience itself is a far cry from what's available in most classified wilderness areas.

Over half the backcountry lakes in the park are within 6 miles of a trailhead and can be reached on day hikes. If you can't get a permit to camp on a lake you really want to see, then consider a day hike. An angler with just a week to spend in the park could probably visit more good lakes by day hiking than by camping in the backcountry.

Glacier is home to more grizzlies per square mile than anywhere else in the U.S. Rockies. Many trails and passes are narrow, so watch for bears and other large game traveling in the opposite direction. Some lakeshores are carpeted with dense willows that make bears and other large game difficult to see. Make plenty of noise when walking in brush. Bears prowl mainly between dusk and dawn. If you camp in the back-country, be close to camp by nightfall. If you day hike, get in and out of the country in decent light.

Dense willows and steep terrain make fishing difficult from many shores, especially on the lush western slope of the park, which receives a lot of precipitation. Lightweight waders and wading shoes will get you out of the brush and make fishing and traveling shorelines easier.

A license is not required to fish in the park. Ask for and read a copy of the park fishing regulations; the use of lead weights for fishing is likely to be banned at some point. All trout populations in the park reproduce naturally, and fisheries are increasingly being managed for limited harvest.

GUNSIGHT PASS REGION

My first backcountry hike in Glacier was a 20-mile trek through the center of the park. My route began near Lake McDonald on the western slope, ran through Gunsight Pass, and exited at St. Mary Lake on the eastern slope.

From Lake McDonald the trail runs up Sprague Creek for about 4 miles before quickly climbing above timber to Sperry Chalet; the eleva-tion gain of 3,000 feet in 6 miles makes this one of the steeper trails in the park. After passing the chalet, you drop 1,000 feet to reach **Lake Ellen Wilson** (5,929 feet) at about the 10-mile mark.

This lake has good fishing for silvery brook trout that mostly run 9 to 12 inches; my biggest was 14 inches and well built, so there are proba-bly some better fish around. I saw my best action by scrambling along the more rugged shores away from the campground. The waterfall at the inlet below Gunsight Pass is a beautiful fishing hole; if you hang around here on a sunny afternoon, you'll see some extraordinary shades of blue, green, and turquoise. As with most park lakes that are near or above tim-berline and provide expansive views, it's worth the hike just to eyeball the country. The timberline in Glacier is around 7,000 feet, but most cirque lakes above 6,000 feet have lightly wooded shores.

Gunsight Pass, just east of Ellen Wilson, sits on the Continental Divide at about 7,000 feet. From the pass the trail drops 1,000 feet in a couple of miles to the outlet of **Gunsight Lake**. Gunsight has good fishing for rainbows. Bring waders, though, because the lake is almost entirely ringed by dense willows that run right to the water's edge. In waders I fished completely around the lake—a distance of about 2 miles—in a day and was forced out of the water by drop-offs only a few times.

At Gunsight the rainbows rose willingly to an Elk Hair Caddis all afternoon, even though there wasn't much natural rising activity. Most of the 'bows were about a foot long, although I did take a couple of solid, acrobatic fish that pushed 17 inches. If you're looking for an extra day of fishing on this trip, schedule two nights for Gunsight, because Lake Ellen Wilson has a one-night camping limit in July and August. There are no other lake-fishing possibilities on this route.

From Gunsight Lake it's 6 miles downhill to the Going-to-the-Sun Road near the head of St. Mary Lake. The trail runs mostly through timber along the upper **St. Mary River.** With some bushwhacking you can dap a fly on seldom-fished river runs and catch some pan-size rainbows.

CAMAS CREEK DRAINAGE

I backpacked into the Camas Creek drainage primarily to fish Trout and Arrow Lakes, which are restricted to fly fishing. **Trout Lake** (4,000 feet), a narrow lake about 2 miles long, is reached by a 4-mile, 900-foot climb from the head of Lake McDonald. It doesn't offer backcountry camping, so I fished here for only a few hours. I took several cutthroats to 14 inches but didn't spot many cruising or rising fish. The lake is reported to fish best in early summer.

Arrow Lake is a couple of miles upstream along **Camas Creek,** which is brushy but beautiful once you're on the water. It holds small cutthroats right through summer and probably pulls larger fish from the lakes at spawning time. The trail between the lakes runs through the best huckleberry patches I've seen, and the berries were peaking when I was there. This valley reportedly holds more than its share of grizzlies, which may explain why I had no company at the campground.

I caught a hard rainfall on my night at **Arrow Lake** (4,070 feet), so I didn't fish much. The action for cutthroats was similar to what I'd seen at Trout Lake, which was mediocre by high-lake standards. I didn't move any bull trout, but Arrow is reputed to hold some good ones.

From Arrow the trail continues up the creek a few miles before ending at Camas Lake, which offers backcountry camping. Lake Evangeline and Roger Lake sit a few miles above Camas Lake at the head of Camas Creek. I found no fish in any of these small upper lakes, but the views get more expansive as you climb along Camas Creek, so it's worth the hike.

HIDDEN LAKE

Hidden Lake (6,375 feet) is just a 3-mile hike from the Logan Pass Visitor Center at the top of the Going-to-the-Sun Road—the most-visited point in the park. Because of its proximity to this popular area, Hidden Lake has no overnight camping, which probably helps its fishing: It's known for challenging cutthroat trout.

If you want to day hike in to Hidden, it's wise to arrive at Logan Pass early to nail down a parking spot before the tourists really get rolling (I can't think of another off-road lake where this is a concern). From the visitor center, follow the boardwalk that runs about a mile to overlook the lake; at the end of the boardwalk, you'll drop 300 feet in 2 miles to hit the lake right at its outlet stream. Mountain goats hang out along this trail. On a nice summer day at least a couple dozen day hikers will make this trip, but they mostly hang around the inlet to picnic, sun, and cast hardware half-heartedly for trout. I just cross the outlet and work the western shore for more than a mile, all the way to the head of the lake. In two hikes in to the lake, I haven't encountered another angler more than ½ mile from the outlet, so I've had the best fishing to myself.

The eastern side of the lake is mostly loose talus sloping down from vertical walls and isn't very fishable. The flatter, flower-strewn western shore is the place to be anyway, because this is where the productive flats are. As you hike toward the head of the lake, you'll cross a couple of small inlet streams. On my first hike in to Hidden, in early August, I found clusters of nice fish hanging in shallow bays off these inlets. The trout were clearly visible cruising the boulder-studded flats. A Fast-Sinking Scud produced more than two dozen cutts to 17 inches and one legitimate 20-incher. Surprisingly, these are Yellowstone cutthroats that were transplanted to Glacier and are well established in the lake.

The second time I day hiked in to Hidden, with my wife, Dawn, was also in late August. That day we lucked into an excellent midday hatch of large mayflies. When the duns started popping, good numbers of fish gorged right against the shoreline rocks in as little as a foot of water. A #12 Adams dropped right into a rise ring and twitched a bit brought a strike on nearly every cast.

There are cutthroat lakes this good and better all over the Rockies, but if you're going to be touring Glacier and want to slip off the road for a taste of productive high-lake fishing, Hidden Lake should deliver.

OLDMAN LAKE

Oldman Lake (6,650 feet) is a pretty cutthroat lake that's reached by a 6-mile hike from Two Medicine Lake. This trip is through the southeastern region of the park, which is considerably drier than the areas west of the divide. The trail climbs better than 1,000 feet through spotty timber and scattered huckleberries. Oldman offers backcountry camping and is within day-hiking range, so it attracts a few anglers. In July and August you're limited to one night of camping here, and because there are no other productive lakes within several miles, this is a one-night trip for most anglers.

The shores of Oldman are sloped but grassy. By working completely around the lake, a distance of about a mile, I enjoyed good angling in solitude, especially off the western end, where an inlet stream enters.

Oldman is classic high-lake fishing. Prowl the shores and watch for cruising fish from high vantages. I took cutts on top with an Elk Hair Caddis and down deep with a Fast-Sinking Scud. These were brilliantly colored Yellowstone cutts that averaged around a foot and topped out at 15 inches.

BELLY RIVER

If you're looking for a backcountry stream in Glacier with decent action for pan-size trout, check out the Belly River. The Belly River Valley is reached by an easy 2-mile hike from a trailhead near Chief Mountain Customs at the Canadian border on the eastern side of the park.

The river offers easy wading over gravel and small cobblestone. Pack waders or hip boots so you can walk right up the channel. Much of the river is shallow riffles. The deepest runs and best cover are tight against the banks, especially on the outside bends, where the current gouges deeper runs.

I didn't see any of the grayling that inhabit the drainage, but I had good action for brook trout and rainbows to 12 inches. The fish were not picky. You only need an Elk Hair Caddis or Adams, and maybe a Woolly Worm or Hare's Ear Nymph for probing the deeper slots.

There's a backcountry campsite right on the river within 4 miles of the road and another site a few miles upstream. I wanted to hike up the river to Elizabeth Lake, 9 miles from the trailhead, but I couldn't land a permit. **Elizabeth** (4,892 feet) is over a mile long and reportedly has excellent fishing for grayling, plus some rainbow and brook trout.

OTHER PROSPECTS

Based on my reading and conversations with a fisheries biologist, here are a few other lakes in Glacier that I'd like to visit.

The **Kootenai Lakes** (4,400 feet) are a collection of potholes a few miles south of Waterton Lake. They're reportedly the best brook trout waters in the park. Mosquitoes and grizzlies are rumored to be abundant as well. There's a backcountry campground at the lakes, but the area is sometimes closed because of bear activity. If you can catch a ride on a cruise boat from Waterton Park to the southern tip of Waterton Lake, it's a short hike to the Kootenais; the entire hike from Waterton Park is about 9 miles. The shortest route through Glacier is a 20-mile pull from Chief Mountain Customs.

Otokomi Lake (6,400 feet) is a small cirque lake that's reached by a steep 5-mile hike from the northern shore of St. Mary Lake. The cutthroat fishing is rated on par with that at Hidden Lake—which would make this one of the better lakes in the park. The trail up Rose Creek climbs 2,000 feet and ends right at Otokomi, which offers a backcountry campground. This sounds like my kind of one-night stand.

The far northwestern reaches of the park are traversed only by dirt roads. I've never been to this area, and I'd like to see it. The main attraction for anglers is **Grace Lake** (4,000 feet), which is said to have big cutthroats. Grace is a 12-mile hike from the inside North Fork Road, which follows the eastern side of the North Fork of the Flathead River. The trail runs up Logging Creek and skirts the northern shore of Logging Lake, a narrow lake about 6 miles long. Grace itself is a narrow, mile-long lake a mile upstream of Logging Lake. The elevation gain from the trailhead is just 600 feet, and according to my topo map, Grace is in the timber, so I'd pack waders. There's a backcountry campground near the outlet of Grace. Logging Creek between Logging Lake and Grace Lake is permanently closed to fishing. I wonder why.

MAPS AND SERVICES

Trails Illustrated publishes a waterproof topo map that covers the entire park and shows backcountry campgrounds.

A booklet titled *Fishing Glacier National Park,* by Paul M. Hintzen, has a brief description of most park waters and is available from the Glacier Natural History Association, (406) 888-5756.

The park's drive-in campgrounds tend to fill early in the day. There are private campgrounds close to the park along most main access roads. Basic supplies can be purchased at various stores in and around the park. Full-service fly shops are scarce in this region.

CHAPTER 45

Rocky Mountain Park (Colorado)

Rocky Mountain Park is an enjoyable place to fish and hike if you happen to live nearby or are visiting the area, but I wouldn't shoot for it as an angling destination. The park is within a short drive of the Denver area, so roads and campgrounds are often congested. There's the usual slew of park regulations to contend with. And the trout in the park are mostly small.

That said, however, the park does provide excellent action in beautiful settings. Self-sustaining populations of trout inhabit about three dozen small backcountry lakes and several creek systems. Brook trout are most common in the backcountry, but populations of native greenback cutthroats have been reestablished in many lakes; all greenbacks must be released.

I've made only two short backcountry trips here. The first was a three-day hike to **Lake Verna** and **Spirit Lake,** which are about 8 miles from Grand Lake on the western side of the park. A string of 13,000-foot peaks rising along the Continental Divide just to the east of the lakes mesmerized me while 7- to 10-inch brook trout sipped my flies willingly.

I also made the 5-mile climb to **Timber Lake** on the western side of the park to catch my first greenback cutthroats. They were small but plentiful.

Based on my reading and inquiries, there is good action for small trout in lakes throughout the backcountry here, but even rumors of large fish are conspicuously absent. I'm sure there are some nice fish secreted away somewhere, but your payback for exploring this park is not likely to be measured in pounds.

Backcountry camping is at designated sites by permit only (most sites don't allow wood fires). Permit reservations are accepted beginning March 1.

A Colorado fishing license is required for fishing in the park. Read park fishing regulations carefully; some waters are closed permanently, and others allow only catch-and-release fishing with barbless hooks.

MAPS AND SERVICES

Earthwalk Press publishes a topo map of the entire park.

Fly Fishing Rocky Mountain National Park, by Todd Hosman, devotes a chapter to describing park waters in and out of the backcountry.

Estes Park, at the east entrance, and Grand Lake, on the west side, offer all services. The five campgrounds in the park usually fill early. There are forest service and private campgrounds throughout the surrounding area.

PART EIGHT

Wild River Canyons

CHAPTER 46

Hiking Down Instead of Up

To reach most backcountry waters in the Rockies, you must climb. But to reach a few superb waters, you must descend—precipitously. In the West descending abruptly almost always takes you into rough terrain and a stark environment. Therein lies much of my fascination with canyon fishing—the contrast between a cold river teeming with trout and hot, desiccated canyon lands is utterly striking.

In canyons I adjust my routines to work around the fierce midday heat. I move camp in the morning, lay up for a few hours around noon, and fish mainly in the late afternoon and evening. In steep-walled canyons the sun may set by early afternoon, leaving hours of deep shade to fish in. Some reaches of canyons receive afternoon shade hours before others. By studying the direction of a river and the surrounding terrain, you can predict where afternoon camping and fishing will be most comfortable.

Dehydration sneaks up on you in arid canyons, especially when you're toiling. Make it a point to drink plenty of water. Munch on jerky or nuts to replace lost salt. Two of the rivers I'll cover in this part of the book are tailwaters that flow from reservoirs. When I drink from a large river that has flowed through ranch lands and civilization, I filter and chemically treat my water. I also add powdered Gatorade to mask iodine or other objectionable tastes.

For better or for worse, in many river corridors, including those discussed here, visitors are now required to pack out solid human waste. Be sure to ask a resource manager (preferably an agency head) to personally demonstrate proper technique.

Arid river canyons are full of things that swoop, slither, and scoot—bats, snakes, lizards, and spiders are common. Watch for prickly pear cactus, whose spines whistle right through nylon boot panels. Poison ivy is plentiful and grows shoulder high; learn to identify western varieties.

After weeks of blustery mountain weather, I always enjoy a stint in a blistering canyon—it warms me right to the marrow. At midday I like to find some shade, prop against my bedroll, and sip from a cold canteen. Doing absolutely nothing has never felt better.

CHAPTER 47

Middle Fork of the Salmon (Idaho)

The Middle Fork of the Salmon originates at the junction of Bear Valley Creek and Marsh Creek some 20 miles northwest of Stanley, Idaho, on the northern flank of the Sawtooth Range. From here the river tumbles north for 100 miles through one of the deepest and most remote gorges in North America before spilling into the main Salmon. En route the Middle Fork flows through the Challis, Payette, and Salmon National Forests, gathering tributary streams that drain much of mountainous central Idaho. The entire Middle Fork lies within the Frank Church River of No Return Wilderness (see chapter 28), which at 2.3 million acres is easily the largest classified wilderness in the lower forty-eight.

Angling for native cutthroat and bull trout in the Middle Fork and its larger tributaries is catch-and-release. Only artificial lures and a single barbless hook are allowed. Excellent numbers of westslope cutthroats averaging 9 to 13 inches provide great action, and I've taken cutts to 17 inches.

The length of the Middle Fork and the sheer size of its wilderness make this country tough to penetrate on your own. Most visitors hire commercial outfitters and float the river in large rubber rafts; I've also seen kayaks and a few drift boats. The Middle Fork has numerous Class III and IV rapids, and most floaters go more for the whitewater thrills than the fishing. Indeed, this is the premier wilderness float in the lower forty-eight, and a lot of groups and families make the trip. The forest service limits the number of float-trip launches to seven per day.

Peak runoff and hazardous floating conditions usually prevail through June. After runoff crests, float trips depart daily right into September. During good flows most floats begin just downstream of Dagger Falls, which is accessible by gravel road. It's a 100-mile float from Dagger Falls to the first road-accessible takeout, at Cache Bar on the main Salmon, a few miles downstream from the mouth of the Middle Fork. Most floats last about six days.

If you choose to hike the Middle Fork, you'll definitely be in the minority. Distances are long, the terrain is rugged, and in the arid lower canyon, summer temperatures soar well into the 90s Fahrenheit. In three backpacking trips along the Middle Fork, I've seen only a handful of other backpackers in the heart of the river corridor.

For backpack anglers the best and easiest way to reach prime fishing on the larger sections of the Middle Fork is to hike down Big Creek to the river (see chapter 53 for a complete route description). From the Big Creek Trailhead, it's 35 miles to the Middle Fork, so you're committed to a 70-mile round-trip before you even begin to explore the river. Still, from the trailhead to the river, you drop only 2,500 feet, and you can enjoy fine angling along Big Creek. The next time I go to the Middle Fork, I'll enter and exit via Big Creek and spend most of my time fishing the creek rather than the river. The Middle Fork and its lower canyon are certainly worth seeing, but because Big Creek can't be floated, the traffic is much lighter and the average fish size larger than on the Middle Fork.

The first time I saw the Middle Fork, I'd come in the hard way—from the Bighorn Crags, a collection of peaks and high lakes east of the river. On that early-July trip, my friend Clark Heindl and I spent a couple of days fishing the Crags before heading for the Middle Fork. On our last night in the Crags, we were treated to high winds, subfreezing temperatures, and several inches of new snow on top of the old snow pack. In the morning we dug out our packs, broke camp, and crossed a little pass above Heart Lake at around 9,000 feet. From there we hiked 13 miles down the Waterfall Creek Trail to strike the lower Middle Fork just opposite the mouth of Big Creek, at an elevation of only 3,300 feet. The transition was as abrupt as any I've seen—in a few hours we walked from a wintery mountain landscape into a parched canyon replete with wild roses, rattlesnakes, and fierce heat.

Climbing out of the canyon on the Waterfall Creek Trail, as Clark and I did, is a considerable pull. If you want to exit by a different route and enjoy fishing all the way, you can cross the Middle Fork on a pack bridge and travel up Big Creek. Or you can hike 80 miles up the Middle Fork to Dagger Falls.

On a solo trip in 1986 I saw as much of the Middle Fork as you can readily see on foot. I began this hike 10 miles above Dagger Falls on Marsh Creek and hiked 90 miles downstream to the mouth of Big Creek; from here to the main Salmon, 20 miles downstream, the Middle Fork flows through a steep-walled canyon that has no foot trails. To exit I hiked up Big Creek for 5 miles, then headed another 35 miles out to the main Salmon through mountains that crest at about 7,500 feet.

A hike down the Middle Fork from Dagger Falls begins at just under 6,000 feet in mostly timbered country. As you near the mouth of Big Creek, nearly 80 miles downstream, the river elevation drops below 4,000 feet and the canyon becomes hotter, drier, and more defined. The timber retreats up the slopes, and much of the river is flanked by sage. Forest service trails parallel the Middle Fork (sometimes on both sides) from Dagger Falls all the way down to Big Creek. There are several pack bridges where horses and hikers can cross the river. In many places you have to scramble down slopes to reach the river from the trail, particularly in the 20 miles upstream from Big Creek. As you work your way downriver into arid country, rattlesnakes become common; I've seen as many as a half dozen in a day. Except for limited wet wading from sand and gravel bars, I do all of my fishing on the Middle Fork in hiking boots and snake leggings. Even if it weren't for the snakes, the terrain is too rugged for wading boots.

Private withholdings are scattered along the Middle Fork, including several small ranches, lodges, and airstrips.

The river gathers size, and the fishing seems to improve, as you progress downstream. You'll fish everything from ½-mile-long riffles to big pools. I have a honey hole where the river undercuts a rock hump. I can stand here for a couple of hours and catch a nice cutt almost every time I swing a Muddler through the cavity. Caddis hatches are abundant, and you should see some mayflies. As with most boulder-strewn western rivers, stoneflies are common, and big nymph imitations drifted near the bottom will usually take fish. Because the trout rise freely, though, it's more fun to prospect with a dry fly.

On a long-distance trek of the Middle Fork, hiking time cuts into fishing time. To get anywhere you have to bypass a lot of appealing water. As a rule I like to hike 10 miles by noon, and then fish and tarry the rest of the day. There are several hot springs conveniently spaced along the river in which you can soak out any muscle kinks; expect company from floaters. A daily dip in the river is a good way to beat the afternoon heat and refresh yourself for an evening of fishing.

The Middle Fork is fine game country. In summer mule deer and elk tend to stick to the forested slopes, but you should see bighorn sheep in the lower canyon. I don't think I've flushed more spruce grouse anywhere, and I've also seen ruffed grouse and chukar partridge.

Open fires are prohibited within the river corridor except in fire pans (the corridor extends ¼ mile on either side of the river). Fire pans are practical for floaters but not for backpackers. If you plan to cook, you must carry a stove or climb out of the river corridor to build a fire— easier said than done in most places. In dry summers open fires are often banned throughout the area, so you may need a stove anyway.

Hikers should be aware that all floaters must use assigned campsites. If you set up camp on a nice, spacious sandbar or terrace right on the river, there's a good chance that a float party will be joining you for the night. I look for smaller sites a bit above or back from the river that obviously won't be assigned to floaters.

MAPS AND SERVICES

The north- and south-half maps of the Frank Church River of No Return Wilderness show the entire Middle Fork and surrounding wilderness. Both maps have a scale of 1½ miles to the inch and a contour interval of 50 meters; they're available in waterproof versions. A special forest service map designed for floaters is also very useful for hikers. This map is printed in a waterproof booklet form called "The Middle Fork of the Salmon—A Wild and Scenic River Map/Guide." It shows the entire river corridor on a scale of 1 inch to the mile. It also lists the mileage from Dagger Falls to dozens of points along the river.

Dagger Falls is easily reached by driving west from Stanley, Idaho, on Idaho 21 for about 20 miles and then turning north on a gravel road that runs right to the headwaters of the Middle Fork.

Access roads to the Bighorn Crags Trailhead are shown on the map of the Salmon National Forest. This trailhead is reached by driving down the main Salmon from North Fork, Idaho, then taking a series of gravel roads up Panther Creek and over Remenclau Saddle. It's about 50 miles to the Crags Trailhead from the main Salmon. The roads are passable with a car, although during an early-July trip we had to park a mile short of the trailhead because of snow pack on the road. I'm not aware of any services once you leave the highway.

As with Big Creek, there are opportunities to fly to dirt landing strips along the Middle Fork and to walk or fly out. Commercial flying services operate out of McCall, Challis, and Salmon.

CHAPTER 48

Black Canyon of the Gunnison (Colorado)

As others have aptly noted, there are deeper and longer canyons in the West. And there are canyons that are as sheer or narrow. But no other canyon in North America combines all of these elements as dramatically as the Black Canyon of the Gunnison in western Colorado.

I'll never forget my first long look over the rim into the somber chasm I was about to enter. Sheer gray walls of schist and gneiss tumbled abruptly to the canyon floor half a vertical mile below. There, grinding ever downward in a pit of rock and nearly perpetual shadow, was a dull pewter gleam and my eventual goal—the Gunnison River. That bright July morning, the opposite rim of the canyon shimmered in the sun just a long rifle shot away. Indeed, there are points at which the depth of the Black Canyon exceeds the distance between its rims, and even in summer direct sunlight penetrates long reaches of the canyon only briefly each day. The sweeping shadows and dark walls combine to give the canyon its brooding countenance and its name.

Much of the legendary Gunnison is impounded, but 26 miles of river are managed as a Gold Medal tailwater fishery that rivals the South Platte as the most productive river in Colorado. The lower 13 miles of Gold Medal water, known as the Gunnison Gorge, see substantial angling pressure. But the upper 13 miles, within the rugged Black Canyon National Monument, are fished only by the few who are willing to scramble more than 2,000 feet down eroded drainage gullies to the river—and then scramble back out. Backpack anglers who camp on the canyon floor within the monument earn the unique opportunity to fish a premier western tailwater in relative solitude.

The Gunnison holds excellent numbers of slab-sided rainbows and browns from 13 to 18 inches, and much bigger trout are occasionally taken. My best was a rainbow that nosed a bit past 22 inches and looked to be pushing 5 pounds. Whirling disease is present. I fished the Black Canyon four times between 1988 and 1994 and saw a definite decline in my rainbow catch over the period, although this could have been coincidental. I did experience my best angling for browns on my last trip, and the river is still well worth fishing.

Within the canyon the river flows 80 to 100 feet wide, with classic freestone structure, including deep, green pools, whitewater chutes, swift runs, and countless productive pockets where fallen slabs of rock momentarily thwart the current. Where the river sweeps away silt and gravel, the bottom is jagged rock slick with algae. Many pools, runs, and pockets can be fished from shore. Waders and high-traction wading shoes are worth packing, but use great caution when you wade.

The river hosts various mayfly hatches, including afternoon *Baetis* hatches. Be prepared to fish caddis hatches, too; one morning I was awakened by the splashing of trout as they chased emerging caddis in an eddy near my tent. Drifting a big nymph along the bottom through the pools and pocket water is an effective way to prospect, especially when the sun is high. On the first cast I ever made in the Gunnison, I caught a leaping 18-inch rainbow on a big Soft-Hackle Woolly Worm. Like a lot of big, brawling rivers, the Gunnison has some water that can be covered only with long casts. I like to probe distant pockets and the far sides of big pools with a Muddler or a big dry fly.

Within the monument there are six undeveloped routes (three from each rim) to the canyon floor. There are no established trails—the routes follow eroded drainage gullies. These gullies are steep and littered with loose dirt and rock, so you have to choose your footing carefully, especially going down. As you descend, the opposite wall looms closer and the river grows steadily. Halfway down you begin to hear the river—a drone that doesn't subside until you exit the canyon. You can gauge your downward progress by looking straight across the canyon to the opposite wall and then lifting your eyes to the far rim. Park literature suggests allowing around four hours for a descent and longer for climbing out. My first descent on the Warner Point route took two and a half hours, and I climbed out in two hours. It's best to descend and climb early in the day to beat the heat.

On the canyon floor, the river surges against sheer walls at numerous points, limiting foot travel along the river. Depending on the route and river level, inner-canyon anglers can work from ½ to 1¾ miles of river.

From the south rim, the Warner Point route provides the longest river access, 1½ miles. This route also has the greatest drop in elevation—2,660 feet in 2 miles. The river in this section offers a good mix of pocket water and productive runs and is flanked mostly by sand and gravel bars that are easily walked. There are a couple of sand campsites with shade trees downstream from the spot where you hit the canyon floor and a few open campsites upstream. My first trip down Warner Point was midweek. I was alone in the canyon for the first two days and saw just one other party, of two anglers, for the final two days. My second trip down Warner Point was over a weekend, and there were three other parties already in the canyon.

From the north rim, the S.O.B. draw route provides the longest river access, 1¾ miles, and drops 1,800 feet in 2 miles. There's a sandy campsite with some shade downstream from the spot where you hit the canyon floor. Here the river has several big, productive pools linked by whitewater chutes. The shoreline is steep and rough—you have to scramble over jumbled boulders to move from pool to pool. During my only trip down on this route, I had the river to myself.

Campfires are not allowed in the inner canyon within the monument. Campsites are so limited that everyone ends up using the same ones, so take extra care not to scar the few trees or leave bits of litter. The canyon looks snaky, but I've been told that rattlers are rare. Do watch for poison ivy, which is chest high and plentiful. Protect your food, too: Big squirrels will crawl right into your pack if you leave an opening. Large birds, including golden eagles, red-tailed hawks, and turkey vultures, can be seen soaring on the updrafts, and there are a few peregrine falcons in the canyon.

Only flies and artificial lures are allowed. A slot-size limit is in effect (check current regulations), but I'd release everything here. Fishing tends to be best in summer and fall, after spring water levels drop and stabilize.

Overall, the Gunnison within the Black Canyon is perfectly suited to the backpacker who seeks solitude and top-notch river fishing for browns and rainbows. After fishing the Gunnison, you'll find yourself wishing that more great tailwaters lay at the bottom of barely accessible canyons.

MAPS AND SERVICES

The south rim is a 15-mile drive east of Montrose, which offers all services. This rim has a visitor center and a paved road to numerous overlooks, and attracts the bulk of the tourist traffic.

The less developed north rim is accessible by a 10-mile drive down a dusty gravel road out of Crawford and sees only limited tourist traffic. There are no services beyond Crawford. Both rims have campgrounds.

All hikers entering the Black Canyon within the national monument need a backcountry permit. On the south rim, permits are issued at the Gunnison Point Visitor Center, which is open daily from 8:00 to 6:30 in summer. On the north rim, permits are issued at a small ranger station that's manned from 11:30 to 2:30 daily and is set up for self-registration when there's not a ranger on duty. Along with your permit, you'll receive a description of your chosen route and be advised of camping regulations. There's a limited number of permits for each route. Permits for all routes are generally available on weekdays; on holidays and weekends some fill up. No firearms or wood fires are allowed.

The Gunnison Gorge has an additional 13 miles of Gold Medal water and lies immediately downstream of the monument. There are four foot trails (Ute, Duncan, Bobcat, and Chukar) on Bureau of Land Management land west of the river. The elevation drop of these trails ranges from 560 to 1,200 feet. For a map of these trails and regulations governing their use, contact the following:

Bureau of Land Management
2505 S. Townsend
Montrose, CO 81401
Phone: (970) 240-5300

CHAPTER 49

Hells Canyon of the Snake (Idaho-Oregon)

At roughly a mile deep, Hells Canyon of the Snake, on the Idaho-Oregon border, is the deepest gorge in North America. Upstream and downstream from the canyon, the Snake is dotted with reservoirs, but in the bowels of Hells Canyon, the river is still carving downward. Within Hells Canyon National Recreation Area, more than 200,000 acres bordering some 30 miles of river corridor are managed as wilderness. From the canyon floor, at just 1,500 feet above sea level, to the 9,000-foot peaks of the Seven Devils Mountains on the Idaho side, it's a land of staggering vistas and dramatic contrasts.

As its name implies, Hells Canyon is a hostile environment. The rocky terrain is more vertical than horizontal. Rattlesnakes are common, and poison ivy is abundant near the river. Summer temperatures reach 110 degrees Fahrenheit. On my six-day trip in July 1992, the thermometer topped 100 degrees every day.

Fly fishing in the river is good for a variety of species, from rainbow trout and smallmouth bass to carp and squawfish. Sturgeon exceeding 10 feet in length and weighing several hundred pounds are frequently caught on cut bait and stout tackle; only barbless hooks are allowed, and sturgeon must be released without being removed from the water.

I never saw another backpacker in a 50-mile round-trip along the river, but I was far from alone. Most people see and fish the canyon by rafting downstream from Hells Canyon Dam (float permits must be reserved in advance). A narrow corridor along the river does not fall within classified wilderness. Commercial jet boats run sightseers up the canyon all the way to the dam; you can expect to see and hear several powerboats daily, although they're pretty much gone by evening.

I considered descending into Hells Canyon the spectacular way—from the Seven Devils Mountains—but to conserve fishing time, I drove to Pittsburg Landing, where a trail heads up the Idaho side of the river. From this landing upstream to Hells Canyon Dam is 32 miles by river and a bit farther by trail. The trail ends in rough terrain about a mile below the dam. I hiked about 10 miles a day, moving camp daily so I could see most of the canyon and fish a different stretch of river. The trail crosses grassy, sage-dotted benches and periodically winds along steep ledges above the river. Rafting parties camp on sandbars right on the water, but I had no problem finding quiet, out-of-the-way sites on grassy benches above it.

My first few days in the canyon, the fishing was slow because of water releases intended to aid the upstream migration of chinook salmon. The river was thundering at 17,000 cubic feet per second; prior to this, flows had been at around 6,000 cfs for some time. Predictably, a 300 percent increase in water volume made for tough fishing. Halfway through my trip, however, the flows were reduced, and judging from the water-mark on the shoreline rocks, the river dropped more than 5 feet. New bars, rocks, and pocket water appeared overnight, and fishing improved immediately. Once the rocks dried, it was also easier for me to work along the river, below the shoreline brush. Because rattlesnakes are common and the riverbank is rocky and brushy, I fished in hiking boots and snake leggings, except for some limited wet wading on sandbars.

The fishing highlight of my first day came while I was eating lunch on a sandbar. A school of carp moved into shallow water; I could see them clearly as they nosed into the current. Just to see how they'd react, I flipped a shelled peanut upstream of them. The peanut sank quickly and tumbled along the sandy bottom. As I watched, a carp tipped and vacuumed the peanut off the sand. I had no doubt they'd take a nymph in the same way—and sure enough, one took a Woolly Worm without hesitation and surged into the main flow, running well into my backing. Even with a 7-weight rod and 2X tippet, I had to use all of my rod butt to force this fish out of the heavy current. I battled carp up to 10 pounds until my arms ached.

Hells Canyon is the only place in the Rockies where I've fished smallmouth bass, and I enjoyed the novelty of doing so in a western setting. The fish were more notable for their quantity than their size: The day after the river dropped, I took more than thirty. Most were under a foot long and my largest was only 15 inches, but these smallies bored hard into the current, and I had a blast. I took a few smallies in boulder pockets, but most came from the back eddies of big pools littered with the best natural riprap I've seen on a river. I caught all of my bass on a Soft-Hackle Bi-Bugger. Big squawfish to 7 pounds also hammered the Bi-Bugger as it drifted through the eddies.

All of the trout I caught were silvery rainbows, and most were lurking just below the mouths of the cold feeder streams that descended from the mountains. At times of the year when water temperatures are lower, trout are probably more dispersed. The rainbows were mostly pan size, although in one run I took four fish that ranged from 15 to 17 inches. Rainbows over 20 inches are considered steelhead and may be kept only during the open steelhead season. Unfortunately, there are no special regulations protecting small trout in the river. Most of my trout were taken on the Bi-Bugger, although I took a few rising fish during late-afternoon hatches of #12 sulfur duns.

Sheep Creek and **Granite Creek** are clean, cold trout streams that enter from the Idaho side. They're high gradient and fishing them entails scrambling along steep, brushy banks. Both hold rainbows and probably help populate the Snake with wild trout. The limit on these tributaries is two trout a day. I camped near tributary streams and filtered my water from them rather than from the river.

Five miles upriver from Pittsburg Landing is the Kirkwood Ranch, which was established as a sheep ranch in the 1880s and is now maintained as a tourist stop. A ranger stationed here told me that cougar sightings are fairly common in the area. I also jumped several coveys of chukar partridge that soared down vertical hillsides, presenting what would obviously be some spectacular shooting; some coasted to the Oregon side of the river before landing.

MAPS AND SERVICES

The map of the Hells Canyon National Recreation Area shows access roads, trails, classified wilderness, and public lands surrounding the river in Idaho and Oregon. The map has a scale of 1 inch to the mile and a contour interval of 200 feet.

Pittsburg Landing is reached by driving west from White Bird, Idaho, on U.S. 95 about 30 miles north of Riggins. The 15-mile gravel road to the river is steep and narrow in places; motor homes and large campers aren't recommended. I left my car baking all alone in the sage where the road terminated. A new trailhead was under construction here. Riggins offers all services and is a hub for whitewater rafting and kayaking.

PART NINE

Premier Westslope Cutthroat Rivers

CHAPTER 50

Our Last, Best Native Rivers

Westslope cutthroat is the common name applied to several cutthroat sub-species native to the westward-flowing drainages of Wyoming, Montana, and Idaho. The story of the westslope cutthroat parallels that of the eastern brook trout. Both require cold, clean water. Both strike readily and are easily overharvested. Consequently, river populations of both have been decimated by decades of environmental degradation and overharvest. Montana, shockingly, has only a single outstanding westslope cutthroat river remaining—the South Fork of the Flathead. Fortunately, several Idaho rivers still provide excellent habitat, and in recent years catch-and-release regulations have allowed the native trout to rebound in numbers and size.

Westslope cutts have finer spots and are usually more silvery than the more heavily spotted cutthroats from the Yellowstone drainage; some are as bright as fresh-run steelhead. Even with the aid of polarized glasses, these light, silvery trout are extremely tough to spot in their transparent rivers, which shimmer over multicolored, cobblestone bottoms.

In the Yellowstone drainage it's not unusual to catch a dozen or more cutthroats a day in the 17- to 20-inch class. Westslope cutthroats of this size are much tougher to come by. In the best river habitats, you're doing well to average one fish a day of over 17 inches, although fish of 12 to 15 inches are common. Though they usually run smaller than Yellowstone cutthroats, westslope cutthroats tend to be stockier and are fine fighters. Anytime you can connect with good numbers of westslope cutts in the 15-inch class, you're in for a lot of fun with a light rod.

In their tumbling headwater rivers, westslope cutts get only a quick look at a passing meal, and as a rule, they must strike quickly or go hungry. During nonhatch periods you can often pick your favorite method for prospecting the water and enjoy steady action. Highly visible dry flies, such as the Royal Wulff or Humpy, can be effective for covering long crystalline runs. I also enjoy watching cutts and the occasional bull trout launch after a swinging Muddler. Nymphing deep with the aid of split shot and a strike indicator produces some of the largest trout and plenty of whitefish. When I want to eat fish on a river from which I can't keep trout, I bake a whitefish.

Westslope cutts tend to feed in quick water. Casting right into the swift throat of a run will often trigger a slashing strike from the biggest trout in it. The tailouts and the smoother midsections of runs often yield mostly juvenile trout and whitefish.

The major westslope cutthroat rivers flow at low elevations by backcountry standards; elevations of 3,500 to 4,500 feet are typical. Spawning is usually completed in June and peak runoff by mid-July, although the timing of both can vary by a few weeks depending on weather and snow pack. Following spawning and runoff, most trout will be high in a given drainage. By late August trout in some streams begin to drop downstream in search of large, deep pools, where they'll winter.

All of the major cutthroat rivers are paralleled by horse and hiking trails for most of their mileage. In spots a trail may climb several hundred feet to skirt a canyon or to cross a ridge, but on balance, river trails are low gradient. Because elevations are also moderate, hiking along rivers is relatively easy compared with hiking in high mountains.

Most anglers camp and fish where rivers break into meadows and open, inviting parklands. Bushwhacking into heavily timbered areas or steep-walled canyons can take you to mother lodes of unmolested fish. I like to move camp a few miles each morning and spend the balance of the day fishing a new stretch of river upstream from camp. After working my way up the stream corridor for the bulk of the day, I cut up to the trail and blow back to camp.

I love the easy rhythm of hiking and fishing my way along sparkling cutthroat rivers—exploring new water each day, sleeping on a different river terrace each night, kicking back in the afternoon in the shade of a big ponderosa while I dig my toes into cool, white sand. Life should have more days like this. The West should have more rivers like these.

CHAPTER 51

Kelly Creek
(Idaho)

Kelly Creek is in the northern part of Idaho's Clearwater National Forest. Like the St. Joe River just to the north, Kelly is born high in the Bitterroot Mountains on the Montana-Idaho border. Similarities between the two waters don't end there. Both offer fine catch-and-release angling for native westslope cutthroat trout. And although the St. Joe is called a river and Kelly is dubbed a creek, the two waters are similar in size and character, especially in their roadless headwater sections. Best of all, Kelly and the neighboring St. Joe can easily be fished in the same week.

Kelly was among the first Idaho rivers to go catch-and-release in the mid-1970s and has developed a following, but in two midsummer trips to its upper reaches, I've encountered only a few other anglers. The creek and its tributaries are restricted to flies or artificial lures with a single barbless hook, so it primarily attracts fly fishers.

The lower 10 miles of Kelly are closely paralleled by a gravel road and receive moderate pressure from anglers based at the forest service campground at Kelly Forks or camped along the road. The water along the road is enticing and worth fishing if you have some time before or after a backcountry trip. There are deep, emerald pools much bigger than any you'll find in the headwaters. My biggest Kelly Creek cutt, a stout fish of 19 inches, inhaled an Elk Hair Caddis in a riffle right behind the forest service campground. In July I've had my best action in the roadless headwaters, but by late summer fish begin to drop downstream in search of large pools to winter in, and I'm told the roadside waters of Kelly can fish very well from late August into September.

About 10 miles above the point where Kelly spills into the North Fork of the Clearwater River, there's a small trailhead on the northern bank where you can leave your vehicle. From here a trail heads east and closely parallels Kelly's northern bank all the way to the Montana border, better than 20 miles. This country is not classified as wilderness, but the trail is suitable only for foot or horse traffic, so the area is wild in character.

From the trailhead upstream to the mouth of **Cayuse Creek** (about 4 miles), Kelly has a lot of broad, shallow runs and riffles that are fished regularly by day hikers. Backpackers are better off bypassing this lower water and fishing Kelly upstream from the mouth of Cayuse. Above the confluence with Cayuse, Kelly loses about half its size but still has plenty of water. The 2 miles just above the junction with Cayuse are among my favorites. Here Kelly is pinched into a fairly narrow canyon; the stream gradient increases, and powerful whitewater chutes gouge a succession of deep pools that all hold good cutts. The North Fork of the Clearwater and its tributaries once had steelhead runs, and Kelly still holds a few resident rainbows. I took a 20-inch rainbow in this section—the only 'bow I've caught on Kelly.

Where they merge, Cayuse and Kelly are about the same size. As a tributary to Kelly, Cayuse is also managed as catch-and-release for trout. I've fished only a couple of miles up Cayuse, but its action was comparable to Kelly's and I'd like to explore further. The lower 10 miles of Cayuse are paralleled by trail. About 5 miles above the mouth of Cayuse, a forest road intersects the stream, so you could also start here and fish either upstream or down. Cayuse has some rugged canyons; if you plan to explore this stream thoroughly, obtain topo maps.

Good campsites are scarce along Kelly until you cut Bear Creek, about 7 miles above the trailhead. At the mouth of Bear Creek, there's an outfitter's camp complete with log corrals, tent platforms, outhouses, and tables; it looks like a base camp that's primarily used for hunting in the fall. At Bear Creek there's also a meadow, which is a good place to pitch camp if you'd like to fish the 2 miles of Kelly upstream to Hanson Meadow. This stretch has scattered pockets of good holding water mixed with shallow riffles that produce few fish.

From Bear Creek the trail climbs out of sight of Kelly. Ten miles above the trailhead, you break out of the timber and descend to Hanson Meadow—the place to base your camp while you fish the headwaters of Kelly. Hanson is a big, grassy meadow where I've seen upward of fifty elk grazing on summer evenings. I've also seen white-tailed deer, mule deer, moose, and coyotes; one morning a pair of sleek river otters clambered onto a midstream boulder to give me a curious once-over before bobbing downstream, probably in search of a trout breakfast.

In Hanson Meadow Kelly is mostly shallow riffle water. There are several good runs at the head of the meadow, and as you work your way upstream into the woods, you'll encounter many beautiful pools and pockets full of eager cutts. About 2 miles above the meadow, where several feeder creeks converge, Kelly loses most of its size. You can continue upstream along several small forks of Kelly for many miles.

I'd rate the action along the hike-in section of Kelly as good. Most days you should be able to land one to two dozen cutts in the 12- to 16-inch range, plus an occasional larger fish. Be prepared to match a variety of caddis hatches. Kelly has good numbers of big stoneflies, too, so stonefly nymph imitations produce all season. The cobblestone bottom supports sculpins, so take some Muddlers. By late summer hopper fishing can be good in the meadows.

The last time I fished Kelly, I was dumped on by heavy rains for two days, but the water in the hike-in section did not rise or discolor significantly. I pack lightweight hip boots for Kelly and can cross the creek in the riffles pretty much at will.

Hiking along this creek is relatively easy. The trail climbs a few hundred feet at a crack in spots but is otherwise mostly level. Elevations along the creek in the hike-in section are around 4,000 feet. Considering the excellent fishing and easy hiking, I've encountered surprisingly few people. Over a Fourth of July weekend in 1992, for instance, I expected some competition, but I met only one other angler in Hanson Meadow.

MAPS AND SERVICES

The forest service map of the Clearwater National Forest (east half) encompasses the entire drainages of Kelly and Cayuse Creeks. Kelly is in a remote area with no commercial services—stock up on gas and groceries before leaving the main highways.

From the east Kelly is reached by taking Interstate 90 to Superior, Montana, which is about 40 miles north of Missoula. From Superior follow Forest Road 250 over Hoodoo Pass on the Montana-Idaho border and descend to Kelly Creek; it's about a 40-mile trip from the interstate.

The gravel road is narrow and winding in places but suitable for two-wheel-drive vehicles. Some years this road is passable by late June; other years the pass is blocked by snow into July.

From the west Kelly is reached by following gravel Forest Road 250 east from Pierce, Idaho, for about 50 miles. This is the better route if you're driving a motor home or pulling a large camper, or if Hoodoo Pass has snow. On either route expect to eat some serious dust in dry weather.

A forest service campground at Kelly Forks, at the mouth of Kelly Creek, is a convenient place to camp the night before or after a back-country trip, or while fishing the roadside waters of Kelly or the nearby North Fork of the Clearwater River.

CHAPTER 52

The St. Joe River
(Idaho)

Wherever excellent river habitat remains intact, catch–and–release regula–tions can allow trout to quickly rebound in numbers and size, even where populations have been depressed by decades of overharvest. Northern Idaho's St. Joe River is a dramatic case in point. Catch–and–release regu–lations, in place only since the late 1980s, have allowed westslope cut–throat trout here to stage a remarkable comeback. Today the upper St. Joe holds far more adult trout in the 14- to 20-inch class than at any time since 1950, and many consider the St. Joe the best cutthroat river in northern Idaho.

The St. Joe is a beautiful freestone river that originates at St. Joe Lake high on the western slope of the Bitterroot Range along the Montana-Idaho border. More than 50 miles of the upper river glide through lush northwestern forest and are managed as catch–and–release water. Only flies and artificial lures with single barbless hooks are allowed.

Of the 50-plus miles of catch–and–release water, the lower 33 miles, from the mouth of Prospector Creek upstream to the Spruce Tree Camp-ground, are paralleled by road. From Spruce Tree upstream, the river is roadless, but it's paralleled by a hiking trail for about 17 miles. On sum-mer weekends local anglers from surrounding areas in Idaho, Washington, and Montana hit the roadside water in considerable numbers. If you want to enjoy excellent cutthroat fishing in solitude, backpack into the roadless area.

In 1992 I backpacked and fished the 17 miles of hike-in water from Spruce Tree upstream to the mouth of Heller Creek. Because of an easy winter and dry spring, runoff was over by late June, about three weeks earlier than normal. I was fortunate enough to be here at the end of June, when the water was in great shape and few other anglers had arrived. I didn't encounter another angler in the heart of the roadless area, even though I covered several miles of water each day. From mid-July through Labor Day, though, you can expect some competition along the hike-in section.

To fish the roadless water, leave your vehicle at Spruce Tree; the trail runs upstream right out of the campground. The first 3 miles of river are heavily fished by day hikers, but there is a beautiful series of emerald runs about 2 miles above the trailhead that are worth working if they're vacant.

Five miles above the trailhead is a private lodge that outfits horseback fishing trips along the river. It sits near a big meadow that's skirted by a log fence. I believe the river within the meadow is on public land, but I left this section to the lodge guests and pushed upriver.

As you continue upstream, the forest and ground vegetation grow dense; you can't see the river from the trail in most places. If you have several days to fish, your best approach is to move your camp a few miles upstream each morning and work a different stretch of river each day. In hip boots I was able to work my way directly up the river channel in most places, and I covered nearly the entire roadless section in four days.

The first two days, I fished the 5 miles of water upstream from the lodge. Here the river is mostly shallow, gravel riffles interspersed with waist-deep runs and pockets. The riffles produce a lot of small fish; the larger fish are in the obvious holding places.

I pitched my third camp near the mouth of Broken Leg Creek. Upstream from here both the water and the fishing grow more interesting. The river canyon narrows a bit, and gradient increases. You'll find many deep plunge pools and more prime holding water.

I made my fourth and final camp near the mouth of Bean Creek and spent a day working upstream to the mouth of Heller Creek. Above the mouth of Bean Creek, the St. Joe loses quite a bit of size, but it still has many good pools and runs. I caught more good fish in the upper half of the roadless section than I did in the larger water downstream. By late summer look for most adult fish to drop downstream.

Above Heller Creek a primitive road follows the river for about 5 miles. Above this the upper 7 miles of river, all the way to St. Joe Lake, are followed by trail. This stretch sees few anglers and looks like it would be intriguing to explore in early summer, when good numbers of adult fish are in the headwaters.

At my last camp on the St. Joe, it rained buckets for most of the night, and I was seriously concerned about flash flooding—but in the morning the river ran crystal clear and had scarcely risen. Apparently it would take a tremendous deluge to muddy the upper St. Joe and ruin the fishing.

If my only trip was representative, the St. Joe certainly ranks in the top handful of westslope cutthroat rivers. I averaged one to two dozen trout a day in the 14- to 16-inch class, plus a few fish to 19 inches. I've also heard reports of some St. Joe cutts that push the 2-foot mark—a westslope cutt of this size is as big as you're likely to catch in any river. I also caught more juvenile trout than I've taken on any other westslope cutthroat river, an indication that natural reproduction in the St. Joe is strong and that the river should continue to flourish under special regulations.

I didn't encounter heavy insect hatches, but the St. Joe has plenty of mayflies, caddisflies, and stoneflies, plus loads of sculpins. I took most of my better fish on a #12 Industrial-Strength Adams.

Hiking along the St. Joe is about as easy as hiking in the Rockies gets. The trail along the river is mostly level, with elevations around 4,000 feet. From my last camp on Bean Creek, I hiked back to the Spruce Tree Campground in less than five hours.

The forest and the ground vegetation are thick, so you may have to search a bit for campsites. There are more good ones in the upper half of the roadless section than the lower. Judging from the lush vegetation, the area gets considerable rain, so pack a good rain suit.

I saw more white-tailed deer along the St. Joe than I've seen while backpacking anywhere else in the Rockies. There are reported to be plenty of black bears around, too, so hang your food.

MAPS AND SERVICES

The entire catch-and-release section lies within the St. Joe National Forest. You'll want the forest service map titled "Idaho Panhandle National Forests (South)." Topo maps aren't needed to backpack along the river.

The upper St. Joe is easily accessible in summer by two-wheel-drive vehicle. To approach from the west, drive upriver from St. Maries, Idaho.

The road along the river is paved all the way to the mouth of Gold Creek; the last 10 miles of road, from the mouth of Gold Creek upstream to the Spruce Tree Campground, are graveled and narrow, but motor homes can make it to Spruce Tree. To approach from the east, take Interstate 90 to St. Regis, Montana (about 65 miles northwest of Missoula). From St. Regis follow gravel Forest Road 282 about 14 miles west to Gold Summit on the Idaho-Montana border. From here a paved road descends another 14 miles to strike the St. Joe at the mouth of Gold Creek. You can't buy gas or groceries along the upper river, so stock up before leaving the highway.

If you've got time, the roadside water of the St. Joe is worth fishing, particularly as summer progresses and fish begin to drop downstream from the roadless headwaters. There are several forest service campgrounds along the river, plus some secluded flats where you can just pull off the road and camp by yourself the night before or after your backcountry trip.

CHAPTER 53

Big Creek
(Idaho)

Big Creek flows due east for over 30 miles through central Idaho's Frank Church Wilderness before spilling into the famed Middle Fork of the Salmon River. Indeed, Big Creek is the largest tributary to the Middle Fork; their confluence is about 20 miles above the main Salmon. Managed as catch-and-release only since the late 1980s, Big Creek has emerged as one of Idaho's top rivers for westslope cutthroats. Biologists report that catches of twenty to forty fish a day are common and that half the trout exceed 14 inches—an outstanding ratio by westslope cut-throat standards.

The main trailhead on Big Creek is on its headwaters. A maintained trail follows the northern side of the creek for 35 miles, all the way to the Middle Fork. As Big Creek drops from an elevation of 6,000 feet at the trailhead to 3,500 feet at its mouth, it picks up many small tributary streams and becomes a small river. With an average drop of 70 feet per mile, Big Creek has inviting stretches of stair-step pools, deep plunge pools, numerous riffles, and long, crystalline runs. Unlike the Middle Fork, which is a superb river for whitewater rafting and kayaking, Big Creek is too rough to be floated. This keeps its traffic very light. Since 1983 I've fished all, or portions, of Big Creek on four trips, and many times I've covered 5 miles of water in a day without encountering another angler.

The easiest way to access Big Creek is to drive to the trailhead on the headwaters and fish downstream as far as you care to go. I've fished all the way to the Middle Fork, but dropping even 5 miles below the trailhead can put you into fast fishing.

The first major tributary, Monumental Creek, enters 10 miles below the trailhead. One of my favorite stretches of Big Creek is the mileage just upstream from the mouth of Monumental. If it rains hard in Monumental's headwaters, Big Creek turns chalky white below the mouth. Then the mileage above Monumental is definitely your best bet.

Just below Monumental the forest opens into scattered parklands. The next 10 miles, downstream to Cabin Creek, offer fine fishing and scenic camping on open river terraces. I've had better fishing in the 20 miles of water above Cabin Creek than in the 15 miles below, perhaps because I've fished the upper half of Big Creek more thoroughly.

In the big meadows around Cabin Creek, I've encountered clouds of mature grasshoppers as early as mid-July. On hot, windy afternoons, hopper fishing is good. The river itself supports good populations of caddisflies, large stoneflies, and sculpins. I like to watch cutts and the occasional bull trout launch after Muddler Minnows.

Any small rainbow trout you catch in Big Creek or the Middle Fork are steelhead parr that should be released with great care. If you happen to catch a brook trout in Big Creek, you can eat it—just make sure you don't mistake a protected bull trout for a brookie. A few chinook salmon spawn in Big Creek in summer, but angling for salmon is prohibited in the Middle Fork and its tributaries—don't disturb any salmon or redds you might encounter. Be sure to observe all fishing laws, including barbless hook regulations. Even in the backcountry, you never know who might be watching; one summer I was checked by Idaho wardens along Kelly and Big Creeks.

Downstream from Cabin Creek, there are about 8 miles of water above Big Creek Gorge. This gorge is just a few miles from the Middle Fork and under 4,000 feet in elevation—low enough, in central Idaho, to be hot and arid. In summer expect midday temperatures in the 90s Fahrenheit. You can fish most of Big Creek quite effectively in hip boots. Given the heat, I wouldn't want to march around in waders. I haven't seen any rattlers on Big Creek, but I've seen them on the Middle Fork right at the mouth.

Wilderness regulations allow camping anywhere over 200 feet from water. There are many fine sites in the woods and on open river ter-races. Firewood is abundant, but campfire bans are often in effect in dry summers.

I'd rate the angling on Big Creek as very good—on a par with Kelly Creek and the St. Joe. Big Creek has more backcountry mileage than Kelly and the St. Joe combined, however, so hiking cuts into fishing time if you want to see the entire creek. As a top-notch cutthroat river that flows through big, wild country and is lightly fished, Big Creek may be Idaho's best.

MAPS, SERVICES, AND A BONUS FISHERY

All of Big Creek is shown on the map of the Frank Church River of No Return Wilderness (north half). This map has 50-meter contour intervals and a slightly larger scale than most forest service maps: 1½ miles to the inch. It's available in a plastic version. The map of the Payette National Forest shows access roads to the Big Creek Trailhead.

The trailhead is a three-hour drive east of McCall, Idaho, on decent gravel roads; you can also approach over gravel roads from the south. Either way, shoot for the small town of Yellow Pine, which is 25 miles from the trailhead. Yellow Pine has gas and limited groceries, and there's a forest service campground near town. From Yellow Pine head for the Big Creek Ranger Station about a mile from the trailhead. A forest ser-vice campground near this station is a handy place to camp if you're interested in day fishing the upper reaches of Big Creek rather than backpacking into the wilderness.

There are few opportunities to legally fly into classified wilderness in the Rockies. Central Idaho is the most notable exception. You'll find a dirt landing strip right at the Big Creek Ranger Station and several strips in the wilderness. You could fly to lower Big Creek from the ranger station and fish your way upstream to your waiting vehicle on your own timetable. You could also fly in to the Middle Fork, fish down that river to the mouth of Big Creek, and then work your way up Big Creek. Commercial flying services operate out of McCall, Challis, and Salmon, and rates are quite reasonable.

If you have an extra day to spend around Yellow Pine and want to sample a different brand of roadside angling, fish the East Fork of the South Fork of the Salmon for bull trout. (At this writing you can still legally fish for bull trout in Idaho rivers on a no-harvest basis, and this area is one of the best.) Fish a big, flashy Marabou Muddler in deep runs just downstream from the mouths of tributary creeks. By August bull trout will be hanging out off the mouths of their spawning creeks. You probably won't see another angler along the dusty roads, and if you work enough runs you'll have a good chance of picking up a 4-pound bull trout. Fish pushing 10 pounds are possible.

CHAPTER 54

South Fork of the Flathead (Montana)

Many Montana rivers offer outstanding angling for imported browns and rainbows, but the South Fork of the Flathead stands alone as the state's last great river for native westslope cutts. Along the wild South Fork, grizzlies still roam stands of virgin timber and trout still rise with reckless abandon to attractor dry flies. In many ways, to travel this river is to step back in time and experience Montana as it was before man so drastically impacted the fisheries, the wildlife, and the landscape.

The South Fork is born at the confluence of Youngs and Danaher Creeks near the southern end of the massive Bob Marshall Wilderness. The river flows north for some 50 miles before spilling into Hungry Horse Reservoir south of Glacier National Park. About 35 miles of river lie upstream of the wilderness boundary, and the best fishing is the upper 25 miles of wilderness water.

Within the wilderness you can possess three cutthroat trout of under 12 inches. Since this slot-size limit was enacted in 1982, catch rates have tripled and average fish size has increased by 2 inches. Biologists report that some wilderness sections hold a thousand trout per mile. I've fished the South Fork three times since special regulations were enacted, and each trip the angling has been significantly better. On my latest trip, in 1993, I caught more westslope cutts of 15 to 18 inches than I have on any other river. Perhaps the South Fork will someday again hold the large numbers of 20-inch cutts it reportedly did as recently as the early 1970s.

You can hike in to the upper reaches of the South Fork from the Holland Lake Trailhead, which is about 25 miles north of the town of Seeley Lake. From Holland Lake you climb 2,000 feet into the Swan Range, to about 7,000 feet in elevation. Then you make a long descent down your choice of creek drainages to the river, which flows at about 4,000 feet. I've hiked from Holland Lake to Big Prairie on the upper South Fork via Gordon Creek in a day—about 25 miles. On that trip I fished down the South Fork to Murphy Flat, about 15 miles, and returned to Holland Lake by the Holbrook Creek Trail. To see 15 miles of water, I carried my pack 70 miles—not the most efficient way to see the river.

The quickest and easiest way to put yourself on the river is to drive to the head of Hungry Horse Reservoir and hike directly up the river corridor from the wilderness boundary. You'll be on the river full-time and won't have to make any significant climbs or descents. A 50-mile round-trip takes you to more good water than you can fish in a week; a 70-mile round-trip takes you all the way to the headwaters around Big Prairie and back. Be warned, however, that during rainy spells pack trains churn long stretches of river trail into calf-deep mud. Take your gaiters and don't expect to make great time in places.

The South Fork can also be floated from its headwaters all the way down to the Mid Creek takeout, just above Meadow Creek Gorge and the wilderness boundary. Outfitters haul float parties and inflatable rafts to the headwaters with mules and horses. Floats last several days and you see the entire river, including the heavily timbered sections and steep-walled chutes that most hikers bypass. Floaters do blow by a lot of water without fishing it thoroughly, however. Hikers tend to camp and fish in the open parklands scattered along the river. I keep hearing about how crowded the South Fork is, but most days here I worked about 3 miles of water without interference from other anglers. If I do bump into somebody, there's plenty of river to work around him.

The trail up the South Fork starts right at the wilderness boundary and follows the eastern bank for 10 miles, staying a couple hundred feet above the river in most places. Overall, the lower 10 miles of wilderness water are not as productive or easily fished as the upper river, although there are some good pools and runs if you want to scramble down to them.

Ten miles above the trailhead, you'll hit the Black Bear pack bridge. Above Black Bear the river gradient eases a bit, the river meanders more, and the fish density improves. From Black Bear trails run upriver along both the eastern and western banks; I've primarily worked the western from here up. About 5 miles above Black Bear, you'll break out of the lodgepole into Little Salmon Park, which offers good fishing and camping. A few miles above this, there's excellent fishing around the mouth of Big Salmon Creek. Fifteen miles above Black Bear (and 25 miles above the trailhead), you'll strike Murphy Flat—a big park with towering ponderosa pines. Here the river braids a bit, and you'll find some fine runs on the sand and gravel flats. White River also enters here from the east, so upstream the South Fork loses a bit of size.

From Murphy Flat to Big Prairie is another 10 miles through timber that affords few looks at the river. Big Prairie is another big, inviting park with a pack bridge on which you can cross the river easily. I've fished downstream from the pack bridge along the eastern side for about 3 miles, into a rugged little canyon; on my next trip I'm going to follow trails down the eastern bank all the way back to Black Bear and check out the various meadows and tributaries on that side. Around Big Prairie I haven't caught as many fish as lower down, but I've caught some of my better South Fork cutts here.

The South Fork is a good-size river by backcountry standards, but not all water is created equal. A long section of riffles will yield only occasional fish, but a short stretch of deeper runs will be stacked with enough cutts to keep you busy all day. Rather than fish too long on marginal water, I keep moving until I hit a productive stretch. Look for runs that are at least waist deep. Most cobblestone runs can be worked pretty effectively in hip boots.

Mayfly hatches are as regular here as I've seen on any backcountry river. In July I often work emergences and spinner falls from midmorning to dark. Pack plenty of dry flies to imitate #12 small green drakes and #14 pale morning duns. On the broad, swift runs of the main channel, heavily hackled flies score well. In some of the slick meadow runs, I've seen fish respond better to no-hackle patterns.

Prior to midday and evening mayfly hatches, a Chocolate Hare's Ear dead-drifted near the bottom can be good for an hour or more of nonstop action. Late afternoons and evenings bring some excellent spinner falls. For clues to mayfly activity, watch the numerous cliff swallows that nest in the earthen riverbanks: Swallows zipping low along the water often signal an emergence, and birds wheeling high above the river are often feeding on spinner swarms that will be on the water shortly.

The South Fork has abundant stoneflies, but adults usually emerge in June when the river is high with runoff. Nymphs, including stone-fly nymph imitations, consistently take some of the larger cutthroats throughout the summer, plus a lot of whitefish.

Two distinct cutthroat populations inhabit the South Fork and are divided by Meadow Creek Gorge, a thundering chute near the wilderness boundary. Cutthroats below the gorge have ready access to Hungry Horse Reservoir; those above are entirely fluvial and stay in the wilderness portion of the river (or its tributaries) year-round. In warm years look for some cutthroats to move into the cooler tributaries in August.

Bull trout, which commonly run 5 to 10 pounds but occasionally exceed 15, are powerful enough to run up the gorge from Hungry Horse Reservoir and spawn in the wilderness headwaters. In summer look for bull trout in deep runs, especially off the mouths of tributaries. By late summer they move into the tributaries. A huge South Fork bull trout once gave me a charge when it grabbed a whitefish I'd hooked and hauled it upstream through heavy current. After a lengthy tug-of-war, the hook pulled out of the whitefish, and the bull trout made off with its prize.

This is prime black bear and grizzly country, and the forest service has implemented strict food-storage regulations. All food must be hung according to specifications or stored in bear-proof containers (which are a more viable option for rafters than hikers).

MAPS AND SERVICES

The map of the Flathead National Forest (south half) shows the entire South Fork and all access roads. The forest service also offers a special topographic wilderness map of the Bob Marshall Complex, which includes the neighboring Great Bear and Scapegoat Wilderness Areas. Detailed topo maps aren't needed for fishing the river, and a lot of the country off the river is too heavily forested to make cross-country travel practical.

From Martin City a gravel road runs south along the eastern side of Hungry Horse Reservoir to the Spotted Bear Ranger Station, about 60 miles. The road is dusty and washboarded but very passable by car. To reach the Meadow Creek Trailhead, cross the South Fork on the bridge just below Spotted Bear and drive 12 miles up its western bank.

There's a forest service campground at Spotted Bear. If you camp here and are looking for a few hours of fishing, try the special-regulation water on the South Fork just above the reservoir. Services at the head of the reservoir are very limited; buy gas before you leave the highway.

Lure of the High Lonesome

I recall with mixed emotions my first backpacking trip, with my father and two younger brothers, into the mountain fastness of Wyoming's Wind River Range. My teenage eyes could scarcely believe what they were beholding—translucent, trout-filled waters, snow squalls in August, sprawling forests, and monumental peaks. After a boyhood of hunting and fishing in the modest hills of southwestern Wisconsin, the Rockies were a revelation. Here was land and sky and water and weather on a scale I hadn't witnessed.

Even on that inaugural trip I was itching to strike off on my own each day—to just grab a rod and go exploring. But it was not to be. Our father was calling the shots. We pretty much hiked and fished together. As rewarding as that trip was, I went home frustrated and harboring an intense desire to return to those mountains and to roam them freely.

I did return to roam the Winds and many other ranges throughout the Rockies. Ironically, in my many summers of wandering alone, when the rod bowed under the strain of a big golden trout, when the light struck the land just so, when I saw the western mountains truly shine, I was to wish countless times for a father or a brother or a friend by my side. Often I hungered to share the splendor of such moments, but always it was an intensely personal passion that drove me.

Without access to vast tracts of public land, my passion for wild places could not flourish. With it I'm a man of ordinary means with access to astounding vistas, forces, and freedoms.

As our population increases and private land is all but cordoned behind one big No Trespassing banner, the value of our public lands will only soar. In wilderness resides the opportunity for each of us to return to the land, at least temporarily, and to discover for ourselves the immensity of nature and the dignity of space.

Resources

NATIONAL FORESTS

National forest visitor maps are generally four-color with a scale of ½ inch to the mile. Lakes and streams are shown in blue. Some visitor maps have contour lines, but most give only scattered elevations. Forested and open areas aren't differentiated. Trailheads and forest service trails are shown. Access roads are shown and classified as paved, all-weather, dirt, or primitive. As of this writing, most forest visitor maps sell for $4 for paper editions or $6 for waterproof plastic editions.

National forest visitor maps can be obtained from individual forests or ranger districts within a forest, but it's more convenient to buy maps for several forests simultaneously by placing an order with regional headquarters. These headquarters can supply you with order forms that list all forest maps and special maps of specific wilderness areas within the region and with a pamphlet that lists the address and phone number of each national forest and ranger district in the region. (For example, the Intermountain Region has sixteen national forests with over eighty ranger districts.) This way you can direct specific questions right to the local officials where you'll be traveling.

For forests in Montana and the Idaho panhandle, contact:

USDA Forest Service
Northern Region
Federal Building
200 East Broadway
P.O. Box 7669
Missoula, MT 59807
Phone: (406) 329-3511

For forests in Utah, Nevada, the southern two-thirds of Idaho, and far western Wyoming, contact:

USDA Forest Service
Intermountain Region
Federal Building
Ogden, UT 84401
Phone: (801) 625-5306

For forests in Colorado and most of Wyoming, contact:

USDA Forest Service
Rocky Mountain Region
740 Simms Street
P.O. Box 25217
Lakewood, CO 80225
Phone: (303) 275-5350

For forests in Oregon and Washington, contact:

USDA Forest Service
Pacific Northwest Region
333 S.W. First Avenue
P.O. Box 3623
Portland, OR 97208
Phone: (503) 872-2750

For forests in Arizona and New Mexico, contact:

USDA Forest Service
Southwestern Region
517 Gold Ave. S.W.
Albuquerque, NM 87102
Phone: (505) 842-3292

NATIONAL PARKS

The national parks listed below all offer excellent backcountry fishing. Contact each park's superintendent for the forms to order maps and books pertaining to that park.

Superintendent
Glacier National Park
P.O. Box 128
West Glacier, MT 59936
Phone: (406) 888-7800

Superintendent
Yellowstone National Park
P.O. Box 168
Yellowstone National Park, WY 82190
Phone: (307) 344-7381

Superintendent
Rocky Mountain National Park
Estes Park, CO 80517
Phone: (970) 586-1206

NATIONAL RECREATION AREAS AND MONUMENTS

Several national recreation areas and monuments in the Rockies have significant backcountry waters. Adjoining national forest maps may cover all or portions of these areas. For maps of specific areas, contact the following:

Hells Canyon National Recreation Area
P.O. Box 832
Riggins, ID 83549
Phone: (208) 628-3916

Sawtooth National Recreation Area
Star Route
Ketchum, ID 83340
Phone: (208) 726-7672

Superintendent
Black Canyon of the Gunnison National Monument
P.O. Box 1648
Montrose, CO 81401
Phone: (303) 249-7036

USGS TOPOGRAPHIC MAPS

Standard United States Geological Survey 7.5-minute topographic quad-rangles have a scale of 1:24,000 (about 2½ inches equals 1 mile) and usu-ally have a contour interval of 40 feet. Standard 15-minute quadrangles have a scale of 1:62,500 (1 inch equals 1 mile) and usually have a contour interval of 50 feet. Most areas are covered by 7.5-minute maps, a few areas are covered only by 15-minute maps, and some areas are covered by both.

USGS topos show various types of water in blue, including lakes, streams, springs, swamps, glaciers, and snowfields. The elevation is printed right on most lakes, which is a great feature for anglers. Forested areas are shaded and nonforested are white, so you can spot meadows and areas above timberline at a glance. Access roads are shown and classi-fied. Boundaries are shown for national forests, national parks, Indian reservations, counties, and other jurisdictions. Buildings, river fords, and forest service trails are shown in black. The last date that a topo map was field-checked is printed on the map. Any physical changes to an area since the last revision won't be reflected. If a topo map hasn't been checked recently, consult a current forest service map for possible trail discrepancies.

Many sport shops throughout the Rockies sell USGS topo maps of the surrounding region. For planning your trips, though, it makes more sense to buy topo maps ahead of time from the USGS, which will send you state indexes on request at no charge. Indexes illustrate the areas covered by standard quadrangles and clearly identify all maps by name and series. The index for each state also lists any special maps available (for instance, the Wyoming Index offers topo maps of Yellowstone and

Grand Teton National Parks). For indexes, a map order form, and current pricing, contact:

U.S. Geological Survey
Information Services
Box 25286
Denver Federal Center
Denver, CO 80225
Phone (800) 435-7627 (HELP-MAP)

OTHER RECREATIONAL MAPS

A few recreational map publishers offer topographic maps that are based on USGS data but cover larger areas than standard USGS quadrangles; many cover an entire wilderness or park. By using larger paper with print on both sides, some maps cover the same area as a dozen or more 7.5-minute quadrangles and still maintain sufficient detail for cross-country travel. Recreational maps are almost always more up-to-date than USGS maps and easier to read at a glance. Hiking trails are boldly enhanced. Features of special interest to hikers, such as designated backcountry campsites in national parks, are often shown. Maps are available in water-proof, tearproof versions.

Earthwalk Press publishes superb, updated topographic maps of various national parks and wilderness areas. Each uses up to eight colors; they're available in paper or waterproof, tearproof versions. For a catalog of maps, contact:

Earthwalk Press
5432 LaJolla Hermosa Ave.
LaJolla, CA 92037
Phone: (800) 828-6277

Trails Illustrated also publishes topographic maps of some wilderness areas and national parks. For a catalog of maps, contact:

Trails Illustrated
P.O. Box 4357
Evergreen, CO 80437
Phone: (800) 962-1643

STATE WILDLIFE DEPARTMENTS

The wildlife department headquarters for each Rocky Mountain state is listed below. Call or write to receive the name, address, and phone number of fisheries supervisors, as well as a copy of the state fishing regulations.

Montana Department of Fish, Wildlife and Parks
1420 E. Sixth Ave.
P.O. Box 200701
Helena, MT 59620
Phone: (406) 444-2535

Wyoming Game and Fish Department
Information Section
5400 Bishop Blvd.
Cheyenne, WY 82006-0001
Phone: (307) 777-4600

Oregon Department of Fish and Wildlife
2501 S.W. First Ave.
P.O. Box 59
Portland, OR 97027
Phone: (503) 872-5268

Idaho Department of Fish and Game
600 S. Walnut
P.O. Box 25
Boise, ID 83707
Phone: (800) 635-7820

Utah Division of Wildlife Resources
Main Office
1596 W. North Temple
Salt Lake City, UT 84114
Phone (801) 538-4700

Colorado Division of Wildlife
Department of Natural Resources
6060 Broadway
Denver, CO 80216
Phone: (303) 297-1192

New Mexico Department of Game and Fish
Villagra Building
P.O. Box 25112
Santa Fe, NM 87504
Phone: (505) 827-7911

Bibliography

Baughman, John. *The Most Complete Guide to Wyoming Fishing.* Cheyenne, Wyo.: Baughman, 1993.

Borger, Gary A. *Naturals.* Harrisburg, Pa.: Stackpole, 1980.

——. *Nymphing.* Harrisburg, Pa.: Stackpole, 1979.

Dennis, Jack. *Western Trout Fly Tying Manual.* Jackson Hole, Wyo.: Snake River Books, 1974.

Hafele, Rick, and Dave Hughes. *The Complete Book of Western Hatches.* Portland, Ore.: Frank Amato Publications, 1981.

Hintzen, Paul M. *Fishing Glacier National Park.* Adelphi, Md.: Hintzen, 1982.

Holt, John. *Montana Fly Fishing Guide,* vol. 1, *West of the Continental Divide.* Helena, Mont.: Greycliff Publishing Co., 1995.

Hosman, Todd. *Fly Fishing Rocky Mountain National Park.* Boulder, Colo.: Pruett Publishing Co., 1996.

Marcuson, Pat. *The Beartooth Fishing Guide.* Billings, Mont.: Falcon Press Publishing Co., 1985.

Mathews, Craig, and John Juracek. *Fly Patterns of Yellowstone.* West Yellowstone, Mont.: Blue Ribbon Flies, 1987; distributed by Lyons Press.

——. *Fishing Yellowstone Hatches.* West Yellowstone, Mont.: Blue Ribbon Flies, 1992; distributed by Lyons Press.

Mathews, Craig, and Clayton Molinero. *The Yellowstone Fly-Fishing Guide.* New York: Lyons & Burford, 1997.

Mitchell, Finis. *Wind River Trails.* Salt Lake City: Wasatch Publishers, 1975.

Schwiebert, Ernest. *Trout.* Vols. 1 and 2. New York: E. P. Dutton, 1978.

Talleur, Richard W. *Mastering the Art of Fly-Tying.* Harrisburg, Pa.: Stackpole, 1979.

Varley, John D., and Paul Schullery. *Yellowstone Fishes: Ecology, History, and Angling in the Park.* Mechanicsburg, Pa.: Stackpole, 1998.

Index